Ionian

Corfu to Zakinthos and the adjacent mainland to Methoni

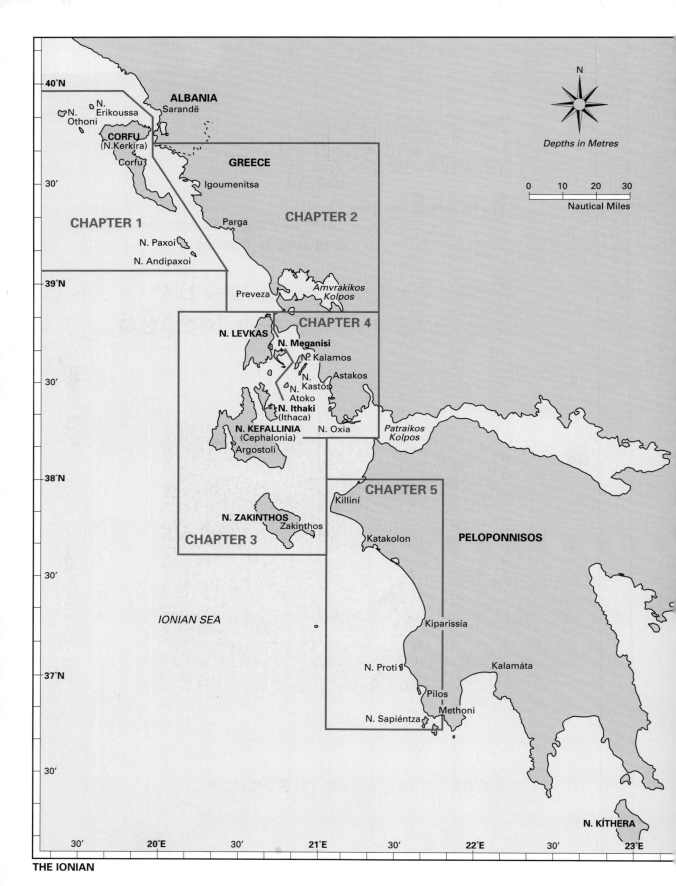

THE IONIAN

Ionian

Corfu to Zakinthos and the adjacent mainland to Methoni

Rod Heikell

Imray Laurie Norie and Wilson

Published by
Imray Laurie Norie and Wilson Ltd
Wych House The Broadway St Ives Cambridgeshire
PE17 4BT England
☎ +(0)1480 462114 *Fax* +(0)1480 496109
Email ilnw@imray.com
www.imray.com
2003

1st edition 1992
2nd edition 1994
3rd edition 1996
4th edition 1999
5th edition 2003

British Library Cataloguing in Publication Data. A catalogue record for this book is available from the British Library.

ISBN 0 85288 733 7

CAUTION
While every care has been taken to ensure accuracy, neither the Publishers nor the Author will hold themselves responsible for errors, omissions or alterations in this publication. They will at all times be grateful to receive information which tends to the improvement of the work.

PLANS
The plans in this guide are not to be used for navigation. They are designed to support the text and should at all times be used with navigational charts.

Printed in Great Britain at
The Bath Press, Scotland

Author's note
Photocopies and downloaded information from my books circulate around the Mediterranean. For those of you sitting and reading a photocopy or information downloaded off internet sites, I suggest you reflect on the fact that you forfeit your own moral basis for objecting to any theft from yourself or your boat. You have after all stolen something from me and my publishers, both in a moral and legal sense, so when you have something stolen, think about how it feels.

RJH

Contents

Chair repairs. Mainland

Eftilia. Levkas

Fisherman. Ithaca

Papas. Levkas

Preface

I've been meaning to write this guide for a long time. I first arrived in the Ionian in 1977, passing through as I thought, but like many others ended up staying for the rest of the summer there. Some of it has changed radically in that time and there are certainly more yachts around, but it retains a charm which brings me back and holds others locked in its geographical fist.

There are good reasons why travellers feel loath to move from the place. It is hard to imagine a more perfect sailing area. In the summer the wind gets up at midday, blows through the afternoon, and dies at night. A perfect gentleman's wind which lets you sail through the afternoon and get a good night's sleep without worrying about the anchor holding. It lets you motor against the prevailing wind direction in the morning calm. I have had the best sailing anywhere in the Ionian and still have my favourite legs where you can rip along on a close reach in near flat water. Ashore this western strip has an Italianate feel to it reflected in Venetian castles, odd belfries, red-roofed houses, a bit of neo-Baroque here and there, and inhabitants who enjoy their pasta as much as their *moussaka*. You have to dig a bit for the Italian connection and travel in other parts of Greece to make comparisons, but it is there though the area is still indubitably Greek.

The name of the area and the sea comes from Io, a priestess to Hera who briefly had a fling with her employer's husband Zeus. Hera found out about the affair and Zeus, worried about what his wife might do, changed Io into a white cow. Cunning Hera sent a gadfly to torment the cow and Io galloped around Europe attempting to escape her persecutor, eventually plunging into the sea now called the Ionian after her. One confusion which sometimes crops up is between the Ionian Sea and the colony of ancient Ionia on the coast of Asia Minor in present day Turkey. The Ionians (properly the Ionics) here were named after Ion, son of Creusa and the Sun God Apollo, and have no mythopaeic connections to the area described in this book.

It has taken me a long time to get around to writing this guide. I hope it provides sound sailing directions and gives a taste of the varied history and geography of the area - if you need more there is a list of a few books which may be useful in the appendix. If things have changed in the time between writing and going to print then please let me know care of the publishers. To those who helped me put this book together my thanks. I would especially like to thank Willie Wilson of Imrays; Julia who re-arranged the text for printing on screen; Debbie who painstakingly perfected the plans; Graham and Katrina Sewell of *Songline* who looked at some of the harbours and read the first proofs; Joe and Robin Charlton of Contract Yacht Services in Levkas who provided a base and good barbecues; Adonis Fotinos of Christo's Boatyard in Levkas; Sotos Kouvaras of Greek Sails; and Odile who did the draft lay-out, compiled the index, read proofs, and crewed *Tetranora* as we pottered around the Ionian.

Rod Heikell
London 1992

PREFACE TO THE FOURTH EDITION

Returning to the Ionian after some time away is like coming home. The landscape is at once familiar but half-remembered: old friends in familiar places with extensions to family and homes;. the sun still hot overhead and the evening sky in pastel hues as the sun goes down. Strange too, to arrive in a new boat, *seven tenths*, both of us still bearing the scars of 8000 odd miles of cruising around Cuba and Haiti and the Leewards before crossing the pond to the Mediterranean.

The area has changed little since the first edition of this book was published and that in itself is a joy. There are new buildings, improvements to harbours and marinas, a new pontoon here and some water points there, but overall the look and feel of the area, the soul of

KEY TO SYMBOLS USED ON PLANS

 depths in METRES

 shallow water with a depth of 1m or less

 rocks with less than 2 metres depth over them

(#) rock just below or on the surface

(2) a shoal or reef with the least depth shown

⤙ wreck partially above water

ⓢ ⓢ eddies

 wreck

(4) Wk dangerous wreck with depth over it

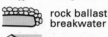 rock ballasting on a mole or breakwater

above-water rocks

cliffs

⚓ anchorage

prohibited anchorage

⚓ harbour with yacht berths

⚓ yacht harbour/marina

⛪ church

☪ mosque

✴ windmill

⌂ chimney

⛫ castle

✈ airport

ruins

▮▮ houses

⚓ port police

fish farm

⊖ customs

travel-hoist

shower

Pc yacht club

water

⚡ electricity

fuel

✉ post office

ℹ tourist information

⋔ pine

trees other than pine

▲ port of entry

Ⓥ visitors' berths

⊕ waypoint

 yacht berth

local boats (usually shallow or reserved)

⊙ beacon

port hand buoy

starboard hand buoy

mooring buoy

Characteristics

light

lighthouse

F fixed

Fl. flash

Fl(2) group flash

Oc. occulting

R red

G green

W white

M miles

s sand

m mud

w weed

r rock

KEY TO QUICK REFERENCE GUIDES

Shelter
A Excellent
B Good with prevailing winds
C Reasonable shelter but uncomfortable and sometimes dangerous
O In calm weather only

Mooring
A Stern-to or bows-to
B Alongside
C Anchored off

Fuel
A On the quay
B In the town
O None or limited

Water
A On the quay
B In the town
O None or limited

Provisioning
A Excellent
B Most supplies can be obtained
C Meagre supplies
O None

Eating out
A Excellent
B Average
C Poor
O None
(*Note* These ratings are nothing to do with the quality of food served in restaurants, but relate only to the number of restaurants.)

Plan
• Harbour plan illustrates text

the place, has not changed radically. It is too easy to criticise some development of the ubiquitous pour-and-fill variety, but in the end the area has escaped lightly from the sort of the development that blights other parts of the world. Let us hope it remains so.

For this edition I would like to thank Barry Nielson of Sailing Holidays, Joe Charlton and Laurie Campbell of Contract Yacht Services, Captain Y Elren of M.Y *Deianeira* for local information, Nigel Patten and Willie Wilson, Julia Knight, Elaine Sharples and all at Imrays who beavered away to get this edition out. My thanks and as ever the mistakes are mine.

Rod Heikell
London 1999

PREFACE TO THE FIFTH EDITION

Over the last three years as I criss-crossed the Mediterranean between Italy and Turkey researching my other pilots I have dipped into the Ionian. Each time I tarried longer than intended and was sad to leave. It is a wonderful cruising area and that is one of its problems in high season. Yachts from all over the Med plot a waypoint arrival in the Ionian, and combined with the resident charter fleets and the private boats based here, it is a very busy place. Consequently I have tried to include a larger number of small harbours and anchorages in this edition as well as updating all the existing harbours in the area. A number of new harbours have been built and some smaller ones significantly enlarged. And for those who want to extend their cruising area a little bit further, I have added another chapter on the southern Ionian from Killini to Methoni.

The Ionian may be crowded in the summer, but with a little effort you can get away to places like the Gulf of Amvrakia, to Astakos and the anchorages around the Dragoneras and Echinades, to some of the mainland anchorages opposite Corfu, as well as to lesser known spots around the islands. If you can sail out of the peak summer months of July and August there are a lot fewer boats around and at the very beginning and end of season it can feel positively deserted. I spent a couple of solitary nights in Fiskardho in early November with not another yacht around. I then sailed across to the Meganisi Channel in shorts and a T-shirt and the only yacht I encountered was at the bottom of the Levkas Canal. It does have a bit of a downside in that nearly everything closes down. Places like Fiskardho become a ghost town and you need to sniff out places where there is enough local life going on for tavernas and bars and shops to stay open – places like Zakinthos, Levkas, Preveza and Corfu.

As I was reading the page proofs for this book an earthquake variously recorded as somewhere between 6·4 and 7·2 hit the Levkas area. There was a fair amount of damage to walls and roofs and to the quay heading in Levkas town and the marina. Thankfully no-one died. First reports indicate there is nothing of any consequence for pilotage in the area, but it would be prudent to keep an eye out for any ballasting that may have moved or fallen into the water near quays in the inland sea.

Acknowledgements

As always a lot of people helped me with this book and if I have omitted anyone, put it down to haphazard filing systems and a peripatetic lifestyle. Lu Michell as always helped me sail *seven tenths*, edit the proofs and took many of the photos for this edition. The book is all the better for her tender ministrations and so am I. Contract Yacht Services helped fix things on the boat and provided much local information – thanks to Jeanette and Via in the office, to Olivier and Pip, and of course to Joe and Robin who provide a home away from home. K & G Marinas, especially Nikitas at Kalamata, provided useful information and the photo of Gouvia. Thanks to Laurie and Kate of Nisos Yacht Charter. Julian of S.Y *Tihama* provided local gastronomic advice. The Cruising Association forwarded valuable bits of information, especially David & Pat Teale of S.Y *Retreat from Battle II*. Conrad Jenkin and the RCC also helped with information. Nigel Patten of S.Y *Magellan* as always climbed the hills to take photos and forwarded information on the area. In addition Steve Miller of S.Y *Ithaca*, Mrs Cas Collins, Paul Braddock, Gerald Keys, Michel Hourcade, Patrick Hontebeyrie, Matthew Hunter of S.Y *Outlandish* and Jeremy Shaw of S.Y *Zingano* contributed information. Willie Wilson and the staff at Imrays put it all together in their usual professional way. To all of you my thanks for your help, though the errors and those typo gremlins that got through are mine.

Rod Heikell
London
September 2003

The Ionian

About Greece

History

One of the problems I constantly encounter in Greece is putting historical events into perspective. When did the Venetians colonise the Greek islands? And which islands? When was the classical period in Greek antiquity? Who were the Myceneans? I am not going to elaborate on any of these, but I have assembled the following historical order of things in Greece (with a slight bias to the Ionian) in order to give some perspective to historical events. For detail, wrangling over dates and places, and for explanations of what went on, the reader will have to consult other sources.

Neolithic period Little is known of early Neolithic life in Greece. Around 6500 BC early stone-age settlers crossed the Bosphorus to mainland Europe and probably used primitive boats and rafts to get to islands close to the Asian shore. Flint tools used by these settlers dating from around 6000 BC have been found on Cephalonia and Zakinthos. Around 4000 BC the Cycladic civilisation was well established and from the wide distribution of their distinctive geometric designs we know that there was communication between the islands on a regular basis.

Minoan period (2000 to 1450? BC) Around 2500 BC new colonists moved down into Greece from the Balkans and Turkey bringing bronze weapons and tools with them. The Minoan civilisation was concentrated on Crete and Thira where the art of pottery and metalwork was brought to a high art. They also seem to have brought the art of comfortable and civilised living to a high art as well. The Minoans colonised few places and appeared happy to police the seas with their vessels and so procure order and peace while permitting other peoples to go about their business. The Minoans are not thought to have colonised any of the Ionian islands. The civilisation ended abruptly around 1450 BC, it is thought from one of the biggest eruptions known, when Thira exploded and tidal waves estimated to be 70ft, earthquakes and ash, destroyed the civilisation overnight.

Mycenean period (1500 to 1100 BC) With the demise of the Minoans, the Myceneans, a Greek-speaking race based at Mycenae in the Peloponnese, stepped into the power vacuum. These are the Aecheans of Homer and the Trojan War, fought around 1200 BC, is thought to be a battle brought about by the Myceneans seeking trade outlets in the Black Sea. Mycenean artefacts have been found on some of the Ionian islands (Levkas, Cephalonia, Ithaca, Zakinthos) and it is likely that the expedition from the Ionian islands described by Homer is derived from real Mycenean settlements, though it is the location of these settlements that causes problems (see the section on Homer and the *Odyssey*). The Myceneans were displaced by the Dorians who invaded from the north bringing with them Iron-Age technology.

Greek civilisation (1100 to 200 BC) This title covers a multitude of sins. From around 1100 to 900 BC the Greek 'Dark Age' wiped out not only culture, but also written language. While the Greek-speaking Dorians existed in this dark twilight, the Phoenicians from the Levant (maybe Syria or Lebanon?) took control of the sea routes. By 800 BC a written language was emerging and Homer, possibly a native of Khios, penned the *Iliad* and the *Odyssey*.

From 750 to 500 BC (the Archaic or Classical period) city-states (*Polis*) sprang up all over Greece, some more powerful than others, some in alliance with others, but all trading with one another and bound together in a loose defence pact. Colonies were established all around the Mediterranean. Corinth, the nearest powerful city-state to the Ionian, colonised most of the major Ionian islands.

The Persian Wars (500 to 478 BC) pulled the city-states together around Athens and cemented the Delian league – though the Ionian was little affected by it all. The Hellenic period arrived with the final defeat of the Persians and the establishment of Athens as the power base. The Ionian islands were effectively under control of Athens and naval bases were established to counter any threat from nearby Sparta. The Peloponnesian War (431 to 404 BC) between Athens and Sparta divided the Ionian islands and caused much hardship for the inhabitants. The war weakened both Athens and Sparta leaving the way open for Phillip II of Macedonia and later his son Alexander the Great to take control, though these tumultuous times hardly touched the Ionian islands.

The Romans (200 BC to AD 295) A weak Greece was easy prey for the Romans and they declared war on Phillip V of Macedonia in 202 BC. The Ionian islands, being closest to Italy, were among the first to fall: Corfu in 200 BC, Levkas in 197, Zakinthos in 191, and Cephalonia in 188. In 31 BC Octavius defeated Anthony and Cleopatra at Actium near Preveza and cemented the Roman Empire into a whole after a decade of infighting. Roman rule had little cultural influence on Greece while things Greek, everything from architectural style to cuisine, had a profound effect on the Roman way of life. Greek cities were largely autonomous owing allegiance to Rome and Greek remained the official language. In AD 295, weakened by attacks from tribes on the edges of the empire and beset by difficulties within, Diocletian split the empire into two.

Byzantium (AD 330 to 1204) The foundation of Constantinople and the rise of Byzantium marks the rise of the first Christian Empire. Byzantine rule of most of its empire, including the Ionian islands, was constantly beset by invasions from the north and south. The Slavs, Avars, Goths, Huns, Vandals and Bulgars came down from the north while the Saracens sailed across from the south. The islands were depopulated and towns and villages contracted in size and moved away from a precarious shoreline. At times the Byzantines drove the invaders out, in the 9th century Emperor Leo VI (the Wise) compacted all the Ionian islands into one province under Cephalonia, but Byzantine power was on the wane and new invaders were afoot.

The Normans (1081 to 1194) In the Ionian the Normans under Robert Guiscard, an obscure Knight with a license to pillage, quickly demolished any Byzantine resistance, but he died of fever before he could enjoy his success. The Normans occupied the Ionian islands until their power base in Italy waned towards the end of the 12th century.

The Venetians (1204 to 1550) In 1204 the Fourth Crusade sacked Constantinople (ostensibly their allies!) and parts of the Byzantine Empire were parcelled out to adventurers from the European nobility. The Venetians, who had transported the crusaders, emerged with a large chunk of Byzantine territory as their prize, including the Ionian

Wherever the Venetians went they stamped their standard, the Lion of Saint Mark, on their castles and forts

3

islands. Most of the Ionian islands were leased out to Venetian families with the Orsini family getting Cephalonia, Ithaca, and Zakinthos. During this period the Venetians established castles and forts at the principal ports along their trade routes. Most of these massive structures remain intact to this day and nearly every fort or castle you come across will be Venetian, at least in origin.

The Turks (1460 to 1830) In 1453 the Ottoman Turks took Constantinople and ended the rule of Byzantium. By the end of the 16th century most of Greece was under Turkish control. In the Ionian and elsewhere the Venetians continued to battle the Turks for territory and managed to hold onto most of the Ionian islands until Napoleon attacked the heart of the empire and by proxy obtained her possessions.

With the British defeat of the French in the Battle of the Nile, the Ionian islands, but not the mainland, came under British and Russian administration. In 1815 the islands came under sole British administration. The mainland opposite and most of the rest of Greece remained under Turkish control.

The War of Independence (1822 to 1830) In 1821 the Greek flag was raised at Kalavrita in the Peloponnese. In 1822 the Turks massacred 25,000 people on the island of Khios and so aroused Greek passions that many took up arms against the Turks throughout Greece. Under British rule the Ionian islands had a neutral status and many Greeks fled here from the fighting on the mainland. The islands also served as a convenient base for Greek resistance groups to operate from and for British and other European eccentrics to hop across to the mainland to aid the cause. Byron was only one of many who used this route, leaving Cephalonia for Mesolongion on New Year's Eve, 1823. The war was effectively won when a combined English, French and Russian fleet destroyed the larger Turkish and Egyptian fleet at Navarino. The Ionian islands remained under British rule.

Modern Greece The newly born republic got off to a shaky start and after a series of assassinations the western powers put a Bavarian prince on the throne. He proved an insensitive and unpopular ruler and was deposed by a popular revolt in 1862. In 1863 a new ruler, George I from Denmark, was chosen and the British relinquished control of the Ionian islands to encourage support. The boundaries of Greece expanded with the acquisition of Thessaly and the Epirus in 1881 and Macedonia and the northern Aegean islands in the Balkan wars (1912–13).

The Greeks fought on the Allied side in the First World War and with the defeat of the Turks on the Axis side, embarked on a disastrous campaign to acquire territory in Asia Minor. When the Greeks were finally driven out the Turkish population remaining in Greece was exchanged for Greeks in Turkey. Greece fought in the Second World War on the side of the Allies and obtained the last of her territory, the Dodecanese, from the Italians at the end of the war. Civil war split the country until 1947 when a Conservative government was elected. In 1967 the army took power with the notorious junta of the Colonels which ushered in seven years of autocratic and harsh rule. Democracy returned in 1974 with Karamanlis. The first Socialist government, PASOK, under Papandreou, was elected in 1981. In 1986 Greece joined the European Community and in common with the other EU members customs and immigration controls no longer apply at the borders for EU nationals.

Homer and the *Odyssey*

With the resurrection of writing after the Greek 'Dark Ages' there appeared, sometime in 800 BC, the two epic poems, the *Iliad* and the *Odyssey*. They are said to have been written by Homer who is thought to have been born on Khios in 800 BC. There is nothing certain about any of this. The two epics survived into later ages in different versions with the words altered and whole passages inserted or missing. Homer may have been one man or the epics may have been the work of a group of poets. The two epics differ intrinsically in style and composition. And the translations available to those of us who don't speak sufficient ancient Greek to read Homer in the raw further complicate the picture. There is plenty of room for speculation and contemplation on the epics and writers of academic tomes and popular reconstructions have plundered the opportunities available to produce literally scores of books on the interpretation of Homer and his epics.

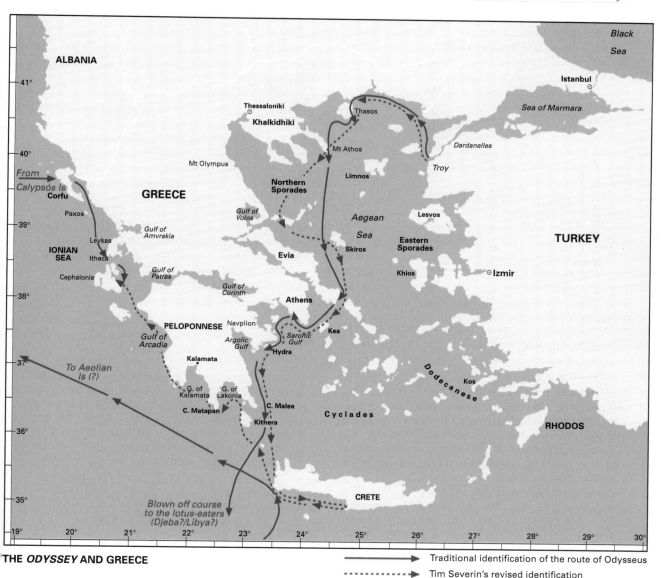

THE *ODYSSEY* AND GREECE

→ Traditional identification of the route of Odysseus

------→ Tim Severin's revised identification

It is the *Odyssey* we are interested in here. Odysseus came from Ithaca and this island most likely existed somewhere in the Ionian. The basic plot of the *Odyssey* concerns the attempts of Odysseus and his men to get home from the Trojan War.

Lineages play a large part in the epic. The Trojan War was ignited when Helen, wife of Menelaus, king of Sparta, eloped with Paris, son of the king of Troy. Menelaus, brother of Agamemnon, king of Mycenae, put together a vast fleet from associated city-states to besiege Troy and punish Paris. Odysseus as Lord of the Kefallenes brings twelve ships to Troy. After ten years a ruse masterminded by Odysseus, the wooden horse, is trundled into Troy and so the city falls. Here the *Odyssey* proper starts following the fortunes and disasters that befall Odysseus on his voyage home. It takes ten years for him to return and he has many adventures along the way before he is re-united with his Penelope on Ithaca.

Dissection and commentary of the *Odyssey* began not long after the mysterious bard died. In the 3rd century BC it reached fever pitch with the great library at Alexandria filled with different

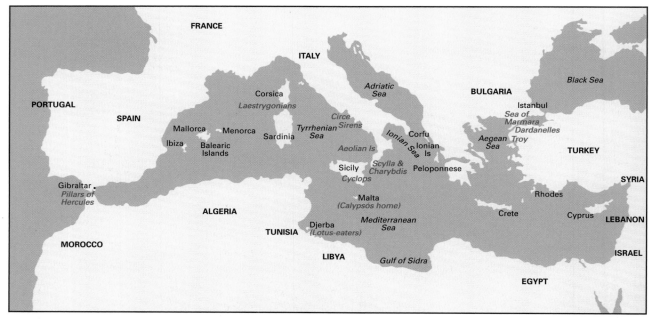

TRADITIONAL IDENTIFICATION OF PLACES VISITED IN THE *ODYSSEY*

versions of the epic and commentaries on it. It was the Alexandrines who divided the epics into the 24 book form that survives today. They were also of the opinion that the two epics were the product of two authors, not one. Despite the wanton destruction of the library at Alexandria, surely one of the greatest losses of the age, the tradition of analysis and commentary survived into the Roman and Byzantine periods before disappearing under the great weight of Christian censorship. Not until the 18th century was there any real revival of interest with a veritable deluge in the 19th and early 20th century as ancient sites were rediscovered and a knowledge of ancient Greece became an essential part of every young gentleman's education. Theories accumulated over just what the *Odyssey* was about – few doubted its obvious literary merits.

So does the *Odyssey* describe a real voyage by a real person? Or is it just an adventure story, a sort of *Buck Rogers* of the 8th century BC plucked from the lay poems of the times. There are many theories which can be roughly divided into the following categories.

1. The events in the epic are a fictional mishmash that do not have any particular geographical location. In effect it is ancient science fiction stroke adventure story and any attempt to identify the places in it would be like trying to locate where a fictional planet or a fictional country was. There may be threads of known geography included but the essence of the geography is fictional. This category also includes all those commentaries that tail off into long diatribes against the futility of trying to locate the geography of the *Odyssey* because it detracts from the literary and mythic qualities of the epic, a position I find difficult to understand when so often a geographical location, however vague, can enhance the poetry.

2. The geography described in the epic belongs not to the Mediterranean but variously to the Black Sea, the Atlantic, the Indian Ocean, the North Sea and the Baltic, or in variations to specific parts of the Mediterranean such as Spain or the Adriatic. Some of these locations are just cranky and are used to bolster theories of previous master-races, some of whom arrived on spaceships, and are recorded in the *Odyssey*. Some of the geographical locations, especially those placing the *Odyssey* in the Atlantic or Indian Oceans are just silly.

3. The geography described in the *Odyssey* is all real and relates to the known world of the time, but the adventures of Odysseus are tailored to

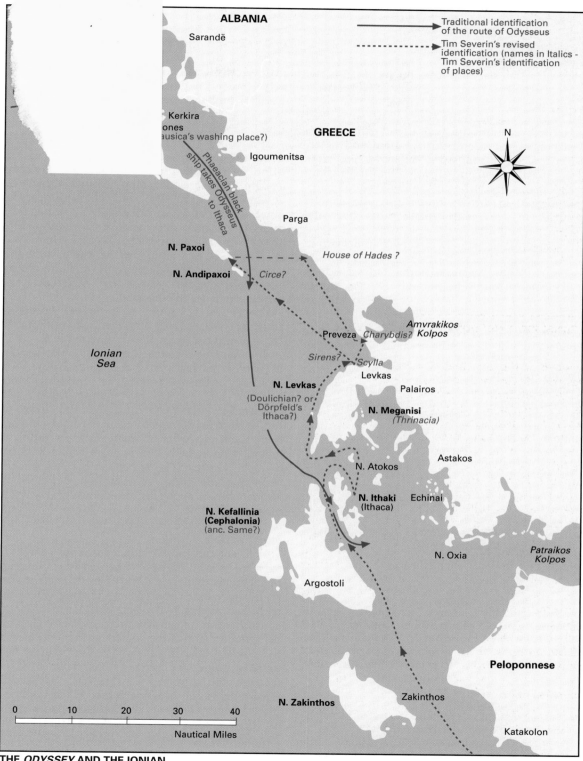

THE *ODYSSEY* AND THE IONIAN

ALBANIA

Sarandë

Kerkira
ones
(Nausica's washing place?)

GREECE

Igoumenitsa

N

Phaeacian black ship takes Odysseus to Ithaca

Parga

N. Paxoi

House of Hades ?

N. Andipaxoi

Circe?

Amvrakikos *Kolpos*

Preveza *Charybdis?*

Sirens? *Scylla*

Levkas

Ionian Sea

Palairos

N. Levkas
(Doulichian? or Dörpfeld's Ithaca?)

N. Meganisi
(Thrinacia)

Astakos

N. Atokos

N. Ithaki
(Ithaca)

Echinai

N. Kefallinia
(Cephalonia)
(anc. Same?)

N. Oxia

Patraikos Kolpos

Argostoli

Peloponnese

| 0 | 10 | 20 | 30 | 40 |

Nautical Miles

N. Zakinthos

Zakinthos

Katakolon

Traditional identification of the route of Odysseus

Tim Severin's revised identification (names in Italics - Tim Severin's identification of places) take us on a tour of the Mediterranean known to Homer and neither he nor his adventures existed as such, but are a fictional web holding the geography together. Thus all the places mentioned exist and can be located in the Mediterranean from the Pillars of Hercules at Gibraltar to Ithaca in the Ionian.

4. The geography and the hero and his voyage are Homers account of real events and a real person, perhaps embellished here and there, but basically a true story. Accounts like Ernle Bradford's excellent *Ulysses Found* take more or less this line. The geography of the *Odyssey* is located in the Mediterranean and can be traced to present-day places that bear the names mentioned in the epic as above.

5. A recent theory propounded by Tim Severin in *The Ulysses Voyage* (Ulysses is the Latinised version of Odysseus) states that Odysseus took the logical route home and all the places mentioned in the *Odyssey* can be located in present-day Greece.

So where does this leave us? There is no definitive proof for any of them. I have sailed around all of the geographical areas described in the various theories (except the silly ones) on numerous occasions and in all sorts of weather and as a personal preference I plump for number three, the rather woolly version that locates the geography in the Mediterranean in specific places, many of which bear the same name to this day, but which allows Homer a bit of license when dealing with his hero. Odysseus may well have existed and one interesting theory paints him as a successful pirate, a sort of Robin Hood from the Dark Ages. As Thucydides (460–399 BC) later commented on piracy in the Dark Ages, it was a respectable profession.

'The leading pirates were powerful men, acting both out of self-interest and in order to support the weak among their own people. They would descend upon cities which were unprotected by walls and indeed consisted only of scattered settlements: and by plundering such places they would gain most of their livelihood. At this time such a profession, so far from being regarded as disgraceful, was considered quite honorable. And in the old poets we find the regular question always asked of those who arrived by sea is 'Are you pirates?' It is never assumed either that those who were so questioned would shrink from admitting the fact, or that those who were interested in finding out the fact would reproach them with it.'

So Homer put together his epic using material from the lay poems and quite possibly from his own experience. There are many references in the *Odyssey* which point to an author acquainted with the sea and travelling upon it. Herodotus (484–420 BC) describes Homer as a travelling man not dissimilar to his hero in the *Odyssey*. He says Homer was born in Smyrna (now Izmir in Turkey) and travelled to many parts of Greece including Ithaca. Later he became blind and penniless and died on the island of Ios.

At the time Homer is thought to have lived there was considerable trading activity from Asia Minor with the Phocaeans from near Izmir leading the way establishing colonies as far away as Marseille (in 600 BC) and doubtless voyaging much further and also bringing back stories from other ships they encountered. We know little about the Phocaeans except that they were excellent seamen and carried out astounding voyages around the Mediterranean. From them a geography could easily be absorbed and implanted in an epic poem.

There are a couple of practical points to consider when mulling over the theories about the *Odyssey* and the geography contained in it.

The first I have touched upon and relates to the details on navigation in the epic. Homer was obviously acquainted with the prevailing winds and the stars to sail by. When Calypso tells Odysseus to keep the Great Bear or the Plough on his left to reach Greece from her island (Malta?) this is exactly what a sailor can do today to maintain an easterly course from Malta or Sicily to get to Greece. The *meltemi* in the Aegean, the wind that still blows, is accurately described by Homer. When distances, directions, and weather matters can be so verified, then it is only reasonable to take Homer at his word for many other matters as well.

The second point concerns the power of existing place names. The erratic Heinrich Schliemann made his discoveries of ancient sites by taking Homer literally and digging where the bard said events had taken place. Much to the consternation of professional archaeologists he discovered many of the ancient sites mentioned in the *Iliad* and the *Odyssey*. We should not underestimate the names that have survived through the centuries to this day: Scylla and Charybdis in the Messina Strait, Circeo (Circe's island) south of Rome, the Aeolian islands north of Sicily, Cape Malea at the bottom of the Peloponnese, and of course Ithaca in the Ionian. The question of Ithaca and the King of the

Kefallenes remains an enduring one and perhaps it is best to leave it at that and accept that the island that bears the name today is the island of the *Odyssey*.

Language

It should be remembered that the Greek spoken today, demotic Greek, is not ancient Greek though it is largely derived from it. Anyone who speaks ancient Greek will be able to pick up a little over 50 per cent of the Greek spoken today, though the pronunciation may not be what you expect. In rendering Greek from the Cyrillic into the Roman alphabet there are very real difficulties and there are no absolutes, just guidelines.

Greek is difficult to master because right from the start you come up against the Greek alphabet which for most people may as well be hieroglyphics. Yet the alphabet can be conquered with a little persistence and common words and phrases to get you by in the tavernas and bars and on the street can be picked up by ear. One of the obstacles to learning Greek is that you so often come across someone speaking English that the need to learn Greek evaporates. However if you can only learn a few phrases, a 'hello' and 'goodbye' and 'how are you?', the effort will be repaid, especially in out of the way places. In Appendix I a few useful phrases will be found.

The Greek Orthodox church

For someone from the west, from the world of Roman Catholicism and Protestantism, the churches and the black-robed priests of the Greek Orthodox church constitute another religious world, and so it is. Up until the last meeting of the Council of Nicaea in 787, the western and eastern branches of the church had stumbled along together, growing apart but outwardly united. Post Nicaea the churches grew apart, partly on doctrinal issues, but mostly one suspects because of the geographical and cultural isolation between Rome and Constantinople. In Rome they spoke mostly Latin, in Constantinople Greek. In the west priests were celibate, in the east they married. In Rome the Pope was infallible, in Constantinople articles of faith were decided by a council of bishops. In the west the spirit of God came from the Father and the Son, in the east from the Father.

The overthrow of Constantinople by the Turks in 1453 scattered the church as far afield as Russia and today the Orthodox church is still spread widely across the Balkans and into the steppes. The church was allowed to continue under the Turks and it became a focus for rebellion against the occupiers of Greece.

Today the church, although much weakened in this secular age, still permeates Greek life. For the Greeks the big event of the year is not Christmas, but Easter, *Pasca*. The date of Easter is reckoned in a different way to that in the west, and the celebration is focussed on the Resurrection rather than the Crucifixion. On Good Friday a service marks the Descent from the Cross and the *Epitafion* containing the body of Christ is paraded through the streets. In some places an effigy of Judas Iscariot is burnt or blown up. This latter can be a spectacular event as all Greek men love playing with dynamite and the effigy is inevitably stuffed with it. All Greek homes brew up a soup from the offal of the lamb which is to be eaten on the Resurrection and depending on your inclination, the soup may be tasty or you may have problems sampling even a spoonful of assorted tripe and other organs.

Cave-like interior of a small orthodox chapel. Unfortunately more and more are being locked because of theft of the icons and ornaments

Late Saturday night there is the *Anestisi* mass to celebrate Christ's return. In the church all the lights are turned out and then from behind the altar screen the priest appears with a lighted candle and proceeds to light the candles of those in the church. Everyone responds with *Kristos Anesti* (Christ is risen) and there is a procession with the lighted candles through the streets to the sound of fire-crackers and sky-rockets, or any other explosive devices that are to hand. This is not a good time to be in trouble at sea as a lot of out-of-date flares are used up – though don't be tempted yourself as it is against the law to do so and there have been prosecutions. The traditional greeting everyone utters at this time is *Kronia Polla* (Many years or Long life). In the home boiled eggs, traditionally dyed red, are dished out and the normal sport is to bet your egg against the others, in the manner of conkers, or to surprise your friends with a solid rap on the head with the egg to crack the shell.

There are many local saints' days in the villages and towns and the whole place will often close down for them even if they are not on the list of state holidays. Greeks normally celebrate not their birthday, but the day of the saint they are named after – their name-day. In some churches there are icons to a saint reckoned to provide an above average service and these will have numerous votive offerings. Many of these are simple affairs, a pressed metal disc showing what blessing is required, whether for an afflicted limb, safety at sea, a new-born baby or a family house. Some of the older votive offerings are more ornate and elaborate, sometimes a painting or a model of a ship where thanks are given for survival at sea, or a valuable brooch or piece of jewellery for some other blessing. Greek churches are wonderful places, the *iconostasis* always elaborate and adorned, and the interior a dark and mystical place. It constantly amazes me that even in the most out-of-the-way places, on a rocky islet or a remote headland, that every church and chapel and shrine will be newly whitewashed and cleaned and will have an oil lamp burning or ready to burn in it.

Food

Greek food is not for the gourmet, rather it is plain wholesome cooking that goes with the climate and the Greek idea that a meal is as much a social occasion as a culinary experience. This is not, emphatically not, to say that Greek food is not enjoyable. I love the unadulterated flavours of charcoal-grilled fish with a squeeze of lemon over it, or a *salata horiatiki*, the ubiquitous mixed salad swimming in olive oil and peppered with *feta* and black olives – the simplicity of the combination of ingredients brings out the best in them. In some restaurants and in Greek family cooking you will come across dishes that have been lost in the tourist areas where either the lethargy of taverna owners or the whingeing of visitors for a bland 'international' cuisine revolving around steak and chips has removed them from the menu. Some of the island tavernas still have a dish or two specific to the island or region such as Cephalonian meat pie on Cephalonia, but for the majority the dishes on the menu are those which are simply prepared and cooked and a few favourites such as *moussaka* and *stifadho*.

The principal meal in Greece is the midday meal and most oven-cooked dishes are prepared in the morning for this meal. In the evening these dishes will simply be partially reheated and served up as an overcooked lukewarm mess. Restaurants in Greece are categorised as either an *estiatorio* (a restaurant), a taverna (a simple tavern), or a *psistaria* (a restaurant specialising in fresh prepared food, mostly grilled meat), but the distinctions between these have now become so

Octopus drying in the sun for charcoal grilling in the evening

Astakos usually means, crayfish as here, and not lobster proper

blurred that most restaurants call themselves a taverna.

The menu in a taverna will have two sets of prices, one with service and one without, and since all food comes with service you pay the higher price. In fact waiters are paid on results and the difference between the two prices goes to them which explains why some waiters work their butts off and others, often family who are not paid on results, loaf about ignoring your frantic pleas for a drink. In most Greek tavernas you will be invited into the kitchen or to a counter displaying the food to make your choice, a handy convention that gets over the problem of knowing what it is you are ordering from the menu. Only in the flasher restaurants will you be requested to order from the menu and there will normally be an English translation on the menu or on a board on the wall to help you out in most places.

A typical Greek meal will be a starter and main course with other side dishes ordered at random. Dessert is not normally served in a taverna although you may get fresh fruit or yoghurt. When ordering don't order everything at the same time as it will all arrive at once or sometimes you will get the main course first and the starter second. Often the food will be just warm, it having been set aside to cool as Greeks believe hot food is bad for you, a belief that has some backing from the medical community. If you get everything in order and hot, and things have improved in recent years, you are on a winner. If you don't, just order another bottle of wine and settle yourself in for the evening like the other Greeks around you – after all, what have you got to do that's so important after dinner.

Below there is a list of the common dishes you will come across though obviously they vary in finesse and taste from taverna to taverna according to the skills of the cook.

Soups, salads and starters

Avgolemono	Egg and lemon soup, often with a chicken and rice broth
Fakes	Lentil soup
Fasolada	Bean soup
Hortosoupa	Vegetable soup
Psarossoupa	Fish soup
Tzatziki	Yoghurt and chopped cucumber dip
Taramasalata	Fish roe dip
Melitzanasalata	Aubergine dip
Patatasalata	Potato salad
Skordhalia	Potato and garlic dip, sometimes accompanies other dishes as a piquant sauce
Salata horiatiki	Mixed salad, usually tomatoes, cucumber, onion, green pepper, black olives, and *feta*
Domatasalata	Tomato salad
Salata marouli	Green salad, usually lettuce
Horta	Spring greens, often including rocket and spinach
Rizospanaki	Rice mixed with spinach
Piperies psites	Baked peppers
Melitzanes tiganites	Fried aubergines, delicious if freshly fried
Kolokithakia tiganites	Fried courgettes
Fasolia yigandes plaki	Giant or butter beans in a tomato sauce
Tiropita	Cheese wrapped in *filo* pastry, mini-versions of the large snack *tiropitas*

Some of the above can accompany the main course.

Main courses

Brizola khirino	Pork chop, normally charcoal-grilled
Brizola mouskhari	Beef chop, normally charcoal-grilled
Paidhakia	Lamb chop, normally charcoal-grilled
Souvlaki	Kebab, usually lamb or beef
Keftedhes	Meatballs in a sauce, usually tomato but may be an egg and lemon sauce
Bifteki	A burger, but usually homemade

Fish and chips and chicken-in-a-basket

Kotopoulo	Chicken, may be oven-roasted or spit-roasted
Kokoretsi	An offal (liver, kidneys, heart, tripe) kebab charcoal-grilled. Can be excellent
Moussaka	Aubergine and mince with a bechamel sauce not unlike a Greek version of shepherd's pie
Stifadho	A meat (usually lamb) and tomato stew
Pastitsio	Pasta with a mince and cheese sauce, baked in the oven
Makaronia	Spaghetti, may be with a meat or tomato sauce
Domates yemistes	Stuffed tomatoes
Piperies yemiste	Stuffed peppers
Kolokithia yemiste	Stuffed courgettes
Melitzanes imam bayaldi	Aubergines baked with tomatoes – a dish left over from the Turkish occupation that literally means: 'the imam fainted'

Fish and seafood

Ohtapodhi	Octopus, may be charcoal-grilled or cooked in a wine or ink sauce
Kalamaria	Squid, normally coated in a light batter and deep fried
Soupia	Cuttlefish, normally deep fried
Psaria	Fish, normally fried or grilled
Barbouni	Red mullet
Fangri	Bream
Sfiritha	Grouper
Tonnos	Tuna
Xsifia	Swordfish
Marithes	Whitebait normally deep fried, you eat them head and all
Garidhes	Prawns, normally fried or grilled
Astakos	Crayfish

Desserts

Normally desserts and sticky sweets are found in a Zakhoroplasteia (patisserie) and in some of the up-market cafés.

Baklava	Honey and nut mixture in filo pastry
Kataifi	Honey and nut mixture in a sort of shredded wheat

Rizogalo	Rice pudding
Galaktobouriko	Custard pie
Loukoumadhes	Small doughnuts in honey
Pagota	Ice-cream

There will also be assorted sticky cakes, though I personally find most of them too sugary.

Wine-making the old fashioned way in Vassiliki – this vintage contained significant quantities of dead wasps and a bit of cigarette ash to give that certain Greek cachet

Wine

Greek wine is a source of mystery to most western oenophiles. There are grape varieties in Greece few have ever encountered before. The production is so inconsistent that wines vary radically from year to year. Most of the wines are oxidised or maderised. Storing wine properly is virtually unknown and most wine is new wine. Until 1969 there was no real government control of wines of a specific origin. To compound all of this wine will often be sitting in a shop window where it gets a dose of sunlight every day. Given all these problems it is amazing that some Greek wine is as good as it is. On the plus side Greek oenology is on the mend and given the climatic conditions, the interesting grape varieties, and the excellent results of a few wine producers who have imported new wine-making technology and nurtured their product, the portent for the future is good. We may well see a renaissance in Greek oenology that will return it to its ancient elevated status.

Vines for wine-making were growing in Greece before anyone in France or Spain had ever seen or heard of the plant or its product. Estimates vary, but probably sometime around the 13th to the 12th centuries BC Greek viticulture was well established. The mythic origins of the introduction of the vine are associated with Dionysis and trace the route of the vine from India and/or Asia to Greece. Dionysis was said to be the son of Zeus and Semele (daughter of Cadmus, King of Thebes) who was brought up in India by the nymphs and taught the lore of the vine and wine-making by Silenus and the satyrs – sounds a wonderful childhood to me. He journeyed from India across Asia Minor to Greece bringing the vine and accompanied by a band of followers.

One can imagine a religious cult growing up around wine, the visions and hallucinations from imbibing it could only have been supernatural, and the introduction of it to Greece would have been unstoppable, hence its incorporation into the mythic universe of the ancients. The Homeric *Hymn to Dionysis* tells of his journey around the islands distributing the vine and describes vine leaves sprouting from the masthead of his ship. Nor is it surprising that the cult of Dionysis was associated with the release of mass emotion, was a fertility cult, and that the Dionysian Festival included wild uninhibited dancing and at times

Greek wine is not helped by a dose of sunlight everyday

violence and sacrifice – all things associated in one way or another with alcohol today.

There is no way we can know what ancient wine was like. It was referred to by its place of origin, thus Pramnian, Maronean, Khian, Thasian, and Koan wine were mentioned by name much as we mention a Bordeaux or Côte du Rhône today. Whether or not it was all resinated as in the ubiquitous *retsina* surviving today is unknown. Most likely amphoras of wine were sealed with a resin mixture to prevent oxidation and this imparted a flavour to the wine. Over time it was assumed that the resin itself, and not the exclusion of oxygen, prevented wine going off and oxidizing and so resin was added directly to the wine to produce *retsina*. It is unfortunate that many people only get to drink bottled *retsina* today as the stuff from the barrel is superior and should be drunk as a new wine. Much of the bottled *retsina* and some of the barrel *retsina* is simply bad wine that can only be made to taste palatable by resinating it.

In the Ionian there are a number of wines that deserve mention, though they are not all easily obtainable.

Mainland

Zitsa AO Good white from Ioannina. Made from the Debina grape by the local co-operative, drink it young.

Corfu

Theotoki Roppa Excellent reds and whites from Kakotriyis, Petrokorintho, Robola, and Sauvignon blanc made near Roppa. Almost impossible to find, but try.

Santa Domenica Good reds and whites from Kakotriyis grapes made near Levkimmi.

Grovino Good red made near Roppa.

Levkas

Santa Maura Red made by the local TAOL co-operative in Levkas.

Cephalonia

Robola of Cephalonia AO Good white produced in Cephalonia as its name indicates. Made from Robola grapes and variable in quality.

Gentilini Excellent whites produced in Argostoli. Made from Chardonnay, Tssaoussi, Robola, and Sauvignon blanc varieties by a small vineyard under Nikolaos Kosmetatos. Difficult to find but worth the effort.

Calliga Good reds and a rosé.

Manzavino Reds and a rosé.

Laguna Good white though variable.

Zakinthos

Verdea A dry astringent white famous in Zakinthos and produced by a number of wine-makers. It is not consistent and should be drunk early.

There are also a number of Muscats that are considered to be good quality, though they are not to my taste. The *Samos Muscat* from the island is considered the best, although *Muscat of Cephalonia* and *Muscat of Patras* produced by

THE REAL GREEK WINE LIST

All rounders
Whites Cambas White, Kretikos White, Asprolithi, Ilioni, Semeli White, Viognier.
Reds Cambas Red, Kretikos Red, Nemea, Porfyros.
Crustacea and fish
Whites Spiropoulos Mantinea, Roditis Alepo, Tselepos Mantinea, Adoli Ghis, Robola of Kefallonia, Thalassitis White, Athiri-Assyrtiko, Tselepos Barrique, Traminer (Averoff), Sauvignon Blanc (Hazimichalis).
Poultry and pork
Whites Strofilia White, Notios White, Megas Oenos, Chateau Julia Chardonnay (Lazardis).
Reds Athanassiadi, Notios Red, Ampellochora, Katogi Averoff, Domaine Mercouri, Satirikon (Oenotekhniki).
Red meat and game
Whites Amethystos (Lazaridis), Minoiko, Antonopoulos Chardonnay.
Reds Naoussa, Strofilia Red, Ramnista, Naousa Grand Reserve, Amethystos, Kava Red, Megas Oenos, Cabernet New Oak (Antonopoulos).

Achaia Clauss also get a mention. Sweet red liqueur wine vaguely resembling port is produced from the Mavrodaphne grape and *Mavrodaphne of Patras* produced by *Achaia Clauss* and *Mavrodaphne of Cephalonia* are passable port-type wines. Many of the local wine shops have a local Mavrodaphne in stock and this is often acceptable.

At *The Real Greek* restaurant in London the owner has put together a fine list of bottled wines that are reproduced here and would be hard to better. The cooking is good too, with the normally robust Greek cuisine refined and fused into one of the best menus in London (book ahead for a table).

Background basics

Getting there

There are good land, sea and air communications to Greece and to the Ionian islands and mainland.

By air

The area is well served by airports and there are numerous scheduled and charter flights to all of them.

Corfu Has scheduled and charter flights every day from many European destinations. Internal flights to Athens.

Aktion near Preveza and Levkas Has charter flights, mostly from the UK. Internal flights to Athens.

Cephalonia Has charter flights, mostly from the UK and Germany. Internal flights to Athens.

Zakinthos Has charter flights from the UK and other European countries. Internal flights to Athens.

Apart from these airports you can fly into Athens and get a connecting flight to one of the regional airports, though as they are often full it pays to book the flight in advance. There are also regular buses to Patras (about 2½ hours) and four buses a day to Levkas (about 4½ hours).

By sea

Ferries run from Trieste, Venice, Ancona, Bari, Otranto and Brindisi. The two places most people aim for are Ancona and Brindisi.

Gaios. Step ashore into the town square – that is if you can get a berth here

Brindisi Has traditionally been the main ferry terminal for western Greece and according to the demand has between four and eight companies operating services. Prices are keen with all the competition and there will always be several services on any one day. Depending on the company the ferries usually stop at several ports in the Ionian, among them: Corfu, Igoumenitsa, Paxos, Vathi (Ithaca), Sami (Cephalonia) and Patras.

Prices for any of the crossings are seasonal with peak prices in July, August and part of September. In the winter and spring the number of crossings is reduced and in some cases ferries may be switched to another service altogether. Out of season it is probably best to make for Ancona or Brindisi.

Getting around

By Land

The drive through France and Italy to catch a ferry from one of the Italian ports to the Ionian can be done in two days, although three is more relaxed. With the introduction of the Euro in 2002 the drive through EU countries is simpler than ever, with little border control within EU countries although there is greater security on borders leaving the EU. Once in Greece a private car can stay on an unlimited basis, provided it is registered in an EU country.

By local ferry

Corfu Regular daily service to Igoumenitsa from Corfu town and Levkimmi (Kavos) in the south of the island. Services to Paxos also run daily, some via Igoumenitsa, and trip boats run from Levkimmi. You may also get connections to Cephalonia on a Corfu to Patras ferry. Weekly ferry and seasonal trip boats from Sidhari to Erikoussa.

Paxos Connections from Igoumenitsa and a *caique* runs daily from Parga in summer.

Levkas Regular service from Nidri to Vathi and Spartakhori on Meganisi. Daily service to Frikes on Ithaca and Sami or Fiskardo on Cephalonia from Vassiliki.

Ithaca Daily connections to Patras, Astakos and Sami from Vathi. Also from Pis'Aitou to Sami.

Cephalonia Seasonal ferries to Patras from Sami, also to Astakos, Vathi and Pis'Aitou (Ithaca). Daily service to Killini from Poros and Argostoli. Connections from Pessades to Ayios Nikolaos on Zakinthos.

Zakinthos Daily connections to Killini from Zakinthos town. Numerous trip boats in summer.

Killini Daily connections to Patras and the Ionian islands listed above.

Some of these routes operate only in the summer and some may disappear altogether if they prove unprofitable. Likewise new services appear if an operator feels he can make a profit.

Water-taxis and tripper boats

In the more touristy areas like Corfu and Paxos water-taxis run trips to nearby beaches or villages. Tripper boats also run from anywhere there is a sizeable concentration of tourists and it is possible to get a one-way trip on one of these. Local *caiques* can also be hired to do short trips across or

FERRY ROUTES THROUGH THE IONIAN

between islands – there is no standard rate and it is up to you and the boatman to come to a mutually agreeable price.

Buses

Local bus services vary widely between the islands, but even the best of the services are infrequent. To get about by bus you will need to check departure times the day before and to exercise a little and sometimes a lot of patience. The larger islands, Corfu, Levkas, Cephalonia and Zakinthos have the best services while smaller islands like Ithaca have an intermittent service. On the mainland opposite bus services are also infrequent and you will have to budget a whole day to get to most places and back.

Taxis

Most of the islands and the mainland towns and larger villages have taxis or you can phone for one. Fares are reasonable as long as there is a meter and it works or the price is roughly agreed upon first. In some of the more touristy spots like Corfu or Argostoli on Cephalonia, tourists are fleeced by drivers, but on the whole little of this goes on.

Hire motorbikes are the cheapest way to get around and can be found on the major islands – just keep your wits about you when dealing with local traffic

Hire cars and bikes

In many of the tourist resorts you can hire a car or jeep, or more commonly a motorbike of some description. Hire cars and jeeps are expensive in Greece and if there are not four people it is not really worth it unless you are feeling frivolous.

Hire motorbikes come in all shapes and sizes from battered Honda 50's to 500cc brutes. Under EU laws many hire shops now ask for a licence and some may refuse you a bike if you do not have a motorcycle licence. And where once it was rare to be offered a helmet, now some hire shops insist that you at least take one with you. The reliability of hire bikes varies considerably with some bikes only a year or so old and others still struggling along after years of battering by would-be TT riders. On the whole I have found the Honda/Suzuki/Yamaha step-through 50's to be the most reliable even when getting on in years and the larger tyres compared to scooters make them safer on gravel roads.

All of the operators charge you for insurance, but read the small print as it doesn't seem to cover you for very much. You are expected to return the bike if it breaks down and to pay for any damage to the bike if you have an accident. Bear in mind that Greece has the highest accident rate in Europe after Portugal and that on a bike you are vulnerable to injury. Even coming off on a gravel road at relatively low speed can cause serious gravel burns, so despite the heat it is best to wear long trousers and solid footwear. Roads on the islands are usually tarmac for the major routes and gravel for the others. Despite all these warnings a hire bike is the best way to get inland and with care you can see all sorts of places it would be difficult for a car to get to.

Walking

There are some fine walks around the islands and on the mainland coast. The main problem is finding a good map as most locally produced maps should be treated with a healthy scepticism. Tracks which have long since disappeared will be shown and new tracks will be omitted. The best policy is to set out with the spirit of exploration uppermost and not plan to necessarily arrive somewhere, rather to dawdle along the away. This mode of walking is encouraged by the energy-sapping heat of the summer. Take stout footwear, a good sun-hat, sunglasses, sun-bloc cream, and most importantly a bottle of water.

Shopping and other facilities

Provisioning

In all but the smallest village you will find you can obtain basic provisions and in the larger villages and tourist areas there will be a variety of shops catering for your needs. Greece now has a lot more imported goods from the other EU countries and you will be able to find familiar items, peanut butter, bacon, breakfast cereals, even baked beans in the larger supermarkets and specialist shops. Imported items are of course more expensive than locally produced goods. Shopping hours are roughly 0800 to 1300 and 1630 to 2000, though shops will often remain open for longer hours in the summer if there are customers around, especially in tourist spots.

Meat Is usually not hung for long and is butchered in a peculiarly eastern Mediterranean way – if you ask for a chicken to be quartered the butcher picks up his cleaver and neatly chops the chicken into four lumps. Salami and bacon are widely available in minimarkets.

Fish Except for smaller fish is generally expensive. Some fish, like red snapper and grouper, are very expensive and prawns and crayfish have a hefty price tag except off the beaten track.

Fruit and vegetables Fresh produce used to be seasonal, but now EU imports mean more is available longer. It is prudent to wash fruit and vegetables before eating them raw.
  Farmed fish provide cheaper alternatives, and farmed mussels are also available.

Bread Greek bread straight out of the oven is delicious, but it doesn't keep well. Bakers are a growth industry in Greece and even small villages often have a good baker with all sorts of bread, from white through all shades of brown. They will also often have mini-pizzas, cheese or spinach pies, bacon and egg pies, stuffed croissants, in fact whatever the baker thinks he can sell. Beware though, most are all but sold-out by lunchtime.

Staples Many items are often sold loose. Some staples, loose or packaged, may have weevils.

Cheese Imported cheeses such as Dutch *edam* or *gruyère* are now widely available courtesy of the

In Greece a supermarket is really a minimarket and a minimarket is very 'mini'

EU. Local hard cheeses can also be found and *feta* is available everywhere.

Yoghurt Greek yoghurt is the best in the world as far as I am concerned. Use it instead of salad dressing or cream.

Coffee and tea Instant coffee is comparatively expensive. Local coffee is ground very fine for 'Greek coffee' and tends to clog filters. Imported ground coffee is available. Good teabags can be hard to find and expensive.

Wines, beer and spirits Bottled wine varies from good to terrible and is not consistent, usually because it is not stored properly. Wine can be bought direct from the barrel in larger villages and towns and at least you get to taste before you buy. *Retsina* is also available bottled or from the barrel. Beer is brewed under licence (*Amstel* and *Mythos* are the most common), is a light lager type and eminently palatable. Local spirits, *ouzo* not dissimilar to *pastis*, and Greek brandy, often referred to by the most common brand name as just *Metaxa*, are good value and can be bought bottled or occasionally from the barrel.

Banks

Eurocheques, postcheques, travellers cheques, the major credit cards (*Access* and *Visa*) and charge cards (*American Express* and *Diners Club*) are accepted in the larger towns and tourist resorts. You will need your passport for identification. Many places now have an ATM, (automatic teller machine) or 'hole-in-the-wall

The ubiquitous *periptero*, a covered stall selling cigarettes, sweets, ice-cream and cold drinks, aspirin and sun-tan oil, useless beach toys, newspapers, indeed anything which can be squeezed into or around a couple of square metres and it will likely have a metered telephone as well

machine', which will give you cash from the major credit cards with a pin number. *Visa* or *Mastercard* generally do the trick and you will be charged at the Euro exchange rate on the day. Most UK banks also charge a handling fee on top.

For smaller places, carry cash. Banks are open from 0800–1300 Monday to Friday. Most post offices and some travel agents will change travellers cheques and Eurocheques.

Telephones

You can direct dial from almost anywhere in Greece. The telephone system is not too bad although it is not unusual to get a crackly line and sometimes to be cut off or find someone else talking on your line. Telephone calls can be made from a kiosk with an orange top to it, a blue-top kiosk is for domestic calls only. In the towns there will be an OTE (Overseas Telephone Exchange) where you can make a metered call and pay the clerk on completion. Telephone calls can also be made from metered telephones in a *periptero* although the charge will be higher than at the OTE.

Telephone cards are now widely available and can be purchased from grocery and other shops, even from the *periptero* that have metered telephones.

Mobile digital phones using the GSM system can be used in Greece as long as your service provider has an agreement with one of the Greek mobile phone companies. You may be required to leave a deposit with your service provider before you leave. In most places the phones automatically lock into the system and coverage in the Ionian is good with this exception: if you are in a bay with high land blocking out the signal then you may not be able to use the phone. Paradoxically the system often works better when you are out sailing around.

Alternatively if you a staying in Greece for longer periods it may be worth while buying a Greek 'pay as you go' SIM card for your GSM phone. You will get your own Greek mobile number with cheap local call charges. Unlike using your UK mobile, you can receive calls from abroad at no cost.

IDD code for Greece 30. IDD code for the UK 44.

Email

There are a number of ways of sending and receiving email while cruising. The following is a brief round-up of ways and means of doing so.

1. Using a laptop computer, a GSM phone and dedicated connection cord you can connect at 9600 baud wherever you can get a signal. 9600 baud is not a very fast speed these days but it is sufficient for text based email. Transmission charges vary not only with your local provider in Greece, but also with your provider in the UK or wherever your phone is registered. Your ISP may have either a local number or a standard international number for use while abroad.

   Improved transmission speeds are claimed for many new phones, but it is worth remembering that these speeds are reliant on the capability of the local network. In practice most networks are a long way from supporting the speeds quoted by the phone manufacturers.

2. Internet cafés. Many quite small places have a cyber-café these days and if you have an internet email provider then it takes little time to download and send mail using a floppy disk. If you do not have a laptop to compile mail on and download it from the desktop in the café then most cyber-cafés will let you print out the mail for a small fee. Costs are low and of course connection rates are high at typically 56K. I use this method of connecting when emailing or receiving large files or when I feel like a coffee with my mail.

3. Acoustic couplers. This sort of connection whereby you use an acoustic coupler onto the mouthpiece of a public phone used to be popular but connection rates are slow and errors can creep in. It is unusual to get connection rates much over 2400 baud.

4. HF Radio. There are a number of companies who will transmit data via HF radio including Sail Mail, Pinoak, GlobeEmail and the Ham Radio Network. Data rates are slow, typically less than 2400 baud, and costs for the service are relatively expensive for the commercial concerns (the Ham network is a co-operative group and you must be a licensed ham operator to use it). In addition you must make a substantial investment in a HF modem and the appropriate software. For the Mediterranean the system is probably too expensive in investment and running costs but does have the advantage of operating in many parts of the world.

5. Magellan GSC 100. This is a combined GPS and email device. The email is sent and received via the ORBCOMM satellite network. Because of the cost of the service it is really only suitable for short messages and besides the small keypad interface would make it tedious to send long messages. Like the HF radio services it does offer near global coverage.

6. Using a satellite system such as INMARSAT you can send and receive email just about anywhere in the world. INMARSAT transmissions vary depending on the system used. INMARSAT B (replacing INMARSAT A) offers fast enough speeds for video conferencing, but is also the most expensive and biggest of the range. The costs of the systems are expensive and transmission charges are expensive, typically $2–6 a minute.

7. Other satellite phone services. A number of new satellite phone services are beginning operation using either high (GEO), medium (MEO) or low (LEO) earth orbiting satellites.

   Iridium The failed Iridium system formerly run by Motorola has been bought by a consortium and is now operational. Data transmission rates are 9600 baud. Coverage is worldwide using LEO satellites.

   Globalstar Coverage over most land areas and the Mediterranean using LEO satellites, but patchy or non-existent (as yet) for offshore waters. Data transmission at 9600 baud.

   Thuraya Using one GEO satellite, covers mid-Atlantic to India except for low latitudes. Another GEO satellite planned. Data transmission and the phone incorporates a GPS receiver.

   Emsat Uses one GEO satellite, giving coverage of northern Europe and the Mediterranean.

8. Plugging in to a conventional socket. If you can find somewhere to plug into a conventional telephone socket ashore with (usually) a meter on the time used, then this is a quick and easy way to send and receive email using your own laptop.

Public Holidays

Jan 1	New Year's Day
Jan 6	Epiphany
Mar 25	Independence Day
May 1	May Day
Aug 15	Assumption
Oct 28	Ochi ('No') Day
Dec 25	Christmas Day
Dec 26	St Stephens Day

Movable
First Day of Lent
Good Friday
Easter Monday
Ascension

In addition many of the islands or regions have local Saints days when a holiday may be declared and some shops and offices will close.

Sailing information

Navigation

Navigation around the islands and along the coast is predominantly of the eyeball variety. The ancients navigated from island to island using prominent features on the coast quite happily and this is basically what yachtsmen still do in Greece. Eyeball navigation is a much maligned art, especially now that electronic position finding equipment has arrived on the scene, but for the reasons outlined below, it is still essential to hone your pilotage skills.

For good eyeball navigation you need the facility to translate the two-dimensional world of the chart into the three-dimensional world around you. Pick out conspicuous features like a cape, an isolated house, a knoll, an islet, and visualise what these will look like in reality. Any dangers to navigation such as a reef or shoal water may need clearing bearings to ensure you stay well clear of them. Any eyeball navigation must always be backed up by dead reckoning and a few position fixes along the way.

Anyone with electronic position finding should exercise caution using it close to land or dangers to navigation. The paradox of the new equipment is that while you may know your position, often to an accuracy of 100m or less, the chart you are plotting your position on is not accurate in terms of its latitude and longitude. Most of the charts were surveyed in the 19th century using astronomical sights and the position of a cape or a danger to navigation, while proportionally correct in relation to the land mass, may be incorrect in terms of its latitude and longitude. Some of the charts carry a warning, and corrections for latitude and longitude, usually the latter, of up to 1M! Consequently you are in the anomalous position of knowing your position to perhaps within 200m, but in possession of a chart which may have inaccuracies of a mile in its longitude. Blind acceptance of the position from electronic position finding equipment can and has lead to disaster.

Navigation and piloting hazards

The comparatively tideless waters of the Mediterranean, a magnetic variation of just over 2° east, and the comparatively settled summer patterns remove many of the problems associated with sailing in other areas of the world. Just having no tidal streams of any consequence to worry about enhances your sailing a hundredfold. Despite this there are hazards to navigation which while not specific to the Mediterranean, should be mentioned here.

Haze
In the summer a heat haze can reduce visibility to a mile or two which makes identification of a distant island or feature difficult until you are closer to it. Sailing from Paxos down to Preveza or Levkas you may not be able to positively identify features until you are two miles or so off. Heavy rain cleanses the air and dramatically improves visibility.

Sea mist
In parts of the Ionian, especially around the north of Corfu and in the Corfu channel, there may be a dense radiation fog in the morning which can sometimes reduce visibility to half a mile or less. The mist will gradually be burned off by the sun and by afternoon should have disappeared.

Reefs and rocks
The Ionian has only a few isolated dangerous rocks and reefs and with care these are normally easily spotted. However this absence of large areas of shoal water or extensive reefs can make the navigator lazy in his craft. The clarity of the water in the Mediterranean means you can easily spot rocks and shallows from the colour of the water. Basically deep blue is good, deep green means its getting shallow, lighter green means watch out, and brown lets you identify species of molluscs at first hand. However with a chop of any sort the whitecaps on the water can make identification of shallow water and reefs difficult and you should give any potential dangers a wide berth.

Fishing nets
Care is needed around local fishing boats or in isolated bays where there may be surface nets laid. Vigilance is needed not to run over a net and incur not just the wrath of a fisherman, but most likely the net wrapped tightly around the propeller.

Fickle winds in the Meganisi channel

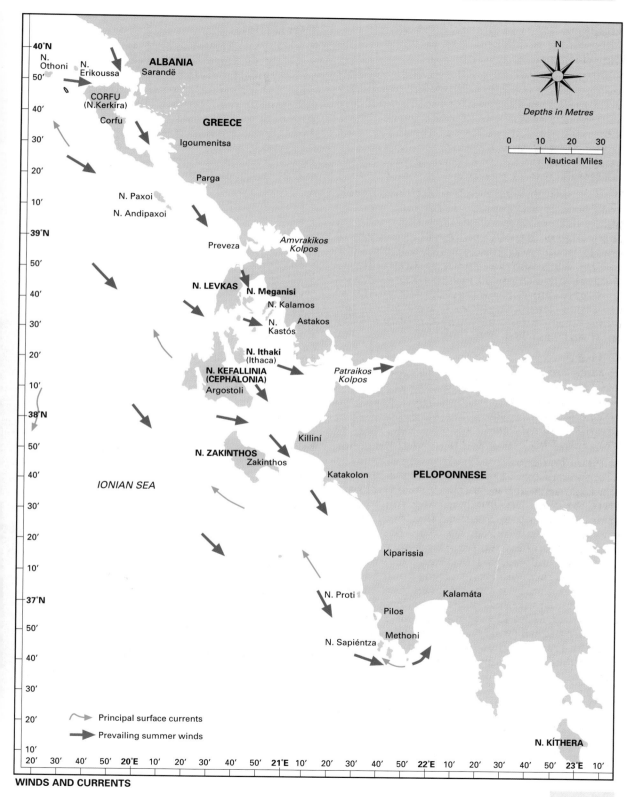

N

Depths in Metres

| 0 | 10 | 20 | 30 |

Nautical Miles

40°N
N. Othoni
N. Erikoussa
ALBANIA
Sarandë
50'
CORFU
(N.Kerkira)
40'
Corfu
GREECE
30'
Igoumenitsa
20'
Parga
10'
N. Paxoi
N. Andipaxoi
39°N
Preveza
Amvrakikos Kolpos
50'
40'
N. LEVKAS
N. Meganisi
N. Kalamos
30'
N. Kastós
Astakos
20'
N. Ithaki
(Ithaca)
N. KEFALLINIA
(CEPHALONIA)
Patraikos Kolpos
10'
Argostoli
38°N
50'
Killiní
N. ZAKINTHOS
Zakinthos
40'
Katakolon
PELOPONNESE
IONIAN SEA
30'
20'
10'
Kiparissia
37°N
N. Proti
Kalamáta
50'
Pilos
40'
N. Sapiéntza
Methoni
30'
20'
Principal surface currents
Prevailing summer winds
10'
N. KÍTHERA
20' 30' 40' 50' **20°E** 10' 20' 30' 40' 50' **21°E** 10' 20' 30' 40' 50' **22°E** 10' 20' 30' 40' 50' **23°E** 10'

WINDS AND CURRENTS

23

Lights

Although the islands and coast are quite well lit, the sheer extent of them means that it is impossible to light any but the most common routes used by ships and commercial fisherman. Navigation at night out of the common routes should be avoided unless you are familiar with the area.

Winds

The winds in the Ionian are remarkably consistent in the summer. From June until the end of September the wind blows down onto the Ionian from the NW to WNW. Generally it arrives around noon, blows between Force 3 to 6 (10 to 25kt), and dies down at sunset. It is a proper gentleman's wind that allows you to motor northwards in the morning calm should you so desire and leaves the evenings calm so you can enjoy an anchorage in comfort. The prevailing wind is channelled and funnelled by the land masses in its way so that it can blow off the land and down channels from anywhere between N and SW. Off the high land there can be strong gusts on the leeward side such as on the E side of Ithaca and Zakinthos. In July and August the wind is at its strongest and the presence of dense clouds hugging the summits of the islands, particularly Cephalonia, Ithaca and Zakinthos, tells you it is going to be fairly strong that day.

In the evening there may be a katabatic wind off the high mainland mountains generally blowing from the NE. This usually gets up around 2000 and can blow up to Force 6 (25kt), but usually less, and normally dies down after 2 or 3 hours.

In the spring and autumn there may be gales from the south when a depression passes over. Sometimes a moderate to strong southerly will quickly turn to the north and increase in strength, so care is needed when sheltering from southerlies. Thunderstorms, usually with an associated squall (winds can be up to 40+kt), also occur in the spring and autumn, but are generally over within 2 to 3 hours. A *scirocco* may also blow from the south, usually in the spring, bringing a sickly humid heat and the red sand of the Sahara from whence it comes.

Berthing

Berthing Mediterranean-style with the stern or bows to the quay can give rise to immense problems for those doing it for the first time, or even the second or third time. Describing the technique is easy: the boat is berthed with the stern or bows to the quay with an anchor out from the bows or stern respectively to hold the boat off the quay. It is carrying out the manoeuvre which causes problems and here a few words of advice may be useful, but will not replace actually doing it.

Everything should be ready before you actually start the manoeuvre. Have all the fenders tied on, have two warps coiled and ready to throw ashore with one end cleated off, and have the anchor ready to run, in the case of a stern anchor have the warp flaked out so it does not tie itself into knots as you are berthing. The manoeuvre should be carried out slowly using the anchor to brake the way of the boat about half a boat length off the quay. The anchor should be dropped about three or four boat lengths from the quay and ensure you have sufficient chain or warp beforehand to actually get there.

Many boats have a permanent set-up for going bows-to so there is not too much scrabbling around in lockers to extract an anchor, chain and

Berthing bows-to: kedge out the back, fenders out, mooring warps ready

A strong *maistro* is often signalled by dense cloud hugging the summits of the islands

warp. This can be quite simple: a bucket tied to the pushpit to hold the chain and warp and an arrangement for stowing the anchor on the pushpit. Boats going stern-to must have someone who knows what they are doing letting the anchor chain go. It should run freely until the boat is half a boat length off the quay. When leaving a berth haul yourself out with the chain or warp using the engine only sparingly until the anchor is up – it is all too easy to get the anchor warp caught around the propeller otherwise.

The good tourist

However much you hate being tagged with the label, we all are tourists, some longer term than others. If you like you can be the good holiday-maker, visitor, yachtsman, or whatever name that doesn't offend you. What is required of those of us who travel upon the water around the Ionian islands, or anywhere else in the world for that matter, is that we do not stain the waters we travel upon or the land we come to. Some tourists regrettably seem not to have any understanding of the delicate relationship between tourist and locals and are so boorish and spend so much time whining about the faults of the country they have come to that I wonder why on earth they bothered – possibly because nobody in their own country could stand them. Which is not to say

that the locals are angels, they can manage to emulate the worst of American and British excesses and can be as boorish as the worst of us, but then this is their country and so I suppose they have more license to do so. Local interaction aside, there are a number of substantive local complaints about us.

Rubbish

Many of the smaller islands are just not geared up to disposing of the rubbish brought in by tourists and on the water you will be visiting some small villages or deserted bays where there are literally no facilities at all. You should take your rubbish with you to a larger island and dispose of it there. Even the larger islands have questionable methods of disposing of rubbish and there is nothing wrong in trying to keep the number of convenience wrapped goods you buy to a minimum. My particular *bête noire* is bottled drinking water as the discarded plastic containers can be found everywhere and when burnt, (the normal way rubbish is disposed of on the islands) produce noxious gases and dangerous compounds.

It hardly needs to be said, you would think, that non-biodegradable rubbish should not be thrown into the sea. Even biodegradable rubbish such as vegetable peelings or melon rind should not be thrown into the water, except when you are five or more miles from land, or it ends up blowing back onto the shore before it has decayed or been eaten by scavengers. Toilets should not be used in harbour if there is one ashore, or they should be used with a holding tank. Holding tanks should not be emptied until you are well offshore.

I don't think most people can quarrel with the above, but sometimes I hear the argument that because the locals pollute the sea and the land, then why bother yourself. It is true that the locals are often the worst offenders, but consciousness of pollution and individual responsibility for it is spreading through the villages and towns and as tourists we have a responsibility to keep the wilder parts of Europe free from pollution when we have made such a tip of our own backyard. Moreover many of the sources of pollution are there to service the tourist trade and if there were no tourists then there would be less pollution.

Noise pollution

This comes in various forms from the simple banality of making your presence known in an anchorage with the tape or CD player turned up full blast to inconsiderate motorboat owners with loud exhausts. Those who play loud music in deserted bays should reflect as to whether they would not be more comfortable in a noisy urban disco, preferably in their own country. Another annoying noise in an anchorage is the puttering of generators and those who need to run their generator all day and night might consider whether they may not be more comfortable in a marina where they can hook up to shore-power – there are a lot of nice marinas along the French and Italian Riviera. Motorboaters with noisy outboards and inboards, and water-bikes which somehow always contrive to have the most irritating whine in their exhaust note as well as the most irritating people driving them, should keep well clear of boats at anchor and keep noise levels to a minimum when they do come into an anchorage or harbour, or anywhere for that matter where they intrude on the peace and quiet most people, themselves included, come for.

Safety and seamanship

In some places small powerboats and inflatables roar around an anchorage without regard for those swimming in the water. This is not just irritating but potentially lethal. If you have ever seen the injuries sustained by someone who has been hit by a propeller, you will immediately understand my concern. Accidents such as these frequently result in death or for the lucky, horrible mutilation. Those on large craft should also keep a good lookout when entering an anchorage where people are in the water or when their own crew is swimming off the back of the boat.

Remember when picking up someone who has fallen overboard to engage neutral or you may replace death by drowning with death by propeller injuries. Although water-bikes do not have a propeller they are just as lethal if they hit someone at speed and injure them – it doesn't take long to drown.

In many bays swimming areas are now cordoned off with a line of small yellow conical (usually) buoys. Although this restricts the area you can anchor in, the swimming areas should be avoided and in fact you can be fined for anchoring in one of these areas. Certainly the locals will let you know in no uncertain terms that you should not be there.

Many of the smaller islands just cannot cope with piles of rubbish from summer-time tourists who apparently cannot read – close by this sign on Kalamos were bags of rubbish left by visiting yachts

Conservation

Under the aegis of organisations like the World Wildlife Fund, Greenpeace, and Friends of the Earth, conservation is coming of age in Greece. Amongst the campaigns being waged two are of especial importance in the Ionian.

The first is the Monk Seal Project. The Mediterranean monk seal, *Monachus monachus*, is numbered amongst the twelve most endangered animals in the world and is the rarest species of seal left. It is specific to the warm waters of the Mediterranean although small numbers are found on the Atlantic coast of Morocco. There are estimated to be only 500 to 800 of these animals left with approximately half the population in Greece.

The Ionian is one of the places where the seal is found and in Fiskardho the Monk Seal Project funded by the World Wildlife Fund is attempting to educate local fishermen and tourists about the species and its habitat. One of the big problems is the encroachment of tourism into the habitat occupied by the seals. Illegal spear-fishing using sub-aqua equipment is eroding the food supply – Italian visitors have been cited as the chief culprits and there have been several convictions, but the blame does not lie solely here. Small powerboats and inflatables with powerful outboards exploit quiet places and the coastal caves where these retiring animals live. Those on the water and the land can help by keeping away from coastal caves and rocky coastlines and at all times should avoid making too much noise – the seals are easily frightened. Any illegal fishing whether by sub-aqua divers or dynamiting should be reported to the port police or any other authority. If you want further information or can help with the project contact Alibi Panou, Fiskardho, Cephalonia, Greece.

The second is the Sea Turtle Project on Zakinthos. The loggerhead turtle, *Caretta caretta*, needs a fine, sandy, south-facing beach to lay its eggs in. Unfortunately one of the principal breeding sites at Laguna on Zakinthos is also a popular tourist beach and unrestricted development along it has made it more difficult for the beleaguered turtles to use the site. The waters around Kolpos Laguna have now been made a restricted zone for any craft on the water and the zone is enforced by the coastguard and local police. (For details on the restricted zones see the relevant section under Zakinthos in Chapter 3.) The restricted zone should give the turtles a bit more of a chance to breed successfully in this area and those on the water should endeavour to stay away from the area during the breeding season.

For more information contact
National Marine Park of Zakinthos
Ktrio Dimotikou Diamerismatos Argasiou,
29100 Argasi, Zakinthos
www.nmp-zak.org

Weather forecasts

Because of the high and large landmasses in Greece it is extremely difficult to predict what local winds and wind strengths will be. The Greek meteorological service does its best but nonetheless it faces an almost impossible task. Fortunately the wind direction and strength in the Ionian is remarkably consistent in the summer. For those who really want to listen to a weather forecast try the following sources, but remember to interpret them leniently.

VHF frequencies

A forecast for all Greek waters in Greek and English is given at 0600, 1000, 1600, 2200 UTC. For local time add 2 hours in the summer. The forecast covers Greek waters for Z+12 hours. Gale warnings are given at the beginning of the broadcast.

Forecast areas to listen to are North Ionian and South Ionian.

A *sécurité* warning on Ch 16 gives all the channels for the different shore stations and you will need to choose whichever shore station is closest to you. In fact the advice notice is garbled so quickly it is almost impossible to decipher, but is worth listening to in case VHF frequencies for the different shore stations are changed.

Ionian shore station list

Corfu (Kerkira)	02
Cephalonia	27
Petalidhi (Kalamata)	83
Kithera	85

A weather forecast from Italy is transmitted continuously on VHF Ch 68 and can be picked up in the Ionian. It is broadcast using synthesised voices and gives a forecast for the whole of the Mediterranean, first in Italian and then in English. The areas of the north and south Ionian are covered by the Italian forecast areas Ionio Settentrionale and Ionio Meridionale.

HF Radio

A forecast in Greek and English is forecast on the following frequency for SSB radios. (Receivers only will need a BFO switch.)
Kerkira   2830kHz   0633, 0903, 1533, 2133 UT

Broadcast Radio

For the eastern Mediterranean a marine weather forecast is given by the Austrian short wave service (in German only) on 6150MHz/49m at 0945 and 1400 local time (from 1 May to 1 October only).

Television

On several of the television channels a weather forecast in Greek with satellite photos and wind forces and directions shown on the map is given after the news around 2100 local time. Many cafés and bars will have a television somewhere and you should ask for *o kairós parakaló*.

Port police and marinas

The port police get a weather forecast faxed to them several times a day. Depending on the inclination of the port police it is worthwhile asking them for a forecast.

Most of the few marinas in Greece post a forecast, often one taken off the internet.

Safety and rescue services

The SAR co-ordinating centre for all rescues is in Piraeus.

PIRAEUS COASTGUARD JRCC
MMSI 237 673 000

VHF Ch 16	DSC VHF
MF 2182kHz	DSC MF 2187·5 kHz
	DSC HF

☎ 210 411 2500 *Fax* 210 411 5798

The regional SAR station covering the Ionian Sea is in Patras. In addition all Greek Port Authorities operate a SAR unit with Coastguard officers. The Hellenic Coast Guard and Olympia radio monitor DSC, VHF, MF and HF frequencies including 2182kHz and VHF Ch16.

USEFUL WAYPOINTS

⊕1 1M S of Othoni SW point light
39°49'.2N 19°23'.2E

⊕2 1M N of Ak Skotini (Erikoussa N end)
39°55'.1N 19°34'.8E

⊕3 ½M N of Ak Ay Aikaterini (Corfu N)
39°49'.85N 19°51'.05E WGS84

⊕4 Mid-channel between Nisis Peristerai and Ak Psaromita
39°47'.29N 19°57'.19E WGS84

⊕5 ¼M E of Ifalos Serpa (Corfu N Channel)
39°46'.24N 19°57'.86E WGS84

⊕6 ½M E of Ak Kommeno (Gouvia N entrance)
39°39'.82N 19°52'.45E WGS84

⊕7 ½M E of Ak Sidhero (Corfu E side)
39°37'.36N 19°56'.61E WGS84

⊕8 1M E of Ak Levkimmi light
39°27'.6N 20°05'.7E

⊕9 1M S of Asprokavos (Corfu S end)
39°20'.7N 20°06'.8E

⊕10 Igoumenitsa Channel (Outer buoys)
39°30'.10N 20°12'.06E WGS84

⊕11 ½M N of Lakki entrance
39°15'.0N 20°08'.0E

⊕12 1M S of Nds Dhaskalia (S end Andipaxoi)
39°06'.8N 20°15'.0E

⊕13 Entrance to Preveza channel (outer buoys)
38°55'.90N 20°43'.66E WGS84

⊕14 N Entrance to Levkas Canal
38°50'.79N 20°43'.27E WGS84

⊕15 ½M S of Ak Dhoukato (Levkas SW end)
38°33'.17N 20°32'.46E WGS84

⊕16 S end of Levkas Canal
38°47'.54N 20°43'.58E WGS84

⊕17 N end Meganisi Channel
38°40'.10N 20°43'.72E WGS84

⊕18 S end Meganisi Channel
38°37'.88N 20°43'.88E WGS84

⊕19 1M SE of Ak Kefali (Meganisi S end)
38°34'.8N 20°49'.8E

⊕20 N end of Ithaca Channel
38°28'.47N 20°35'.73E WGS84

⊕21 ¼M N of Ak Marmara (Ithaca N end)
38°30'.47N 20°38'.93E WGS84

⊕22 ¼M E of Ak Ay Illias (Ithaca NE end)
38°26'.07N 20°42'.91E WGS84

⊕23 ¼M E of Ak Ay Ioannis (Ithaca SE end)
38°19'.20N 20°46'.36E WGS84

⊕24 1M S of N.Vardhianoi light (Cephalonia SW end)
38°06'.9N 20°25'.6E

⊕25 ½M W of Ak Ay Theodhoroi (Kolpos Argostoliou)
38°11'.5N 20°27'.5E

⊕26 2¼M E of Ak Mounda (Cephalonia SE end)
38°03'.20N 20°49'.97E WGS84

⊕27 1M N of Ak Skinari light (Zakinthos N end)
37°56'.9N 20°42'.2E

⊕28 1M S of Ak Marathis (Zakinthos SW end)
37°37'.9N 20°50'.0E

⊕29 ½M E of Ak Krioneri light (Zakinthos E side)
37°48'.26N 20°54'.89E WGS84

⊕30 ½M S of Ak Kamilavka (Mitika)
38°39'.77N 20°55'.21E WGS84

⊕31 Mid-channel Stenon Kalamou (N end)
38°37'.01N 20°56'.26E WGS84

⊕32 Mid-channel Ak Tourkovigla – N. Kaloyiros (SW approach to Astokos)
38°29'.83N 21°01'.90E WGS84

⊕33 ½M S of Ak Oxia
38°16'.60N 21°05'.95E WGS84

⊕34 1M N of Ns Kavkalidha (Killini)
37°57'.5N 21°07'.3E

⊕35 ½M S of Ak Katakolon
37°37'.38N 21°21'.63E WGS84

⊕36 N end of Proti Channel
37°04'.14N 21°33'.87E WGS84

⊕37 ¼M W N. Pilos light
36°54'.08N 21°40'.09E WGS84

⊕38 ½M N of Ak Karsi light (N. Sapientza)
36°48'.23N 21°42'.24E WGS84

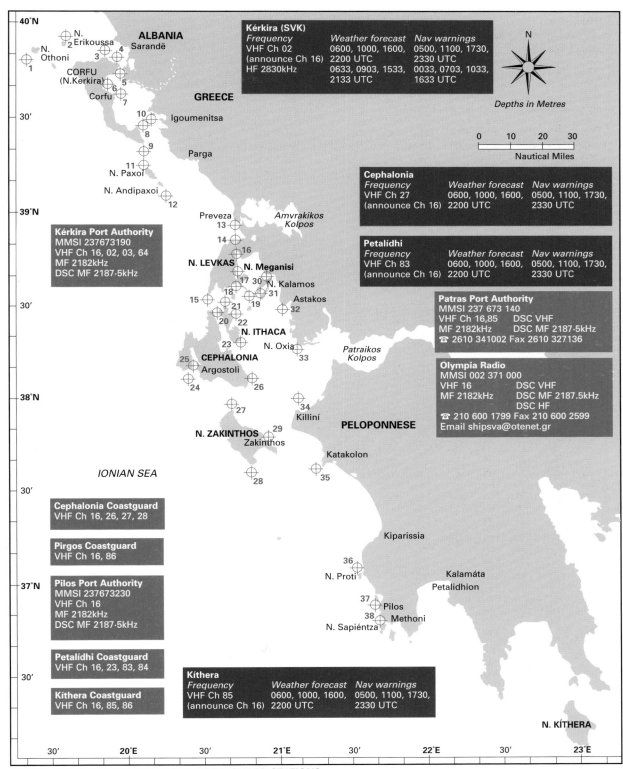

Kérkira (SVK)

Frequency	Weather forecast	Nav warnings
VHF Ch 02	0600, 1000, 1600,	0500, 1100, 1730,
(announce Ch 16)	2200 UTC	2330 UTC
HF 2830kHz	0633, 0903, 1533,	0033, 0703, 1033,
	2133 UTC	1633 UTC

ALBANIA
Sarandë
N. Erikoussa
N. Othoni
CORFU
(N.Kerkira)
Corfu
GREECE

Igoumenitsa
Parga
N. Paxoí
N. Andipaxoi

Preveza
Amvrakikos Kolpos
N. LEVKAS
N. Meganisi
N. Kalamos
Astakos
N. ITHACA
N. Oxia
Patraikos Kolpos
CEPHALONIA
Argostoli
N. ZAKINTHOS
Zakinthos
PELOPONNESE
Killiní
Katakolon

IONIAN SEA

Cephalonia

Frequency	Weather forecast	Nav warnings
VHF Ch 27	0600, 1000, 1600,	0500, 1100, 1730,
(announce Ch 16)	2200 UTC	2330 UTC

Petalídhi

Frequency	Weather forecast	Nav warnings
VHF Ch 83	0600, 1000, 1600,	0500, 1100, 1730,
(announce Ch 16)	2200 UTC	2330 UTC

Kérkira Port Authority
MMSI 237673190
VHF Ch 16, 02, 03, 64
MF 2182kHz
DSC MF 2187·5kHz

Patras Port Authority
MMSI 237 673 140
VHF Ch 16,85   DSC VHF
MF 2182kHz   DSC MF 2187·5kHz
☎ 2610 341002 Fax 2610 327136

Olympia Radio
MMSI 002 371 000
VHF 16   DSC VHF
MF 2182kHz   DSC MF 2187.5kHz
                  DSC HF
☎ 210 600 1799 Fax 210 600 2599
Email shipsva@otenet.gr

Cephalonia Coastguard
VHF Ch 16, 26, 27, 28

Pirgos Coastguard
VHF Ch 16, 86

Pilos Port Authority
MMSI 237673230
VHF Ch 16
MF 2182kHz
DSC MF 2187·5kHz

Petalídhi Coastguard
VHF Ch 16, 23, 83, 84

Kíthera Coastguard
VHF Ch 16, 85, 86

Kíthera

Frequency	Weather forecast	Nav warnings
VHF Ch 85	0600, 1000, 1600,	0500, 1100, 1730,
(announce Ch 16)	2200 UTC	2330 UTC

Kiparissia
N. Proti
Kalamáta
Petalidhion
Pilos
Methoni
N. Sapiéntza

N. KÍTHERA

N
Depths in Metres

0   10   20   30
Nautical Miles

USEFUL WAYPOINTS/WEATHER AND COASTGUARD STATIONS

WEATHER FORECASTS ON THE INTERNET

There are a number of good sources for weather on the internet. If there is a cyber café around half an hour should be plenty to get a forecast.

Poseidon weather for Greece

http://www.poseidon.ncmr.gr/weather–forecast.html
Up to 72 hour surface wind forecasts for Greece. The best source of weather for Greek waters. The chart gives wind direction with colour coding for the wind force in Beaufort (the colour bar is on the right hand side of the chart) On the left hand side is a table for current and up to 72 hours forecast.
Choose the one you want and press DISPLAY

Mediterranean sailing

http://www.medsail.nildram.co.uk
Rod Heikell's site for sailing in the Mediterranean with a weather page and links to those sites he considers most useful in terms of content and download time. Includes 36 hour surface charts from NEMOC, satellite loops, wind and sea forecasts from a number of sources.

University of Athens

http://weather.noaa.gov/weather/GR–cc.html
Weather observations at Greek Airports.

DWD Mediterranean Forecast

http:www.dwd.de/forecasts/seemm.htm

3-day text forecasts for a number of Mediterranean areas including the eastern Mediterranean. In German only, but easily read in table form.

Weather Online

www.weatheronline.co.uk/sail.htm
Current satellite and radar imagery and text forecasts.

Jcomm by Meteo-France

weather.gmdss.org/III.htm
A text only forecast identical to the NAVTEX forecast.

SMS text message forecast

Poseidon provide a web based weather forecast and can now send a basic forecast by text message to your mobile phone. Text: W GPS (co-ordinates of position for forecast) and send to 4264

eg *W GPS 38 50 20 43* requests a forecast for the area around Levkas.

The message gives wind strength and direction for 24 hours in three 6 hour intervals.

eg *24/9 15 4B (NW)* indicates Force 4 NW wind at 1500 hours UTC on 24 September

The service costs around 25 cents per message.

SAFETY OF LIFE AT SEA REGULATIONS (SOLAS)

From 1 July 2002 skippers of craft under 150 tons are required to conform to the following SOLAS V regulations. The regulations will almost certainly be applied in piecemeal fashion in the Mediterranean countries. What follows is very much my précis of the regs and at the time of writing clarification is ongoing.

R19   A radar reflector (3 & 9 GHz) must be exhibited.

R29   A table of life saving signals must be available to the skipper/helmsman at all times.

R31   Skippers must report to the coastguard on dangers to navigation including (R32) wrecks, winds of Force 10 or more and floating objects dangerous to navigation.

R33   Vessels must respond to distress signals from another vessel.

R34   Passage planning is now mandatory. If a vessel involved in an incident can be shown not to have engaged in detailed passage planning the skipper can be prosecuted. This is a very messy regulation and may involve having corrected charts and up-to-date pilotage instructions on board and keeping a ship's log.

R35   Distress signals must not be misused.

All Hellenic Coastguard and Olympia Radio stations for the area are shown on the plan.

A number of harbours operate patrol boats which while not strictly lifeboats are often heavy weather craft. A number of lifeboats and a number of large RIBs are also operated around the coast. For major operations the navy and air force will be called up and rescue helicopters, aircraft and large offshore vessels can be called out.

About the plans

The plans which accompany the text are designed to help those cruising in the area to get in and out of the various harbours and anchorages and to give an idea of where facilities are to be found. It is stressed that many of these plans are based on the authors sketches and therefore should only be used in conjunction with the official charts. They are not to be used for navigation.

Waypoints

Waypoints are given for all harbours and anchorages. The origins of the waypoints vary and in a large number of cases the datum source of the waypoint is not known. Where I have taken waypoints for a harbour or anchorage it has a note after it reading WGS84. All these waypoints are to World Geodetic Survey 1984 datum which, it is intended, will be the datum source used throughout the world. Most GPS receivers automatically default to WGS84.

It is important to note that plotting a waypoint onto a chart will not necessarily put it in the position shown. There are a number of reasons for this:

1. The chart may have been drawn using another datum source. Many of the Imray-Tetra charts use European datum 1950 (Europe50). There are many other datum sources that have been used to draw charts.
2. All charts, including those using WGS84, have errors of various types. Most were drawn in the 19th century and have been fudged to conform to WGS84 (the term 'fuzzy logic' could aptly be used).
3. Even when a harbour plan is drawn there is still a significant human element at work and mistakes easily creep in, as I know to my cost.

The upshot of all this is that it is important to eyeball your way into an anchorage or harbour and not just sit back and assume that all those digits on the GPS display will look after you. In the case of waypoints I have taken and which are appended WGS84, the waypoint is indeed in the place shown. In the case of other waypoints it can be derived from the light position, from reports in my files, or from other sources.

In this edition I have also included useful waypoints which are listed at the beginning of the relevant chapter and included on the location maps. As above, any that are appended WGS84 are from my own observations using the radar for distance off and a compass bearing for the direction. Given that some radar distance off readouts can be a bit of a guesstimate, these should be used with every caution. In most cases I have endeavoured to keep a reasonable distance off so that an error of say, 50m, should be unimportant when the waypoint is 0·5 NM from the land. There are other occasions when I have shaved a cape or islet and the distance off is considerably less.

All waypoints are given in the notation:

degrees   minutes   decimal place of a minute

It is important not to confuse the decimal place of a minute with the older 60 second notation.

Levkas
Lu Michell

I. Corfu and nearby islands

Quick reference guide

	Shelter	Mooring	Fuel	Water	Provisions	Tavernas	Plans
Corfu							
Limin Kerkira (Corfu)	A	AB	A	A	A	A	•
Nisis Vidho	C	C	O	O	O	O	•
Mandraki (POIATH YC)	A	A	B	A	A	A	•
Ormos Garitsas	B	C	O	O	A	A	•
NAOK Yacht Club	A	A	O	B	A	A	•
Gouvia Marina	A	A	A	A	A	A	•
Ipsos	C	A	O	O	A	A	•
North coast							
Sidhari	O	C	O	B	C	C	
Rodha	O	C	O	O	C	B	
Ay Aikaterina	C	A	O	O	O	O	
Ormos Imerola	C	C	O	O	O	O	•
Kassiopi	B	A	B	B	B	A	•
Ormos Vroulias	C	C	O	O	O	O	•
North Corfu Channel							
Ay Stefanos (E coast)	B	C	O	B	C	B	•
Ormos Kouloura	C	C	O	O	O	C	•
Ormos Kalami	C	C	O	O	C	C	•
Ormos Agni	C	C	O	O	O	C	•
East coast							
Benitses	O	C	B	B	B	B	•
Voukari	O	C	O	O	C	C	•
Petriti	B	AC	O	B	C	C	•
Ak Levkimmi	O	C	O	O	O	C	
Kavos (Levkimmi)	C	AB	O	O	O	C	•
West coast							
Ay Stefanos (W coast)	B	AB	B	B	B	B	•
Ormos Ay Yeoryiou	C	C	O	O	O	C	•
Palaiokastrita	B	AC	B	B	C	A	•
Pentati	C	C	O	O	C	C	•
Ay Yeoryios	B	C	O	O	B	B	
Othoni							
Ormos Ammou	B	C	O	B	C	C	•
Ormos Fiki	O	C	O	O	O	O	
Errikousa							
South Bay	B	C	O	O	C	C	•
Mathraki							
Plakes	B	A	O	B	C	C	•
Paxoi and Andipaxoi							
Lakka	B	AC	O	A	C	C	•
Longos	C	AC	O	O	C	C	•
Limín Gaios	A	A	B	A	B	A	•
Mongonisi	A	AC	O	O	O	C	•
Andipaxoi	C	C	O	O	O	C	

Corfu

(Nisos Kérkira)

Ask anyone to name three Greek islands and Corfu will invariably be one of them – Mikonos and Rhodes will probably be the other two. It is famous and infamous as a resort island. Aircraft are continually landing and taking off at the small airport, ferries churn in and out of Corfu harbour from Italy and Patras, car ferries shuttle back and forth from Igoumenitsa, all helping to swell the population from its normal 100,000 to over half a million in the summer months. It is impossible to ignore this congestion, parts of the island have wall-to-wall concrete hotels as awful as any in the Mediterranean, but surprisingly enough it is possible to escape the crowds – though it takes a little effort.

Corfu's popularity is derived largely from its geography. The sickle-shaped island lying just off the mainland coast of Greece and Albania has three times the rainfall of the islands in the central Aegean and consequently is a verdant green place even through the hot summer months. It has good beaches and a typically sunny Mediterranean climate, the necessary ingredients along with the green and shaded interior for an idyllic holiday island. Couple this with a recent history of comparatively benign English administration leaving familiar architecture and natives used to English peculiarities, and it was inevitable that the crowds would flock here.

Numerous invaders throughout the known history of the island have probably prepared the Greeks for the invasion of sun-starved northerners at the end of the 20th and into the 21st century. The name of the island that most people know it by is not even the official one. Properly it is Kerkira after the ancient name Corcyra, but this was changed during the Byzantine occupation to Corypho (peaks) after the twin peaks in the town, which was then bastardised by the Venetians to Corfo or Corfu.

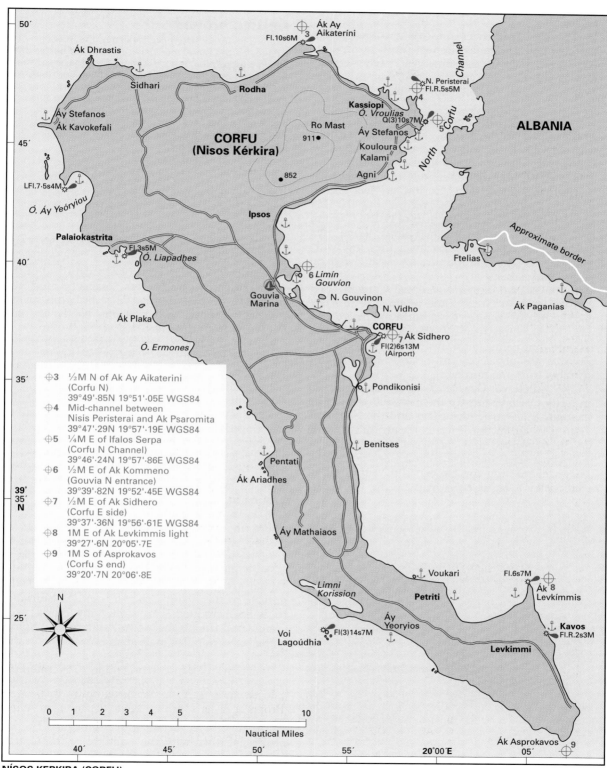

50′

Ák Dhrastis

Sidhari

Ák Ay
Aikateríni
Fl.10s6M 3

Rodha

Kassiopi
O. Vroulias
Q(3)10s7M

N. Peristerai
Fl.R.5s5M
4

North Corfu Channel

ALBANIA

Áy Stefanos
Ák Kavokefali

Ro Mast
911

CORFU
(Nisos Kérkira)

Áy Stefanos
Kouloura
Kalami

Agni

5

45′

LFl.7·5s4M

Ó. Áy Yeóryiou

852

Ipsos

Palaiokastrita

Fl.3s5M
Ó. Liapadhes

Approximate border

40′

Gouvia
Marina

Limín
Gouvíon
6

N. Gouvinon

N. Vidho

Ftelias

Ák Paganias

Ák Plaka

CORFU

Ák Sidhero
7
Fl(2)6s13M
(Airport)

Ó. Ermones

Pondikonisi

35′

Benitses

39°
35′
N

Pentati

Ák Ariadhes

Áy Mathaiaos

Voukari

Fl.6s7M

Ák 8
Levkímmis

Kavos
Fl.R.2s3M

Limni
Korission

Petriti

25′

N

Áy
Yeóryios

Levkimmi

Voi
Lagoúdhia
Fl(3)14s7M

0 1 2 3 4 5   10

Nautical Miles

Ák Asprokavos
9

40′   45′   50′   55′   **20°00′E**   05′

NÍSOS KERKIRA (CORFU)

History

In 734 BC Corinth established a colony called Corcyra with the main site just south of present-day Corfu town. In the same year a sister-colony was established at Syracuse on Sicily and trade from the south of Italy flowed into Greece via Corcyra, virtually guaranteeing its prosperity. A few remains of the ancient city can be found south of present day Corfu. The ancient harbour was most likely the lagoon next to the airport. It is now very shallow, probably due to silting.

In 665 BC the upstart colony rebelled against Corinth and defeated the Corinthian fleet sent to quell it in what Thucydides recorded as the first naval battle in Greek history. In 433 BC Corinth and Corcyra again clashed and when the Corcyrans asked Athens for help, they indirectly sparked off the Peloponnesian War between Sparta and Athens.

In 200 BC the Romans occupied Corcyra, their first conquest in Greece, and retained it until the decline of the empire. Byzantium inherited it as part of the territory of the Eastern Roman Empire, but being so far away from the centre of power it was neglected and became easy prey for invaders from the north.

Like much of Greece, Corfu was trampled underfoot by invaders for the next 800 years. The Vandals, the Ostrogoths, Slavs and the Normans were the significant invaders until finally the Venetians arrived and claimed Corfu as part of their prize after they had sacked Constantinople. They did nothing for almost 200 years, but in 1386, after a request for help by the Corfiotes,

Corfu old harbour – picturesque but smelly

Getting around

There is an intermittent bus service to the major villages on the island, but generally you are better off hiring a motorbike or a car. One of the legacies of the British was a good road system and the major roads are tarmac and mostly in good condition. Hire motorbikes are a reasonable price, there being some competition between the numerous hire-shops, so check out a few before you hire. Car hire is expensive and really only worthwhile if you have four people to cram into the car or jeep.

Unless you want to mingle with the crowds I suggest you head south towards Ay Mat Theos, Aryirades, and Levkimmi, villages that have more to do with things Greek than things British or German and are also near some of the best and least crowded sandy beaches.

they established a garrison at Corfu town that was the start of more than four centuries of occupation. Venetian control of Corfu and of the other Ionian islands was essential for the protection of their trading fleets bringing spices, especially pepper, and precious goods like silk and ivory, from the east.

When the Turks swept through Greece in the 15th century they left Corfu alone, but in 1537 they turned their attention to the island and landed a large force backed up by cannon. The Turks failed to take the citadel, but sacked the other villages on the island and took nearly half of the population captive. After the siege the Venetians decided the west of Corfu needed extra defences and built the fort above the old harbour which became known as the 'new castle' as opposed to the 'old castle' on the peninsula terminating in Ak Sidhero.

In 1716 the Turks tried again, landing 30,000 troops to take Corfu town. After six weeks of bloody assault on the two forts, the Turks mysteriously gave up and sailed away when it seemed all was lost for the defenders and the capital would fall. The Greeks attributed the miracle to the island's patron saint, St Spiridon, he is also credited with saving the island from famine and the plague, so not surprisingly Spiros is the most popular male name on Corfu to this day.

Venetian rule came to an end in 1797 when the republic fell to Napoleon. French rule brought with it much democratic reform and a good deal of building and re-building around the island. Corfu town was turned into a lookalike French provincial town with the building of the Liston, Corfu's version of the Rue de Rivoli, and a

Myth

Corfu is traditionally identified as Skheria, the island of the Phaeacians, where Odysseus was washed ashore naked and exhausted after his raft broke up on voyage from the island of Calypso to his home on Ithaca. Homer does not mention Corfu in the *Odyssey*, but it has been identified as Skheria since commentaries on Homer began.

There are some silly traditions, many of them recent inventions or reinventions for tripper boat commentaries, associated with the story. The Phaeacians provided a ship to take Odysseus to Ithaca and on its return Poseidon, angry at Odysseus for blinding his son the Cyclops, turned the ship and crew to stone. The stone ship is usually identified as Pondikonisi, the small island off the lagoon to the south of Corfu town, and sometimes as the islet off Ormos Liapadhes at Palaeokastrita.

Palaeokastrita is often identified as the site of the capital of the island under the Phaeacians, a marvellous steep-to site perfect for an acropolis, with a natural harbour below. Homer tells us that Odysseus was washed ashore at the foot of steep cliffs and only escaped being dashed against them by swimming into a river mouth. Such a site exists at Ermones just over 4M down the coast and is popularly identified as the place mentioned in the *Odyssey*. Here Nausicaa, daughter of the king, arrived with her handmaidens to do the family washing in the river and discovered Odysseus. It's a touching story but you have to wonder why Nausicaa struggled all the way from Palaeokastrita to Ermones to do the washing. And if the capital of Skheria was sited around present day Corfu town then it seems unlikely Odysseus would have been rescued from Ermones at all.

Mysteriously the Phaeacians disappeared without trace, no pre-Greek city has been discovered, and the verifiable history of the island begins with a colony from Corinth.

rationalised street plan and construction for the rest.

After the defeat of Napoleon in 1813 Corfu passed to the British and a year later all of the Ionian islands were incorporated into a protectorate under their control. British control was by turns benevolent and repressive. The Corfiotes got good roads, a hospital and university, and importantly religious freedom so they could practice Greek Orthodoxy again. But when Commissioner Maitland refused to let the Corfiotes go to help in the struggle for independence on the mainland in the 1820's, local feelings were embittered against the English and a nationalist movement was formed to agitate for union (*enosis*) with the Greek mainland.

In 1863 Corfu and the other six Ionian islands became part of the newly reborn Greece. The British left behind them not only roads and buildings, but a fondness for cricket and ginger beer amongst the local population. Ginger beer is still brewed and cricket is played on the Esplanade (*Spianada*) every Wednesday and on weekends. During the Second World War Corfu was occupied by the Italians, though it was a benign occupation as acts of war go. When the Germans attempted to move in the Italian forces fought off their erstwhile allies though they were doomed against the superior German forces. In 1944 the Germans left and the British were back

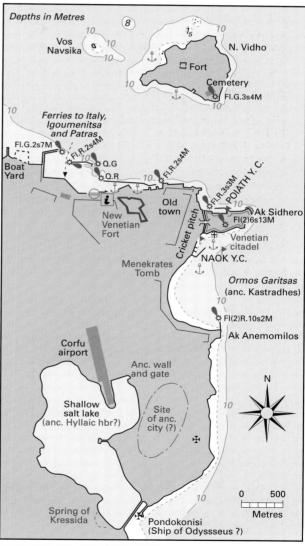

CORFU TOWN AND ENVIRONS

in Corfu to the delight of the Corfiotes. They have been there ever since, an army of tourists that occupy the beaches and bars, though now the Corfiotes are paid handsomely for being occupied.

Limin Kerkira

(Corfu Harbour)

Corfu Harbour is the port for Corfu town, the principal town on the island and with a resident population of 30,000, the largest town in the Ionian islands. Some of the ferries running between Patras and Italy stop here so travellers can get to Patras or across the Adriatic to Brindisi or Ancona. The airport is one of the busiest outside of Athens (and also ranks as one of Europe's top five most dangerous airports) with charter and scheduled flights all over Europe and internal flights to Athens. The car ferries from Igoumenitsa bring in land travellers. And many of the yachts arriving in Greece make this their first stop after crossing from Italy or coming down from the Dalmatian coast. Not surprisingly therefore, Corfu town is many peoples' first introduction to the Ionian islands.

Pilotage

Approach From the north Nisis Vidho obscures most of the buildings in the town. Closer in the huddle of buildings of the old town, the 'old castle' and the lighthouse on Ak Sidhero, and the urban sprawl of Greater Corfu to the west, will be seen. There is a safe passage between Nisis Vidho and Vos Navsika, the rock above water approximately 750m west of Vidho. From the south the 'old castle' on Ak Sidhero stands out well. Normally the large ferries in the commercial port and the car ferries from Igoumenitsa will be seen arriving or leaving.

Mooring If you have to clear in make for the customs quay inside the western breakwater. The shelter here is not always good with a strong NW breeze (the prevailing wind) so it is best to arrive in the morning and aim to be off the quay by midday. Yachts normally go alongside in the E basin and despite the fact

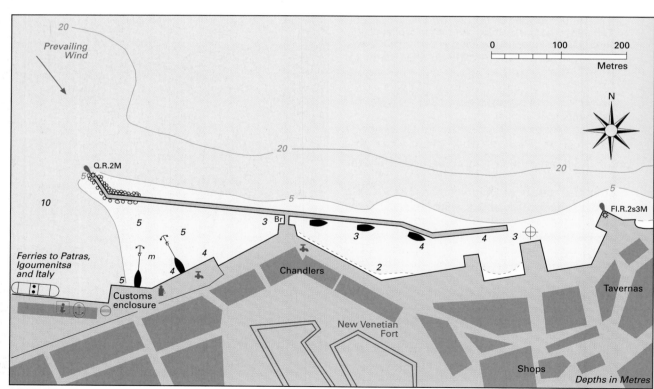

LIMIN KERKIRA (Palaio Limani)
⊕39°37'·66N 19°55'·15E WGS84

Corfu old harbour. There is talk of cleaning it up and making a small yacht harbour close to Corfu town. *Lu Michell*

try *The Venetian Well Bistro* in a courtyard in the old quarter.

Other Internal and international flights. Ferries to Patras and Brindisi. Banks. PO. Hospital. Dentists. Hire cars and motorbikes.

General

Corfu town is a place to wander around rather than one in which to visit monuments, though it has some of those. The streets of the old quarter running off the Esplanade are mostly given over to tourist boutiques selling bad onyx chess sets, T-shirts from China and Korea emblazoned with something along the lines of *I love Corfu* or worse, and tacky local pottery. There are no bargains to be had in the tourist boutiques, but bowls turned

that it is very smelly in here, it is crowded in the summer. Shelter inside is good.

There are plans in the pipeline to smarten up the harbour to encourage more yachts to stay, moving the commercial boats along into the commercial port, sorting out the sewerage and generally cleaning up the quay. This project is likely to take considerable time to come to fruition, indeed if at all.

Yachts wanting to escape the unsavoury E basin can anchor in Ormos Garitsas or berth at the NAOK Yacht Club or you may find a berth at the POIATH Yacht Club in Mandraki harbour. Alternatively head up to Gouvia Marina, where you can also complete entry procedures.

Facilities

Services Fuel and water on the quay in the W basin of the old harbour.

Provisions Ashore there are all the facilities you would expect in a big town. Good shopping for all provisions once you have found your way to the shops and markets behind the 'new castle' out of the touristy part of the town.

Eating out Restaurants and bars everywhere. The *Averoff* behind the E basin is as good as any or for a quiet and slightly more up-market meal

Corfu old town   *Lu Michell*

The unmistakable outline of the old citadel on Ak Sidhero, Corfu

from olive wood and gold and silver are worth looking at.

Away from the tourist alleys the old quarter is a warren of alleys between the Italianate houses and here the sights and sounds approach something closer to everyday Corfiote life. There are a few restaurants and bars tucked away from the mainstream that are worth exploring. On a Wednesday or on weekends an hour or two can be pleasantly wasted sitting in one of the bars on the Esplanade watching a cricket match on the green.

If you feel in need of a little edification about the history and life of Corfu there are several interesting museums.

Archaeological Museum Is situated just south of the Esplanade at Vraila St 5. There are numerous interesting finds from the island, but two stand out. The Gorgon Pediment dating from around 500 BC is a Medusa head with wings on her back and serpents at her head and waist. It is a brilliant piece of Corinthian sculpture that needs no ancient pedigree to vouchsafe it. In an adjacent room is the sculpture of a lion from the same period, probably from the tomb of a warrior.

Museum of Far Eastern Art Situated in the Palace of St Michael and St George on the north side of the Esplanade. Not the sort of museum you might expect to find on a Greek island, but this extensive eclectic collection by a Greek diplomat, Grigorios Manos, was bequeathed to Corfu, and well repays a visit.

Paper Money Museum Situated in the Ionian Bank building on N. Theotoki St. Again not the sort of museum you might expect to find here, but well worth a visit to look at a history of the stuff we all use and are constantly short of.

Museum of Byzantine Art Situated in the Church of the Virgin Mary Andivouniotissa just off Arseniou St which runs around the coast on the N side of the old quarter. Contains a small collection of icons from churches around the island.

The Achillion Not actually in Corfu, but 16km S near the village of Gastouri. However Corfu is the easiest place to arrange a trip to this monument to bad taste. It was built by Empress Elizabeth of Austria, dedicated to Achilles hence the name, and like much Germanic neo-classical architecture, is an awful amalgam of different styles hedged about by bad statuary, the whole being a monument to kitsch that is so awful it is almost good. It is now a casino operated appropriately by a German consortium.

Nisis Vidho

With the prevailing NW winds the anchorage on the S side of Vidho can be used. The bottom comes up very quickly so you will have to anchor in 5–15m where convenient. In calm weather it is possible to anchor in the cove on the west side in 2–10m.

The island was fortified by the Venetians and then by the British. Before the British forces left in 1864 they blew up most of the defensive works on the island to the anger of Corfiotes. Later it became a prison island and then a borstal. Tripper boats run excursions across to the island in the summer and usually include a tour around the eroded rock of Vos Navsika to the west.

Mandraki yacht harbour near Corfu old town   *Lu Michell*

Mandraki (POIATH Yacht Club)

The harbour in Mandraki on the N side of Ak Sidhero is home to two yacht clubs. POIATH is the Hellenic Offshore Racing Club and IOK is the Corfu Sailing Club. You may be able to find a berth in here if there is room. The best bet is to go by land to contact the *marinero* in charge or alternatively try approaching the entrance and see if you are directed to a berth.

An L-shaped mole protects the harbour and the masts of the yachts inside are easily identified. There are 3–4m depths in the entrance and mostly 1·5–3m depths inside off the outer mole. Laid moorings tailed to the quay or to buoys. Good shelter inside. A charge is made.

The harbour is in an enviable situation under the steep walls of the fort on Ak Sidhero and it is a short walk into the centre of town.

Ormos Garitsas

The bay on the S side of Ak Sidhero. Anchor in 5–12m on mud, good holding. Good shelter from the prevailing wind but open to the S.

NAOK Yacht Club

The yacht harbour on the W side of Ormos Garitsas belongs to NAOK: the Nautical Club of Corfu. There are a limited number of berths for visiting yachts in the summer.

There are 3–4m depths in the entrance and 3m depths on the outer end of the mole, decreasing

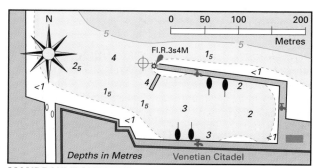

MANDRAKI (POIATH YC)
⊕39°37'·6N 19°55'·7E

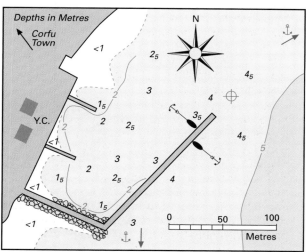

NAOK YC HARBOUR
⊕39°37'·32N 19°55'·65E

further into the harbour. Off the W quay and piers there are a number of shallow patches. Go stern or bows-to the mole where directed or where convenient. The bottom is mud and weed, poor holding in places. Good shelter from the prevailing NW winds. In strong southerlies the harbour is reported to be untenable. A charge is made by the yacht club.

Ashore there are restaurants and bars and there are shops for provisions nearby. Water and showers at the yacht club. The Esplanade is just above the anchorage.

Garitsas or Kastradhes is assumed to have been the Harbour of Alkinoos for ancient Corcyra. The ancient city is scattered over the hill to the south and although the remains of the city wall, several temples, and the possible site of the *agora* have been identified, there is little to see since most of the ancient stone has been 'quarried' over time by the Corfiotes for building materials.

Pondikonisi

S of Garitsas off the end of the shallow lagoon is one of the most photographed places in Corfu, the twin islets of Vlacherna and Pondikonisi. Pondikonisi is the outermost islet and is traditionally said to be the Phaeacian ship that ferried Odysseus home and was turned to rock by Poseidon. Vlacherna is connected to Kanoni on Corfu by a causeway and has the Monastery of Vlachernas on it.

What most guide books neglect to mention is that the peninsula of Kanoni is now irrevocably scarred with some of the worst modern architecture on Corfu and that planes thunder in overhead continually throughout the day – Kanoni and the islets are begrimed with spent aviation fuel and you can't hear yourself speak most of the time. Why anyone would want to come on holiday here is difficult to understand and after looking at the twin islets from seawards, I recommend anyone on the water to desert the flight path and head N or S.

Limin Gouvion and Gouvia Marina

This large landlocked bay lies just over 3M WNW of Limin Kerkira and Corfu town. At the S end of the bay Gouvia Marina has been established and this has become the base for several yacht charter companies in the North Ionian.

Pilotage

Approach Nisis Gouvion in the southern approaches and Ak Kommeno and Vrakhos Foustanopidhima on the N side of the entrance are readily identified. Two large hotels on the N side of the entrance are also conspicuous. Once up to the entrance to the

Pondikonisi before the age of instant hotels and jet engines. Old postcard

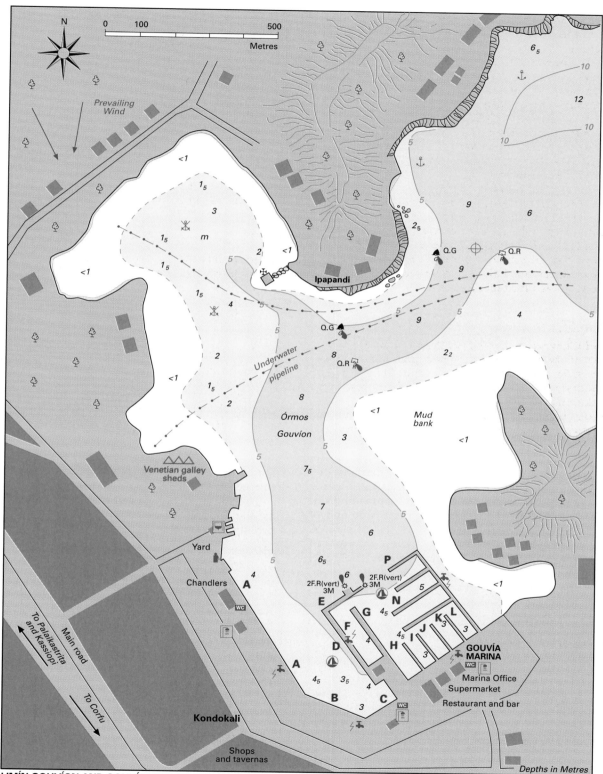

N

0   100   500
Metres

Prevailing
Wind

<1

1₅

3

m

1₅

<1

1₅

1₅

1₅

4

2

2   <1

5

Ipapandi

2₅

Q.G

Q.R

9

9

9

4

5

Q.G

Underwater
pipeline

8

Q.R

2₂

2

1₅

2

<1

8

Órmos

Gouvíon

3

5

Mud
bank

<1

7₅

7

5

6

Venetian galley
sheds

Yard

6₅

P

Chandlers

A

4

2F.R(vert)
3M

6

2F.R(vert)
3M

N

5

E

G

4₅

K **L**

F

4₅

J 3   3

D

4

H

3

**GOUVÍA
MARINA**

A

3₅

4

To Palaikastrita
and Kassiopi

Main road

B

4₅

3₅

C

3

Marina Office
Supermarket
Restaurant and bar

To Corfu

Kondokali

Shops
and tavernas

Depths in Metres

LIMÍN GOUVÍON AND GOUVÍA MARINA
⊕39°39′·53N 19°51′·35E WGS84

Gouvía Marina looking SE   *K & G Marinas*

bay the red and green buoys marking the channel into the bay are readily seen. Care is needed to avoid the mud bank spreading out over half of the channel on the S side and of the shoal water and rocks on the N side. A course of 231° from the S tip of Foustanopidhima bearing towards the hotel above the old galley sheds shows the way in, though with the buoys in place there is little room for confusion.

Mooring Gouvia Marina can be contacted on VHF Ch 69 (call sign *Gouvia Marina*). Berth where directed in the marina where you will usually be assisted by marina staff on the quay. There are laid moorings tailed to the quay.

Shelter in the marina is now much improved with the construction of new piers and is generally good. However some berths are still uncomfortable with the prevailing wind, especially those on the far west quay, and in some cases berths may become very uncomfortable here.

The south anchorage can no longer be used as the marina berths cover the area. It is prohibited to anchor in the north of the bay.

Facilities

Services Water and electricity at all berths. Potable water by tanker. Shower and toilet blocks. Laundry. Fuel dock. Sewage pumpout. 65-ton travel-hoist. Chandlers and yacht repair facilities.

Provisions There is a supermarket in the marina and others in Kondokali high street.

Eating out Restaurant and café at the marina. Others in Kondokali.

Other Banks and PO. Hire cars and motorbikes. Intermittent bus to Corfu town.

General

Gouvia is a bit like a giant Butlins transported to Corfu. This stretch of coast with Kondokali, Gouvia, Dasia, and Ipsos along it has little to do with things Corfiote or even things Greek apart from its geographical location. This area is mostly devoted to cheap package holidays and the means of making those here feel they never left home – English breakfasts, English roasts on Sunday, English pubs, English newspapers and magazines – most of the signs are in English and most of the people you meet will be English apart from a few Continentals who inadvertently booked a holiday here. Many of the buildings are new and nearly all are villas or small hotels and pensions built in the last ten years for the trade in tourists.

Kondokali and Gouvia, small villages as recently as fifteen years ago supported by a little fishing and local agriculture, have disappeared under the onslaught of reinforced concrete. There are still a few spots where things Greek can be found, but its a hard slog finding them.

The old Venetian galley sheds at the N end of the marina are worth a walk though they have not been restored or even protected from the elements. Corfu along with Levkas further south was previously a centre for cigarette smuggling with conspicuous high-powered motorboats berthed in the town centres, but the smuggling days are over and the ex-smugglers are captains of tripper boats or prop up the counters in bars telling stories of derring-do.

Nisos Gouvinon

In calm weather or when the prevailing wind is not blowing strongly you can anchor off the S side of Gouvinon. Care needs to be taken of a shallow patch off the middle of the island and another off the small pier on the SW corner.

Akra Kommeno

The bay on the S side of Ak Kommeno sheltered from the E by Vrakhos Foustanopidhima provides good shelter from the prevailing northwesterlies. Anchor in 5–12m on mud and weed and take a long line ashore if possible. There are several hotels with associated restaurants and bars scattered around the headland.

Ipsos

Part of the ribbon development of holiday complexes that have sprung up around the coast to the north of Gouvia in an attempt to accommodate some of the tourist overflow from Corfu town.

A small harbour has been built towards the south end of the beach, used mainly by small fishing boats and trip boats. To the north of the harbour is a watersports platform that extends out for some distance from the beach. There are 2–3m depths in the entrance to the harbour and 2–2·5m further in. Depths off the rough stone breakwater are not sufficient to go close to. Go stern or bows-to taking a long line to the breakwater. You will need to use your dinghy to get ashore. Adequate shelter from the prevailing NW–W wind but open N–NE.

Tavernas and bars ashore. Good shopping for provisions. Ipsos is a noisy resort area and if you are looking for peace and tranquility then head elsewhere.

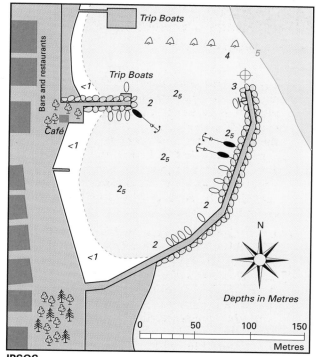

IPSOS
⊕ 39°41'·72N 19°50'·38E WGS84

Ipsos near Gouvia. The harbour is the best thing about Ipsos which has otherwise become a by-word for package-holiday-ville on Corfu
Lu Michell

North coast of Corfu

There are few sheltered places for a yacht to go along the N coast until past Ak Ay Aikaterini.

Note

The advent of new fast ferries running between Greece and Italy has brought with it the problem of massive ferry wash. At speed these ferries push a massive wall of water that crashes into what were otherwise protected anchorages and harbours causing damage to yachts and other small craft. When the ferries first began running they caused a lot of damage and there were thousands of claims against the ferry companies involved. This has caused the ferries to slow down in coastal waters with the exception of the northern approaches to Corfu. What this means is that places like Kassiopi and some of the northern and northeastern bays will experience the wash from these ferries.

If you do experience damage from one of these ferries document the time, damage, etc and make a claim. If possible take photographs and if you

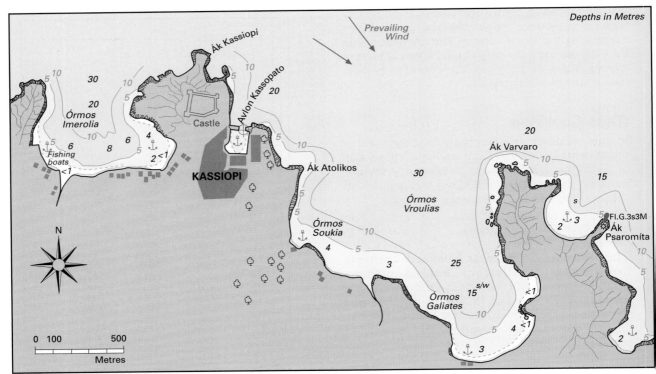

ÓRMOS IMEROLA TO ÁK PSAROMITA
⊕39°47'·48N 19°55'·40E WGS84

get no satisfaction, get in touch with the Greek Tourist Board. Eventually the ferry operators will get the message that speeding in coastal waters is not only environmentally damaging, but it is also going to cost them.

Sidhari

There is a good beach at Sidhari and a short mole where local *caiques* berth, but the anchorage off the beach can only be used in calm weather or light southerlies. Care is needed of rocks and reefs and shoal water bordering the coast. Restaurants and bars ashore.

Rodha

A good sandy beach, but like Sidhari the anchorage can only be used in calm weather. Restaurants and bars ashore.

Ay Aikaterini

⊕ 39°49'·07N 19°50'·59E WGS84

At the NW end of Almiros beach in Ormos Ay Yeoryios is a tiny fishing harbour west of Ak Ay Aikaterini. Depths are mostly <1m and in any case is too small for all but the smallest yachts.

Care is needed of shallows extending northwards off the cape Ak Ay Aikaterini for some distance.

Ormos Imerola

⊕ Fishing boat quay 39°47'·44N 19°54'·56E WGS84

A bay with two sandy beaches close west of Kassiopi. Some shelter from the prevailing westerlies can be found on the W side of the bay. Anchor in 3–5m on mud, sand and weed.

In the SW corner of the bay a concrete apron has been built out to provide a quay for local fishing boats. There may be space to go alongside here, but you will need to move if you take a fishing boat berth. In strong westerlies the bay may become untenable. The overspill of buildings from Kassiopi comes across the isthmus to the bay. Restaurants and bars ashore.

Kassiopi (Avlon Kassopeto)

A small harbour tucked under the east side of the headland with a Venetian castle on the summit.

Pilotage

Approach From the W the castle on the headland and the buildings around Ormos Imerola are readily identified. From the E the houses of Kassiopi will be seen.

Mooring Go stern or bows-to on the E quay. Depths are irregular along the quay and some care is needed. The bottom is mud and weed, adequate holding once the anchor is in. Reasonable shelter from N–NW winds although some swell enters. If the wind goes around to the NE it can get very uncomfortable.

Facilities

Services Water ashore and a petrol station on the outskirts of the village.
Provisions Good shopping for provisions nearby.
Eating out Restaurants and bars around the waterfront.
Other Bank. PO. Hire motorbikes. Tripper boats run around the coast.

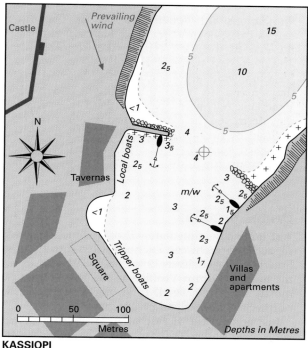

KASSIOPI
⊕39°47'·48N 19°55'·40E WGS84

Kassiopi yacht quay   *Lu Michell*

General

The original small fishing village here has been pretty much swamped by the new buildings, mostly self-catering villas and apartments and small hotels. The place still has a sympathetic feel to it outside of July and August and it is possible to get away on some pleasant walks.

The castle on the hill has Byzantine foundations with Venetian top works. There has been a castle or fort here since Hellenic times. At the end of the 11th century the Norman fleet under Robert Guiscard based themselves at Kassiopi while they sacked the island, though they failed to take the capital. When the Venetians retaliated and the island was retaken they destroyed the fort at Kassiopi so it could not be used by hostile forces again. The inhabitants dispersed throughout the island and the once prosperous town dwindled in size to a small village.

Ormos Vroulias

The large bay immediately E of Kassiopi. In light westerlies a yacht can anchor tucked into Ormos Soukia, a cove halfway down on the W side, or at the head of Ormos Vroulias itself. The bottom is mostly sand and weed. In strong westerlies and northerlies the bay can be untenable.

Just around the E side of Ak Varvaro a yacht can shelter under Ak Psaromita or in the cove just S of it. The latter anchorage is the best and can be

used in moderate to light westerlies – wonderful deserted surroundings and clear water.

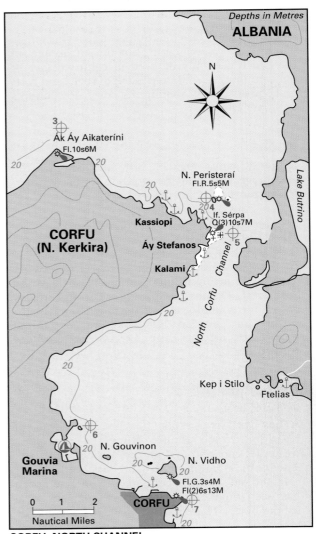

CORFU: NORTH CHANNEL

⊕3   ¼M N of Ak Ay Aikaterini (Corfu N)
      39°49'·85N 19°51'·05E WGS84
⊕4   Mid-channel between Nisis Peristerai and Ak Psaromita
      39°47'·29N 19°57'·19E WGS84
⊕5   ½M E of Ifalos Serpa (Corfu N Channel)
      39°46'·24N 19°57'·86E WGS84
⊕6   ½M E of Ak Kommeno (Gouvia N entrance)
      39°39'·82N 19°52'·45E WGS84
⊕7   ½M E of Ak Sidhero (Corfu E side)
      39°37'·36N 19°56'·61E WGS84

North Corfu Channel

This channel between Corfu and the mainland opposite divides Greece from Albania. Albania is just one mile away from Corfu and in the channel it is less than a mile to this sad, battered country attempting to shrug off its communist legacy.

In the approach from the NW Nisis Peristerai with a small lighthouse on it is easily identified. The passage between Peristerai and Corfu is clear of dangers in the freeway. The danger in the channel is Ifalos Serpa, a reef extending E from a headland just above Ay Stefanos. The reef is marked by a stone cairn in the middle and by a platform and light structure (Q.3s7M) near the end of the reef.

A number of yachts have ripped their bottoms out on the reef including *Carinthia V*, a super yacht built for Helmut Horten, a German department store tycoon. On her maiden voyage the yacht went from Cannes to Athens where the owner and his wife left, ordering the yacht back to Cannes. Speeding up the Corfu channel the yacht hit Serpa and went to the bottom, taking the John Bannenberg interior with it but fortunately not the crew. Herr Horten promptly commissioned *Carinthia VI* though the skipper now tends to avoid Corfu.

On the other side of the channel Albania poses a problem of another sort. Many stories circulate about the dastardly deeds of the Albanian authorities, but these are mostly from people who aren't even sure where Albania is. At present the confused situation in Albania means it should be avoided.

In the past there have been a number of incidents of piracy off the Albanian coast and some off the nearby Greek mainland coast and in Corfu. Albania now appears more settled and recent reports are that there is less anarchy ashore. Even so yachts should keep well off the coast and when approaching the North Corfu Channel keep as close as practicable to the Greek coast. Yachts on passage from Italy can head around the south end of Corfu and then up to Gouvia if there is a real need to get there or alternatively it makes more sense to head for Paxos, Preveza or Levkas. Given the prevailing winds are NW in the summer this presents few problems. At present there is a strong Greek

Ay Stefanos in the North Corfu Channel

Naval presence and this should ensure the safety of craft in the area. However it would pay to keep an eye on developments and act accordingly.

Charter yachts should listen to advice from the area manager or flotilla leader. Generally the advice has been to avoid the area on the mainland side of the North Corfu Channel although in recent years a number of yachts have been returning to the anchorages here. See what the local advice is and follow it.

For the future it is necessary to keep an eye on developments here. One thing that is for sure is that predicting the political path of a newly emerging country such as Albania is next to impossible. After the demise of communism in Albania it was thought the country would soon open up to yachts and tourism to help out the ailing economy. How wrong we were.

Ay Stefanos

A small inlet tucked in S of Ifalos Serpa. Once into the entrance the buildings around the head of the inlet will be seen. Anchor in 2–7m where convenient on mud, sand and weed. Some tavernas have short jetties off the beach where yachts can go bows-to, although you are rightly obliged to use the taverna. Although there are sufficient depths for a small yacht to go bows-to the outer half of the small mole inside, there is rarely room in the summer and anyway you are better off anchored out. This is especially true now because of the wake from the fast ferries which can penetrate the bay. Good shelter from the prevailing winds.

There are numerous restaurants and bars ashore and some provisions can be obtained. Around the slopes are villas built for the more

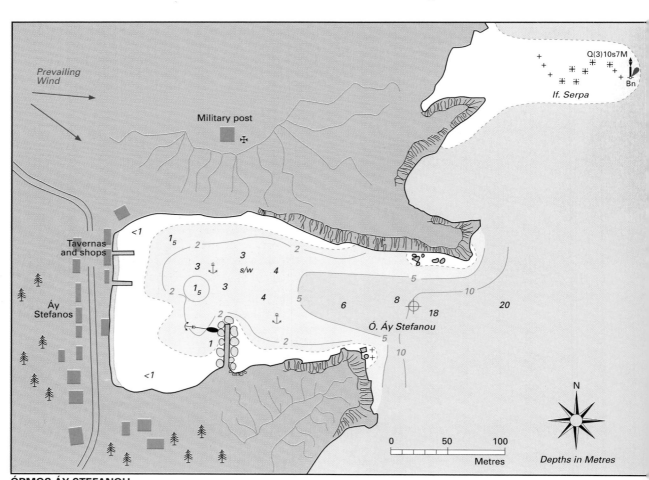

ÓRMOS ÁY STEFANOU
⊕39°45'·90N 19°57'·09E WGS84

discerning self-catering visitors. The bay retains a relaxed and uncrowded feel to it despite the number of restaurants which attract customers from as far away as Corfu who seem undeterred by the winding road down to the village.

Ormos Kouloura

A small bay S of Ay Stefanos. It is immediately recognisable from the small church perched on the edge of a miniature harbour, though from the S you won't see it until close-to. Only very small boats can get into the harbour, there is just over a metre in the entrance and about 1·5m in the middle. Even if you get in there is little room to berth. Care should be taken of the shoal water and reef with less than a metre over it bordering the breakwater for nearly 100m to the N and E.

Yachts can anchor to the W of the entrance to

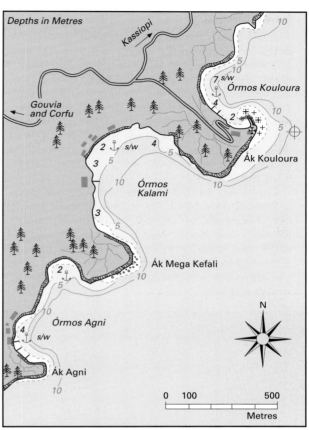

ÓRMOS KOULOURA, KALAMI AND AGNI
⊕39°44'·60N 19°56'·50E WGS84

the harbour and take a long line ashore. Alternatively anchor in 8–15m in the bay. Good shelter from the prevailing winds.

There is a taverna immediately above the harbour which is popular in the day, but by evening the bay is a peaceful place. The surroundings are simply enchanting.

Ormos Kalami

A large bay immediately S of Kouloura. Anchor in 4–10m where convenient. The bottom is sand and weed, good holding. This bay is subject to gusts off the hills with the prevailing northwesterlies so make sure your anchor is well in. Some provisions and tavernas ashore.

The miniature harbour at Ormos Kouloura – only accessible to craft drawing less than a metre

Ormos Agni

The last of the trio of bays from Kouloura. Yachts normally anchor in the S end in 4–10m on mud and weed. However there is no reason why a yacht cannot anchor at the N end. Tavernas ashore at the S end. Off the tavernas here there are wooden jetties where it is possible to go stern-to. Because of the wash from the high speed ferries it is really better to anchor off. If you do go on a jetty make sure you go stern-to and keep the yacht pulled well off the jetty to avoid damage from the wash.

The slopes around Kalami and Agni are steep-to but cultivated with olives though there are the tall silhouettes of cypress and pine in places. Recently the slopes haves been carved up for villas and villa complexes, a sort of pastoral extension to greater Corfu. Down on the water you are in the best place away from the coast road and its incessant traffic.

East coast of Corfu town

Benitses

Benitses was once a small fishing village, but that was long ago. Now it resounds to the sound of amplified *bouzouki* and disco music and is host to considerable numbers of tourists in the summer.

A large white hotel complex is conspicuous immediately N of the resort proper. There is a small harbour, but it is occupied by resident tripper boats and you will be lucky to find a berth. If there is room go stern or bows-to on the end of the breakwater in 2–2·5m. Otherwise anchor off in 3–10m. This can only really be a lunch stop (should you desire it) as the prevailing wind makes it very uncomfortable and usually untenable here. Tavernas and bars ashore everywhere.

Petriti   *Lu Michell*

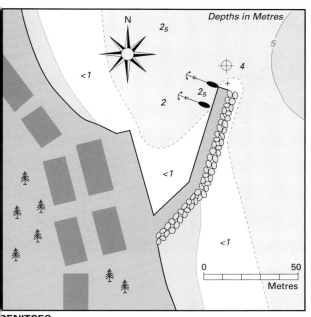

Voukari

⊕ 39°27'·57N 19°58'·68E WGS84

A small village and harbour situated approximately 1½M W of Ak Voukari. The tiny harbour is very shallow (mostly <1) and there is little room in here. In calm weather you can anchor off the tiny harbour, although like Benitses the prevailing wind sets in from the N here so it can only be used as a lunch stop. The hamlet and the harbour are enchanting and miles away from the awfulness of Benitses. If the weather is calm stop over here. Several tavernas ashore.

Petriti

A bay with a small harbour where reasonable shelter from the prevailing wind can be found.

Pilotage

Approach Immediately S of Ak Voukari an eroded escarpment is easily identified. Closer in the mole of the small harbour and the buildings of the hamlet will be seen. From the E care needs to be taken when rounding Ak Levkimmi. The cape itself is very low-lying and shoal water extends up to ½M off.

Vourkari on the east coast of Corfu   *Lu Michell*

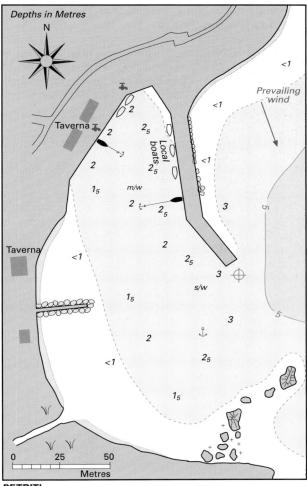

Mooring Enter the bay of Petriti slowly as it is quite shallow. Anchor off in 2–3m on mud, sand and weed. Alternatively go bows-to the quay on the west side taking care of irregular depths in places. The mole on the E is used by the local fishing boats and care is needed to avoid their permanent ground tackle when going bows-to the village side of the harbour. Reasonable shelter from the prevailing wind at anchor and good shelter in the harbour.

Facilities

Several tavernas and bars ashore. *Stamates Taverna* on the waterfront is a popular haunt for flotilla boats stopping here. Some provisions.

General

The hamlet has a few visitors by land, a few tripper boats call briefly for lunch, and a few yachts stop here, but otherwise Petriti is pretty much a sleepy hollow. The bay is attractive, a shaded green place with a stream running down through reed beds to the sea, a group of wind-sculpted knobbly rocks in the sea at the S end of the bay, and shallow water near the beach providing a safe swimming area in translucent water.

Ak Levkimmi

⊕8 1M E of Ak Levkimmi light 39°27'·6N 20°05'·7E

The low-lying cape on the W side of the southern Corfu channel. The cape is difficult to pick out from the distance and the first thing you are likely to see is the light structure hovering in the haze above the sea. Shoal water extends for up to ¾M N of the cape and ½M E. Although the shallows are readily identified in calm weather, with the prevailing wind kicking up a chop the shoal water can be difficult to spot. Keep a good distance off the light structure and if in doubt over how far off to go, head even further out. One of the flotilla operators calls it the Venus flytrap of the Ionian and that is a pretty fair description.

In calm weather yachts often anchor on the W or E side of the cape. Close the coast slowly as depths come up quickly from 15–20 metres to 2–5 metres. Anchor where convenient on mud and sand, good holding. If the prevailing wind gets up it is better to move on to somewhere more sheltered.

Levkimmi Canal   *Lu Michell*

Levkimmi Canal
Skala Potamou (Canal entrance)
⊕ 39°26·11N 20°05'·16E WGS84

1·5M south of Ak Levkimmi is the mouth of the canal which leads a mile or so inland to Levkimmi town. A training wall extends out from the beach on the south side, with a light structure on the extremity. The canal is liable to silt and depths are uneven, reported to be just 1–1·5m. In calm weather yachts can anchor off the beach in 4–10m, but with the prevailing northerlies this anchorage is not tenable except in the morning calm. Taverna on the beach at Skala Potamou, more choice in Levkimmi town.

Levkimmi is the administrative centre for the south of Corfu and is the second largest town. More amazingly, it is seemingly immune from the onslaught of tourism which happily has missed this sleepy gem of a town.

Kavos (Levkimmi)

A new harbour constructed for the ferries from Igoumenitsa. The ferries berth on the west quay, smaller trip boats use the southwest corner. The harbour has been dredged to 4–5m and yachts can go alongside the quay on the north side. Good shelter in this corner although the prevailing northerlies blow into the entrance and can set up a surge and strong northerlies may make the harbour untenable. Some yachts use the harbour as a refuge when beating northwards to

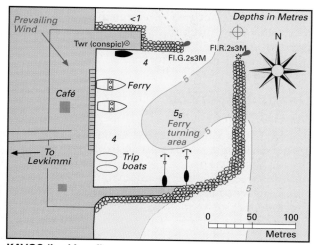

KAVOS (Levkimmi)
⊕39°24'·96N 20°06'·09E WGS84

Ay Stefanos near Avliotes on the west coast of Corfu
Lu Michell

Corfu town. The new main road to the north runs out of the port and bypasses Levkimmi town centre, 1½km away. The port itself is pretty isolated, with just a café in the ferry ticket office providing drinks and snacks. Although the port is known as Kavos, it shouldn't be confused with the package tour resort of the same name further to the south.

Ak Koundouris and Ak Asprokavos

Off these two capes at the S end of Corfu an area of shoal water extends for more than ½M in places and a yacht should keep well off.

West coast of Corfu

There are few safe anchorages on the W coast as the prevailing wind sets directly down onto it and the only really secure shelter is at Ay Stefanos and Palaeokastrita.

Ay Stefanos (W coast)

This Ay Stefanos is not to be confused with Ay Stefanos on the northeast coast. It is a small harbour on the north side of Ak Kavokefali where a breakwater has been built out from a natural bight to shelter it from the prevailing westerlies.

Approach The approach should be made from the north. Care is needed at the entrance which silts and it would be wise to reconnoitre in the dinghy to see if depths are adequate. With the normal N–NW winds this can be difficult so if possible arrive here early in the morning before the prevailing wind gets up.

Note In 2003 depths in the entrance channel were around 2·5m.

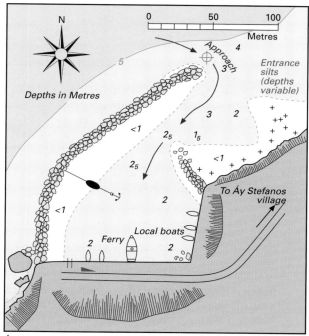

ÁY STEFANOS (AVLIOTES)
⊕39°45'·24N 19°38'·00E WGS84

Mooring Most of the quay space is occupied by local craft and it is unlikely you will find a berth here. Anchor and take a long line to the rough breakwater or go bows-to on the S quay. The bottom is sand and good holding. Good all round shelter.

Several tavernas nearby and the village of Avliotes is about a mile away. Villas are being built around Avliotes and the surrounding slopes, but if you can get in here the harbour is removed from the villa sprawl nearby.

Greek place names are often repeated which is why you will find Vathi (deep), Ay Nikolaos (the Patron Saint of Sailors), Ay Yeoryios (Saint George, the same one as our dragon slayer), used for different geographical places, even places quite close to each other as here with Ay Stefanos.

St Stephen (Stefanos) was the first Christian martyr who was accused of blasphemy and stoned to death. Why this proto-martyr should be so popular in Greece is a bit of a mystery, but you will find places named after him all over Greece.

Ormos Ay Yeoryiou

(Ag Georgiou)

A large bay situated under Ak Arilla. Reasonable shelter from light westerlies can be found tucked up into the N corner off the beach, but in a brisk onshore breeze it becomes untenable.

A narrow isthmus separates a narrow inlet on the west side of Ormos Ay Yeoryiou from Port Timoni on the outside of the promontory which ends in Ak Arilla. The inlet provides excellent shelter from the prevailing NW winds, although there is very little room and it is best to anchor

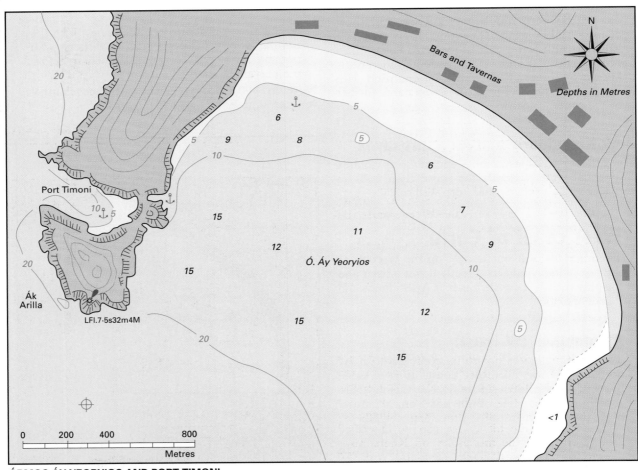

ÓRMOS ÁY YEORYIOS AND PORT TIMONI
⊕39°42'·45N 19°39'·3E

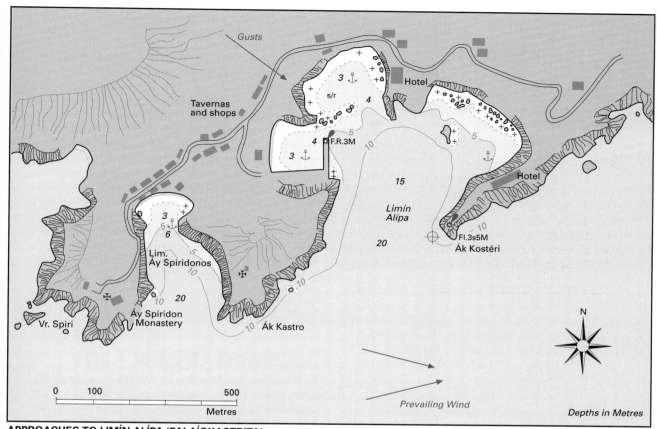

APPROACHES TO LIMÍN ALÍPA (PALAÍOKASTRITA)
⊕39°40′·24N 19°42′·75E

and take a long line ashore to the N side.

In Port Timoni there is more room to anchor, but the bay is open to the prevailing winds and should only be used in calm weather.

The beach is marvellous and tavernas and bars open in the summer.

Palaiokastritsa

(Ormos Liapadhes, Limín Alípa)

Pilotage

Approach With the prevailing wind setting onto the coast there can be big seas in the approaches and care is needed. If possible make the approach in the morning before the prevailing wind gets up. The village of Lakones on the hill above can be identified and closer in the monastery on Khersonisos Monis Palaiokastritsa, the headland to the W of Ormos Liapadhes, will be seen.

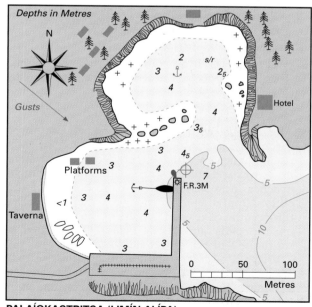

PALAÍOKASTRITSA (LIMÍN ALÍPA)
⊕39°40′·45N 19°42′·58E

Palaíokastritsa harbour looking SW. Note the rocks off the N side of the entrance

Once into the bay some of the hotels around the slopes will be seen and the harbour mole on the W of the bay is easily identified. Care is needed of the above and below-water rocks across the entrance to the N cove and also partially obstructing the entrance to the harbour.

Mooring Go stern or bows-to in the harbour if there is room or anchor in the N cove. The bottom is mud and sand, good holding. Good shelter in the harbour from the prevailing winds but dangerous in southerly gales.

Facilities

Water ashore. Most provisions can be found. Restaurants and bars nearby. Intermittent bus to Corfu town.

General

The site is without doubt one of the most spectacular in the Ionian. From seaward the cliffs rise up in jagged pinnacles, eroded here and there into caves and arches, with small sand and shingle beaches tucked into coves at the bottom of the cliffs. From the land you get wonderful views through the olives and cypress of the sea crashing on the cliffs and rocks below. The water is turquoise and azure over sand and rock.

With all of this it should be no surprise that Palaeokastritsa is besieged with tourists in the summer. The landscape has been adulterated with hotels that mar the landscape. Yet for all that it is possible, especially outside of July and August, to appreciate something of the natural beauty and not even tour operators have been able to remove all the natural charm of the spot.

Where the monastery now stands on top of a rocky bluff is the supposed site of the Phaeacian capital mentioned in the *Odyssey* with the bays below serving as harbours. Whether or not there is any substance to this assertion is doubtful – no trace of a civilised pre-Hellenic culture have ever been found here or anywhere else on Corfu. The monastery is well worth a visit despite the crowds visiting it. A sign at the entrance asks you *Not to enter the monastery in bathing suits or shorts* and a gnarled old lady at the entrance provides scarves and wrap-around skirts for a donation to the monastery. The monks inside tolerate the visitors amazingly well and it is one of those divine mysteries that the courtyards and buildings somehow retain a semblance of peace and serenity despite the whirring video cameras and babble of different languages.

Southwest coast of Corfu

Much of the coast south of Paliokastritsa running right down to Ak Asprokavos has devoted itself entirely to package holidays. Every inch of sandy beach is filled with sun worshippers and there is little authentic Corfiot life to be found. Some larger resorts, notably Pink Palace at Ay Yeoryios have built miniature harbours to shelter watersports facilities but there is nothing of use to yachts. The hamlet of Pentati is relatively untouched by the mass tourism, but the tiny fishing harbour is packed with local craft and in any case is shallow, mostly <1m.

Othoni, Erikoussa and Mathraki

Nisos Othoni

Othoni is the precipitous outer island of the group of islands lying to the N of Corfu. At one time when sea levels were lower it would have been joined via Nisos Mathraki to Corfu by a narrow land bridge that can be traced on the depth contours of a chart. Although Othoni is a high bold island, some 393m (1289ft) in the SW

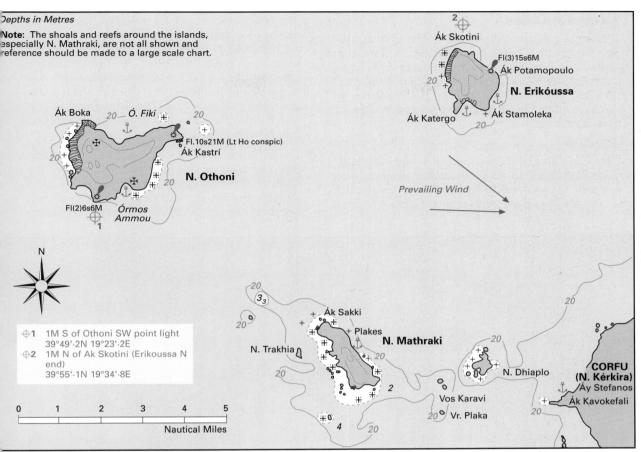

Depths in Metres

Note: The shoals and reefs around the islands, especially N. Mathraki, are not all shown and reference should be made to a large scale chart.

Ák Boka   20   *Ó. Fiki*   20
Fl.10s21M (Lt Ho conspic)
Ák Kastrí
N. Othoni

Fl(2)6s6M   *Órmos Ammou*
1

Ák Skotini   2
Fl(3)15s6M
Ák Potamopoulo
N. Erikóussa
Ák Katergo   Ák Stamoleka
20

Prevailing Wind

N

⊕1   1M S of Othoni SW point light
      39°49'·2N 19°23'·2E
⊕2   1M N of Ak Skotini (Erikoussa N
      end)
      39°55'·1N 19°34'·8E

20
3₃
20
Ák Sakki
Plakes   **N. Mathraki**
N. Trakhia
20   20
2   N. Dhiaplo
CORFU (N. Kérkira)
Áy Stefanos
Ák Kavokefali
Vos Karavi
0   Vr. Plaka   20

0   1   2   3   4   5
Nautical Miles

SOI OTHONI, ERIKOUSSA AND MATHRAKI

corner, it is often obscured by haze and sea mist in the summer, so much so that yachts crossing from Italy to Corfu will often not see it until a mile or two off. The island is much used by yachts as a stepping stone en route to or from Italy and no doubt has been so used since antiquity.

The Italian name for the island is Fano, probably a corruption of *faro*, 'lighthouse'. The name indicates it had a lighthouse in Venetian times. There is a Medieval fort on the top of Kastri, in the NE, where the present lighthouse stands, and it is likely a lighthouse existed here in the Middle Ages. As well as the fort there is reported to be an acropolis on the island certifying its importance as a stepping stone in ancient times. Othoni is sometimes mentioned as Homer's *Ogygia*, the island where Calypso seduced Odysseus and he, not surprisingly, tarried for seven years. Though one should never

dismiss local folklore out of hand, it is probable that Malta or one of the islands around Sicily is more likely to be Homer's *Ogygia*.

In this century Othoni has served as a stepping stone for a more nefarious trade, cigarette smuggling to Italy. On several occasions when on passage between Italy and Othoni I have seen high speed motorboats scudding across the horizon and in Ammou on Othoni there used to be a variety of exotically powered craft, the sort that have three 300 HP outboards on a 12m light planing hull. Its not something you enquire about, but presumably the boats couldn't get back to the Italian base port because of the *guardia di finanza* or bad weather, and Othoni provided the nearest convenient port of refuge. These days it is rare to see such craft around as it seems immigrants and not cigarettes are the new cargo of choice for the smugglers.

Ormos Ammou

The only village on the island is scattered around the shores of a bay on the S side. A ferry runs irregularly from Corfu in the summer and *caiques* carrying the islands' needs run from Corfu and Sidhari. Most visitors to the island arrive by yacht, usually en route from or to Santa Maria di Leuca in Italy.

Pilotage

Approach Though Nisos Othoni is high and bold, it is difficult to pick out in the summer haze until 1½–2M off. The lighthouse on the NE corner is conspicuous and the light tower on the SW corner can be identified closer in. In the approach to the bay care needs to be taken of Ifalos Aspri Petra, a rock with less than 2m over it, lying directly in the southern approaches. Care is also needed in the approach from the SE of rocks and shoal water extending off the coast. The fishing harbour on the E side of the bay is rock bound and should not be approached.

Mooring Anchor in 2–10m where convenient keeping clear of the ferry turning area off the end of the breakwater. The bottom is sand outside the 5m line and sand and rock inside it – care is needed of the rocks which can snag an

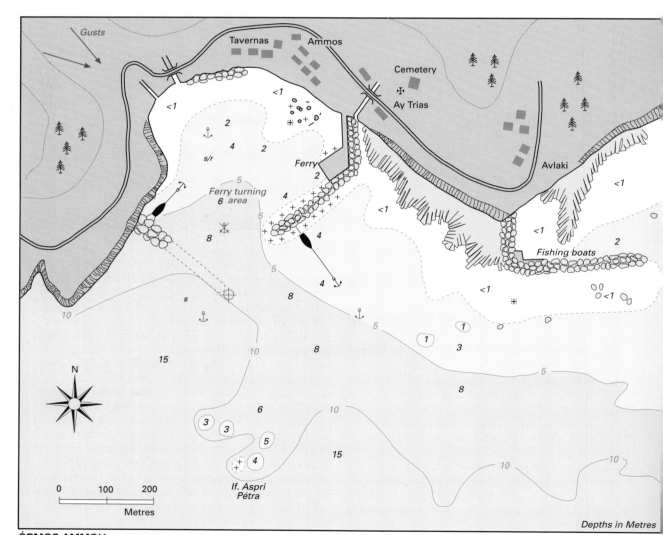

ÓRMOS AMMOU
⊕39°50'·2N 19°24'·2E

anchor. A yacht can also anchor off the outer end of the harbour breakwater with a long line to it. Small yachts can berth on the W side of the quay when the ferry or supply *caique* are not due, but most yachts will be better off anchored out. In the summer the prevailing wind blows out of the bay and shelter is good, though some swell works around into the anchorage making it a bit rolly. The bay is open to the S.

Facilities

Limited provisions from a shop attached to one of the tavernas where small amounts of money can be changed and there is a metered telephone. Several tavernas open in the summer and locally caught fish is often available. A small hotel and village rooms available.

General

Everything on Othoni revolves around the small village of Ammou and its harbour. Communication is mostly by *caique* although there is a rough road used by tractors and the few motorbikes. The rough interior offers some interesting cross-island trekking though it would be wise to let someone in the village know where you are setting off for.

Ormos Fiki

The bay on the N side can be used to shelter from southerlies or explored in calm weather. It is untenable with the prevailing northwesterlies. From the W the approach is free of dangers, but from the E there are several underwater rocks off Ak Kastri. In the bay there are above and below-water rocks off the beach, though these are easily spotted. Anchor in 4–10m on sand and rock.

The bay is a wild forlorn place, stunted *maquis*, a few shepherds' shelters, and a messy pebble beach dotted with tar washed down onto it from the Adriatic.

Nisos Erikoussa

Nisos Erikoussa, also called by its old name, Merikha, lies 7M due E of Othoni and 6M off the NW tip of Corfu. It is a lower island than Othoni, less craggy and bold. The only village, really a hamlet, is in the large bay on the S side of the island. The long sandy beach around the bay and its proximity to Corfu attracts tripper boats which

charge over here in the summer, drop their queasy-looking cargo off on the beach, and a few hours later charge back to Corfu town with them.

South Bay

The large bay in the S between Ak Katergo and Ak Stamoleka on the SE tip of the island.

Pilotage

Approach The approach is free of dangers except for above and below-water rocks off Ak Katergo and Ak Stamoleka. The white cliffs of Ak Katergo are conspicuous and closer in the small electricity generating plant at the E end of the beach will be seen as well as the houses around the W end.

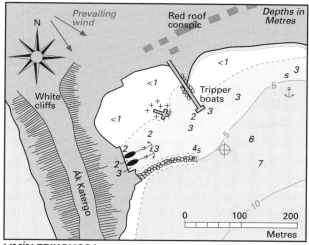

LIMÍN ERIKOUSSA
⊕39°52′·6N 19°34′·8E

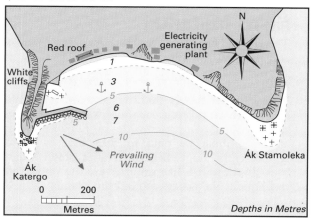

ERIKOUSSA SOUTH BAY

Mooring The bottom slopes gradually to the beach. Anchor in 3–6m where convenient, although care must be taken of a cable, presumably for electricity or telephones, lying approximately 150m off the shore. The bottom is sand and rock, mostly good holding.

A yacht can enter the harbour on the W side of the bay although care is needed of the remains of the mole on the north side. Go stern or bows-to the south or west quays taking care of depths close to the quay where the bottom is irregular in places. Shelter in the harbour is good from the prevailing northwesterlies and the harbour should also afford some protection from southerlies. If there is room you may find a place on the pier running out from the shore closer to the village although it is much used during the day by the tripper boats. Good shelter in the bay from the prevailing NW winds.

Facilities

Limited provisions. Several restaurants ashore where locally caught fresh fish is available. Village rooms available. Communications mostly seems to be by the tripper boats from Corfu and Gouvia which also carry goods over to the island.

General

From midday until the mid-afternoon the bay buzzes with trippers from Corfu, but by four o'clock they have all departed and quiet descends. On the E side of the island a yacht can find shelter from the prevailing winds in some idyllic coves and bights with excellent snorkelling in the clear water. Inland, like Othoni, the island promises some good trekking.

Nisos Mathraki

The jagged island lying S of Othoni and Errikousa and 5M W of the NW tip of Corfu. It is surrounded by above and below-water rocks, islets, and shoal water. The small island of Dhiapolo lies nearly midway between Mathraki and Corfu on a bridge of shoal water. There are safe channels on either side of Dhiapolo, but attention must be paid to the chart to avoid several reefs. Local fishermen after crayfish and rock-dwelling fish like grouper are the only craft to frequent the waters around the islands.

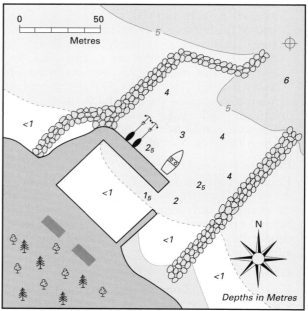

PLAKES (MATHRAKI)
⊕39°46'·9N 19°31'·3E

Plakes

The harbour lies on the east side of the island somewhat more towards the northern end. Make the approach from a northerly direction as shoals extend out from the shore to the SE of the harbour. There are depths of 5m in the entrance to the outer harbour and 2–3m along the central pier. Go stern or bows-to the pier leaving space on the end free for the ferry. The harbour is very small so you will need to have everything ready before you enter. Good shelter and open only to the NE.

There are several tavernas nearby and basic provisions can be found. Wonderful sandy beaches nearby.

Nisoi Paxoi and Andipaxoi
(Paxos and Anti-Paxos)

Paxos and its diminutive Anti-Paxos lie some 7M S of Corfu, two small islands offering refuge between Corfu and Levkas further S. Paxos itself is only 5M long by 2½M wide and has a permanent population of around 2,000, including some eccentric British residents who discovered the tiny island years ago. Anti-Paxos lying just over a mile S is 2½M long and 1M wide with a permanent population of just 50.

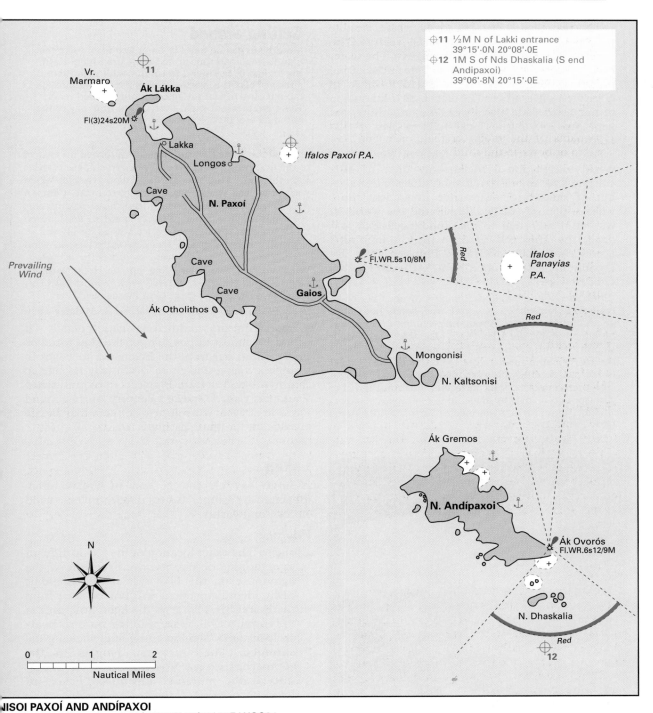

⊕**11** ½M N of Lakki entrance
39°15'·0N 20°08'·0E
⊕**12** 1M S of Nds Dhaskalia (S end Andipaxoi)
39°06'·8N 20°15'·0E

Vr. Marmaro

Ák Lákka

⊕ 11

Fl(3)24s20M

○ Lakka

Longos ○

Cave

N. Paxoí

⊕ Ifalos Paxoí P.A.

Prevailing Wind

Cave

Cave

Cave

Ák Otholithos ○

Fl.WR.5s10/8M

Gaios

Red

Ifalos Panayías P.A.

Red

Mongonisi

N. Kaltsonisi

Ák Gremos

N. Andípaxoi

Ák Ovorós
Fl.WR.6s12/9M

Red

N. Dhaskalia

⊕ 12

N

0   1   2
Nautical Miles

NISOI PAXOÍ AND ANDÍPAXOI
⊕ 100m N of Ifalos Paxoi 39°13'·72N 20°10'·27E WGS84

The two islands are still idyllic places despite the large numbers of waterborne visitors who descend on them in July and August. The water here is that almost unbelievable blue and green of picture postcards set off by the dull sheen of cultivated olive groves. In fact until the invasion of the last decade olives were the only thing that kept Paxos going – local folklore has it that Harrods sells only Paxiot olive oil.

Paxos has few claims to fame in the ancient world except for a melancholy one, of little consequence in our rigidly monotheistic universe, but of shattering importance in ancient times when a panoply of gods inhabited the world. It was off Paxos that it was announced Pan was dead, the only god to have died in our time according to Robert Graves. Plutarch gives this account in his sadly titled *Why the Oracles Cease to Give Answers*.

'Epitherses told me that, designing a voyage to Italy, he embarked himself on a vessel well laden both with goods and passengers. About the evening the vessel was becalmed about the Isles Echinades, whereupon their ship drove with the tide till it was carried near the Isles of Paxi; when immediately a voice was heard by most of the passengers (who were then awake, and taking a cup after supper) calling unto one Thamus, and that with so loud a voice as made all the company amazed; which Thamus was a mariner of Egypt, whose name

was scarcely known in the ship. He returned no answer to the first calls; but at the third he replied, Here! here! I am the man. Then the voice said aloud to him, When you are arrived at Palodes, take care to make it known that the great God Pan is dead. Epirtheses told us, this voice did much astonish all that heard it, and caused much arguing whether this voice was to be obeyed or slighted... Being come to Palodes, there was no wind stirring, and the sea was as smooth as glass. Whereupon Thamus standing on the deck, with his face towards the land, uttered with a loud voice his message, saying, The great God Pan is dead.'

Plutarch *The Moralia* transl. by R. Midgley 1870

Apart from the muddled navigation details – it would be almost impossible for the ship to travel under sail or oar from the Echinades to Paxos in a single evening and there is virtually no tide in this area – and despite Plutarch's account, when Pausanias visited Greece a century later he found Pan still actively worshipped, so there may be life after death for pantheists after all.

Getting around

Motorbikes can be hired in Gaios and from there the island's only road runs up to Lakka, branching off in the middle of the island to Longos. Although there is just one road, it is worth an excursion inland through the old olive groves set amongst grey eroded rocks. There are pleasant walks everywhere from any of the harbours around the island.

Lakka

A large bay on the N end of Paxos much inhabited by tripper boats, dinghy sailors, wind surfers, and yachts.

Pilotage

Approach The exact location of the bay is difficult to determine despite its size. From the W the lighthouse on the NW side of the island is easily identified, but it will not be seen from the E and SE. Closer in the light structures at the entrance will be seen. In the summer boats are constantly coming and going, showing the entrance. There are no dangers in the approaches except Vos Marmaro off the W side of the entrance and Ifalos Paxoi off Longos.

Mooring Anchor where convenient in the middle or anchor and take a long line ashore in the NW corner. There is some room on the quay for small and medium-sized yachts, though do not obstruct the ferry berth or berths for local

Paxos cat waiting for the next customer.

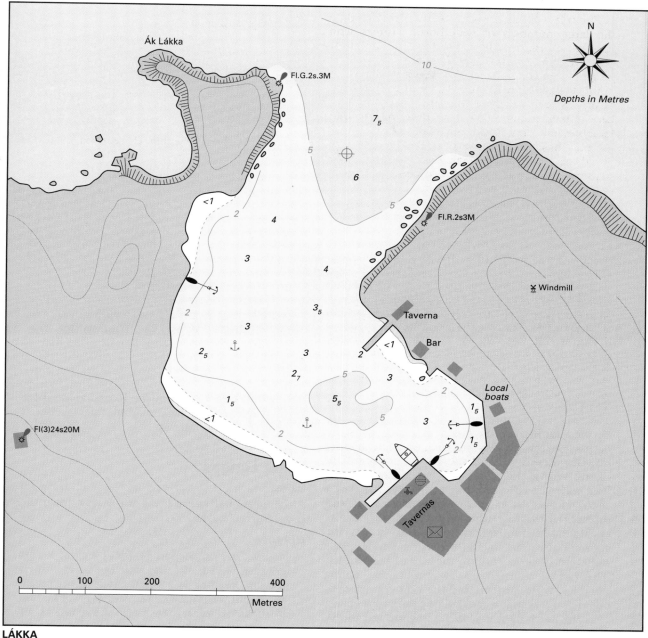

LÁKKA
⊕39°14'·65N 20°07'·75E

boats. With care parts of the quayed area E of the town quay can be used though it is best to go bows-to. The bottom is sand and weed, good holding. Good shelter from the prevailing winds but prolonged N–NE winds cause a very uncomfortable swell.

Facilities

Limited water on the quay although it may be turned off altogether in the summer. Most provisions ashore. Tavernas and bars. PO.

Ormos Lakka   *Nigel Patten*

General

The bay is picturesque. The slopes about are covered with the dull green of olives with the occasional tall cypress sticking up. The hamlet huddles at the head of the bay, a collection of earthy brown tile roofs and faded pastel walls. The water, mostly just four or five metres over a sandy bottom, is a patchwork quilt of blues and greens. Inevitably this combination attracts considerable numbers of people to it. In the summer the quayside is a noisy bustling place quite out of proportion to the size of the hamlet. The bay is churned up by speedboats, sailing dinghies, wind surfers, and the odd tripper boat coming and going, a cocktail of colour and chaos.

In the morning it is worth going around the W side of the island where there are several impressive sea caves eroded into the equally impressive cliffs. At one time a small colony of monk seals lived here, but no more – these shy animals have moved elsewhere since the tourist presence increased. Local myth also has it that a Greek submarine sheltered in one of the caves during the Second World War, but this is a common bit of Homeric myth-making throughout Greece and in the Ionian alone there are two other caves where submarines sheltered according to local folklore.

Limin Longos

(Logos)

A miniature harbour a third of the way down the E coast from Lakka.

Pilotage

Approach Care is needed of Ifalos Paxoi, a reef less than ½M E of Longos. It can be identified in calm weather as a small patch of turquoise water, but is difficult to see otherwise. The line of rocks running out from the coast S of Longos are easily identified and close in the houses of the hamlet and a chimney of the old soap factory will be seen.

Mooring There are no really comfortable berths here. The small harbour is reserved for local boats and tripper boats. Go stern-to the outside of the mole with a long line to it or anchor and take a long line ashore to the N side of the bay. With the prevailing wind you roll around most uncomfortably with the ground swell.

Just under a mile S of Longos, S of the conspicuous line of rocks running out from the coast, there is a quiet anchorage off a sandy beach suitable in calm weather or light northwesterlies.

Facilities

Most provisions ashore and tavernas and bars. *Vassili's Taverna* on the waterfront has been there forever and still has excellent food.

General

The little fishing port is a beautiful spot, a huddle of houses around the miniature harbour. Formerly it relied on fishing and olives for its livelihood. It still has a small fishing fleet though much of the catch goes straight into the fish tavernas on the island. The old soap factory on the shore that turned the leftovers from olive oil production into soap has been disused for years. Now the inhabitants have a thriving trade in tourists though it is all quite sympathetic and the village retains a pleasant feel to it.

Disused soap factory at Longos on Paxoi

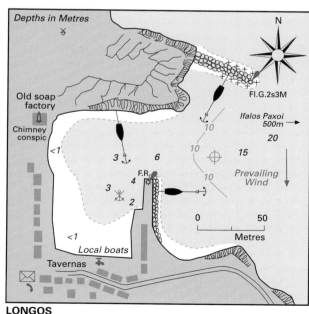

LONGOS
⊕39°13′·61N 20°09′·75E WGS84

Ifalos Panayias

A reef just under the water lying approximately 2½M E of Nisis Panayia, the islet at the entrance to Limin Gaios. Some dispute the charted position and say it should be closer to the mainland, but it looks about right to me. An area of shoal water lies to the E and S of the reef. It is difficult to see with the prevailing winds which whip up chop over it, so it should be given a wide berth. Unfortunately the reef lies very close to the course between Gaios and Parga so care is needed and a dogleg course should be made to keep well clear of it.

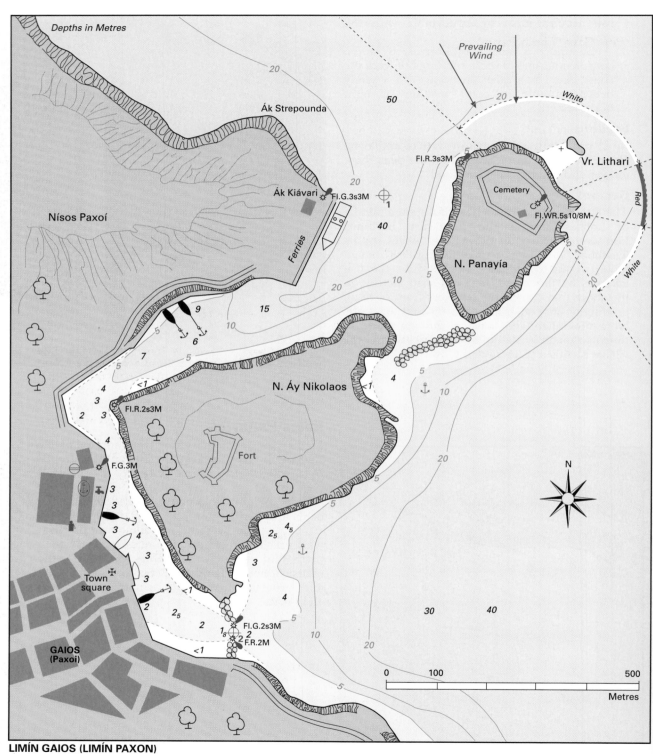

Depths in Metres

Ák Strepounda

50

Prevailing Wind

20

White

Ák Kiávari

Fl.G.3s3M

Fl.R.3s3M

5

Vr. Lithari

Nísos Paxoí

Ferries

40

Cemetery

N. Panayía

Fl.WR.5s10/8M

Red

White

20

20

10

5

20

10

15

10

5

9

6

5

7

5

5

4

5

<1

10

N. Áy Nikolaos

<1

4

5

4

2

3

Fl.R.2s3M

4

Fort

F.G.3M

3

3

3

4

20

N

3

4

5

3

Town square

3

2

5

30

40

2

2 5

<1

Fl.G.2s3M

2

1 8

2

F.R.2M

GAIOS (Paxoi)

<1

5

10

20

5

0   100   500

Metres

LIMÍN GAIOS (LIMÍN PAXON)
⊕1 39°12·22N 20°11′·47E WGS84
⊕2 39°11·80N 20°11′·32E WGS84

Limin Gaios

(Port Gayo, Limin Paxon)

The main harbour on the island tucked in and completely hidden behind the islet of Ay Nikolaos. This is where all ferries and tripper boats arrive or leave and in the summer there are a large number of them testifying to the tiny islands popularity. Ferries and excursion boats run from Corfu and Parga on a daily basis and some of the large ferries from Italy also stop here.

Pilotage

Approach It is difficult to see the entrance to the harbour from the N although closer in the small lighthouse on Nisis Panayia will be seen. Care is needed in the N entrance as tripper boats and small ferries charge in and out of here and it is impossible to see if anyone is coming in the opposite direction where the channel curves abruptly to the S.

From the S it is easier to identify where the harbour is as some of the buildings of Gaios can be seen. In the S entrance there are barely 2m depths in the middle and no room to manoeuvre out of the channel, so wait until the way is clear.

Mooring The harbour is so crowded in the height of summer that anyone arriving after two or three o'clock is unlikely to find a berth on the

Gaios looking up the south channel

town quay. Go stern or bows-to wherever you can find or negotiate a berth keeping well clear of the ferry quay. Crossed anchors are a fact of life here and something you will just have to live with. The new quay in the north channel doesn't have the cache of being on the town

Gaios looking in through the south entrance. If you draw anything close to 2 metres use the north entrance

quay, but does have some peace and quiet and even better, you can usually find a berth here. Go stern or bows-to where there is room, but remember you may be dropping your anchor in quite deep water in the channel. Larger yachts can anchor off under the breakwater between Ay Nikolaos and Panayia. Shelter in Gaios is good from the prevailing summer westerlies, but not as good as it looks from strong southerlies when there can be a considerable surge in the harbour.

Facilities

Services Water near the quay though it can be in short supply in the summer. Water can also be obtained by mini-tanker. Contact the *Kirki Bar* near the southern entrance. Fuel near the quay.

Provisions Provisions available in the town though things here are a little more expensive than elsewhere as nearly everything is brought in by ferry.

Eating out Tavernas and bars in the town. Any of the tavernas in the square will take your money. There are a number of good tavernas on the road out of town well away from the hubbub of the centre. A friend of mine recommends *Dodo's* just in from the southern entrance to Gaios, or *Mambo* on the waterfront just past the central square if heading towards the southern entrance.

Other Bank. PO. Hire motorbikes.

General

Gaios is chaos in the summer. Yachts and their owners are running around in circles searching for berths, those already berthed are defending their patch against newcomers, water-taxis carve up the water going about their business, and landlubbers sit in cafes on the square and watch bemused. The square itself, hedged in by buildings on three sides and by the harbour on the other, is always buzzing with conversation and waiters' shouted orders. Despite all this, or perhaps because of it, Gaios is a beguiling spot where once you have gone to so much trouble to secure a berth, it seems a pity to move on too quickly.

There is nothing here you must go to see for your education. On the island of Ay Nikolaos that shelters the harbour a medieval fort and a chapel sits on the summit. In the town there is some pleasing architecture from the 19th century. And there are pleasant walks out of town through the ubiquitous olive groves of Paxos. Like Corfu, many of the olive groves were planted under Venetian occupation and some of the old gnarled trees on the island are said to be four or five hundred years old and still bearing.

One other inhabitant of Gaios has to be commented on and that is the taverna cat. At every taverna there are as many cats as there are tourists, hordes of cats, some attractive and some battle-scarred with minor bits of anatomy like an eye or an ear missing, but all intent on sharing your meal with you.

Mongonisi

(Spuzzo)

Just over a mile SE of Gaios is the enclosed bay of Mongonisi. The approach is straightforward although it can be difficult to determine exactly where the bay is until close-to.

Go bows-to on the N or E side if there is room. Alternatively anchor off where convenient. The

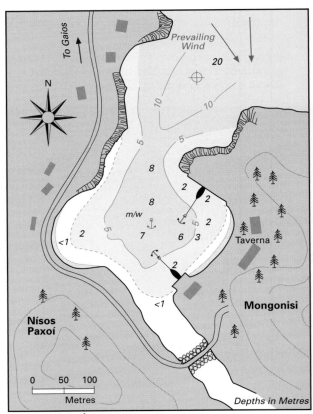

MONGONISI (ÓRMOS SPUZZO)
⊕39°11'·0N 20°12·3E

bottom is mud and weed, good holding once through the weed. Good all-round shelter.

Ashore there is *Theo's Taverna* and bar set amongst gnarled old olives. Depending on the night it can be low-key and relaxed in here or a riotous and rowdy party. You can walk around the rough road to Gaios or in the summer water-taxis run back and forth. Mongonisi is actually the name of the small islet forming the E side of the bay and joined to Paxos by a rough causeway.

Nisis Kaltsonisi

A small islet just off Nisis Mongonisi. In the narrow gap between the two islands a yacht can anchor with care. It is mostly very deep shelving quickly. Clear water and an oasis of peace on this crowded island.

Nisos Andipaxoi

(Anti-Paxos)

The small island lying to the S of Paxos. It is popular with yachts and tripper boats who charge over here to the sandy beaches (Paxos doesn't have many good sandy beaches) and the wonderful clear water.

There are two bays on the NE side of the island popular as day anchorages. Approach the coast with care as there are numerous fringing reefs. The north bay here is known as Emerald Bay and the next bay down is Ormos Agrapidhia. Anchor where convenient. When the NW wind gets up it can get uncomfortable in here and may become untenable.

There is a miniature harbour at Agrapidhia but it is really too small for most yachts and in any case is usually full of local boats.

Numerous tripper boats run to and from Paxoi, but after the hordes have departed it is a peaceful spot. Several tavernas are reported to open in the summer.

Care is needed of above and below-water rocks off the southern end of Andipaxoi and yachts should keep well out from Nisis Dhaskalia off the southern tip.

Andipaxos *Nigel Patten*

2. The mainland coast
Pagania to Preveza

This stretch of coast forms the western edge of Northern Greece with the Epirus and the start of the Pindus mountains, these towering, ragged sheets of rock, arching across mainland Greece to the northern Aegean. For the most part the mountains drop abruptly into the sea except where a river mouth has deposited silt to create a coastal plain as at Igoumenitsa and around Preveza. The Epirus has always exercised a powerful hold on those who have visited it. The Pindus are the mountains that Homers 'rosy fingered dawn' touches. Eccentric travellers as diverse as John Morrit on his 'Grand Tour', Lord Byron looking for Ali Pasha, and a melancholy Edward Lear tramping the mountains to record them in watercolours and in his *Diary of a Landscape Painter in Greece and Albania*, all came this way. Recently the region was highlighted in Nicholas Gage's *Eleni*, the tale of terror in the mountains during the Second World War and the bloody civil war that followed.

Yet despite this sort of eminent reporting over the years, it remains very much an out of the way region compared to the islands across the water. Any trips inland will be repaid tenfold. It may surprise many to know that this mainland region was Turkish right up until the end of the Second Baltic War when the Greek Army finally captured Ioannina in February 1913. There are still a few old folk alive who were born under Turkish occupation and memories are long in the mountains so tread lightly on their memories.

Quick reference guide

	Shelter	Mooring	Fuel	Water	Provisions	Tavernas	Plans
Ftelias	B	C	O	O	O	O	
Pagania	A	C	O	O	O	O	•
Sayiadha	B	AB	O	B	C	C	•
Ormiskos Valtou	A	C	O	O	O	O	•
Igoumenitsa	B	AB	B	B	B	B	•
Platarias	A	A	B	A	B	C	•
Mourtos and nearby islands	A	AC	B	B	B	B	•
Ormos Paramithas	C	C	O	O	O	C	
Parga	B	AC	B	A	B	A	•
Ormos Ay Athanasiou	C	C	O	O	A	A	•
Ormos Ay Kiriakis	C	C	O	O	O	O	
Ormos Ay Ioannou	C	C	O	O	O	O	•
Ormos Fanari	AB	BC	B	B	C	B	•
Two Rock Bay	C	C	O	O	O	O	
Ligia	B	A	O	B	C	C	•
Preveza	B	AB	A	A	A	B	•
Ormos Vathi	A	C	O	B	O	C	•
Amvrakikos Kolpos (Gulf of Amvrakia)							
Vonitsa	B	AC	B	B	B	B	•
Loutraki	C	C	O	O	O	O	
Amfilokhia	O	AC	B	B	B	B	•
Menidhion	B	AC	B	B	C	B	•
Nisoi Vouvalo and Koronisia	C	C	O	O	O	O	•
Salaora	C	C	O	O	C	C	•

Note

The warning regarding the situation for anchorages close to Albania mentioned in Chapter 1 applies to mainland anchorages and harbours close to Albania. It bears repeating here. In the past there have been a number of incidents of piracy off the Albanian coast and some off the nearby Greek mainland coast. Albania now appears more settled and recent reports are that

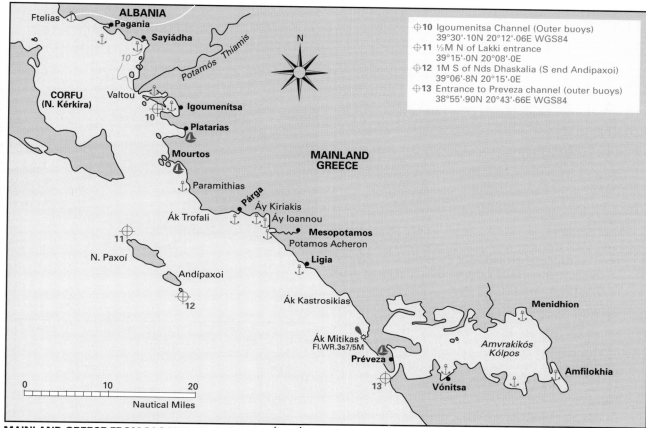

MAINLAND GREECE FROM PAGANIA TO AMVRAKIKÓS KÓLPOS

Map legend:

⊕10 Igoumenitsa Channel (Outer buoys)
39°30'·10N 20°12'·06E WGS84
⊕11 ½M N of Lakki entrance
39°15'·0N 20°08'·0E
⊕12 1M S of Nds Dhaskalia (S end Andipaxoi)
39°06'·8N 20°15'·0E
⊕13 Entrance to Preveza channel (outer buoys)
38°55'·90N 20°43'·66E WGS84

Map labels:
Ftelias, ALBANIA, Pagania, Sayiádha, CORFU (N. Kérkira), Valtou, Potamós Thiamis, N, Igoumenítsa, Platarias, Mourtos, MAINLAND GREECE, Paramithias, Párga, Áy Kiriakis, Ák Trofali, Áy Ioannou, Mesopotamos, Potamos Acheron, N. Paxoí, Ligia, Andípaxoi, Ák Kastrosikias, Menidhion, Amvrakikós Kólpos, Ák Mitikas Fl.WR.3s7/5M, Préveza, Amfilokhia, Vónitsa

Scale: 0 10 20 Nautical Miles

---

there is less anarchy ashore. Even so yachts should keep well off the coast and when approaching the North Corfu Channel keep as close as practicable to Corfu. Yachts on passage from Italy can head around the south end of Corfu and then up to Gouvia if there is a real need to get there or alternatively it makes more sense to head for Paxos, Preveza or Levkas. Given the prevailing winds are NW in the summer this presents few problems. At present there is a strong Greek Naval presence and this should ensure the safety of craft in the area. However it would pay to keep an eye on developments and act accordingly.

Charter yachts should listen to advice from the area manager or flotilla leader. Some care is certainly needed on the mainland side of the North Corfu Channel, although in recent years a number of yachts have been returning to the anchorages here. See what the local advice is and follow it.

Ftelias

⊕ 39°41'·4N 20°00'·5E

A small bay tucked up under the Albanian border. In the approaches a high rugged island on the Albanian side and a low rocky island on the Greek side will be seen. Leave the Greek island to starboard and enter the bay. There are fish farms in the bay. Good depths in the entrance decreasing to 10m off the fish farm on the north side and 3m around the dogleg. Anchor where convenient on mud. No facilities.

Pagania

An enclosed bay 4M ESE from Ftelias.

Approach From the south it is difficult to see the entrance. From the distance the road cut into the hill appears to disappear where Pagania headland obscures it. Once into the entrance the farm buildings will be seen.

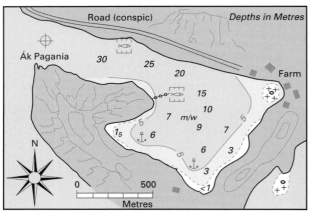

PAGANIA
⊕39°39'·8N 20°06'·0E

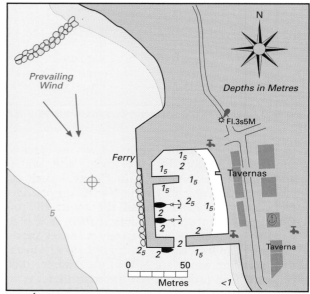

Sayiadha   *Lu Michell*

SAYIÁDHA
⊕39°37'·52N 20°10'·88E WGS84

Note A fish farm extends out from the west side of the bay. It is easily seen by day. There are also other fish farms in the bay.

Mooring A yacht can anchor in the SW or SE corner in 3–6m on mud and weed. Good all-round shelter.

This remote corner of Greece is about as close to Albania as you can get, the border is just over ½km away, so don't stray too far.

Note

In the past there have been a number of incidents concerning yachts and Albanians at or near Pagania and even a gun battle between the Greek navy and some stray Albanians. At the time of writing things appear settled, but do take some local advice before coming here.

Sayiadha

(Sagiadha)

Like Pagania, Sayiadha is not too far from the Albanian border, although at the time of writing things appeared settled here apart from the locals wondering where the yachts had gone to.

Approach The buildings of the hamlet can be identified from the distance and closer in the harbour will be seen. The old entrance on the NW side has been closed off and a new entrance on the SE side opened.

Mooring Only shallow draught yachts should attempt to enter. The bottom inside the harbour is uneven, but most yachts up to 11 metres or so should be able to get in here depending on draught. The entrance is narrow so care is needed negotiating it. In calm weather yachts can go alongside on the outside of the mole, although it can be a bit bumpy with the prevailing wind blowing down into the bay.

Shelter inside the harbour is excellent if you are small enough to get in.

Facilities Water near the quay. The hamlet ashore is a little visited place where the tavernas serve simple but good fare, including good fresh fish caught locally.

General

Citrus orchards surround the village where agriculture still dominates the hinterland, and salt marshes fringe the coast. It is also quite close to the tiny village of Lia up in the mountains which would have remained entirely unknown but for the success of Nicholas Gage's *Eleni*, the semi-autobiographical account of his search for the murderer of his mother in the bitter civil war following the Second World War. This region, close to communist Albania, was a stronghold of the Greek communists who committed the sort of awful atrocities described in *Eleni*. The book is a fascinating read, describing the sort of hand-to-mouth existence that was the lot of many of these remote villages, and the awfulness of family set against family and brother against brother as sides were taken for communist or nationalist.

Note

Care must be taken of the shoal water extending out from the coast S of Sayiadha. There are reports that this area is greater than that shown on the charts.

Ormiskos Valtou

The somewhat bleak anchorage, sometimes known as Igoumenitsa Creek, is on the N side of the entrance to Igoumenitsa. Make for the innermost cove on the S side where the fish farm cuts off further access to the inlet. Anchor in 3–5m on mud and weed, good holding. Good all-round shelter in splendid isolation.

From the inlet there is a pleasant walk over the sand dunes and beach to the N side of Igoumenitsa Bay. The land around the river mouth was formerly a group of small islands until river silt fused them into the mainland. They are believed to be the ancient Sybota (demotic Sivota) Islands where the Corinthians and Corcyreans fought a naval battle in 433 BC that indirectly led to the Peloponnesian War. The name has now passed to a group of islands to the S of Igoumenitsa (see below) which has interesting implications for the theories of Dörpfeld and his quest for Homer's Ithaca discussed in Chapter 3.

Nesting stork near Sayiadha   *Lu Michell*

Igoumenitsa

The large enclosed bay lying under the flat marshy land, the river delta built up by the Potamos Thiamis, opposite the middle skinny part of Corfu. Igoumenitsa is the mainland ferry port for Corfu and at all times of the day and night there are ferries churning in and out of the large port.

Pilotage

Approach In the approach, Nisis Prasoudhi, although only 50m high, stands out well against the flat river delta to the N. Closer in the buildings of Igoumenitsa will be seen and the light buoys marking the channel into Ormos Igoumenitsa show the channel into the bay. In practice the numerous ferries coming and going pinpoint where the harbour is.

A VTS (Vessel Traffic Service) is in operation. Listen out on VHF Ch 14 for instructions although the VTS is really for ships using the port. Yachts are sometimes

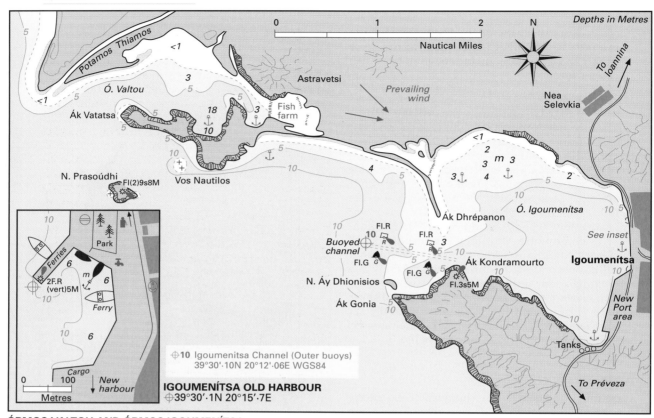

ÓRMOS VALTOU AND ÓRMOS IGOUMENÍTSA

Map labels:

Depths in Metres

N

To Ioannina

Potamos Thiamos

Astravetsi

Prevailing wind

Nea Selevkia

Ó. Valtou

Ák Vatatsa

Fish farm

N. Prasoúdhi Fl(2)9s8M

Vos Nautilos

Ák Dhrépanon

Ó. Igoumenítsa

See inset

Buoyed channel

Fl.R

Fl.R

Igoumenítsa

Fl.G

Fl.G

Ák Kondramourto

Fl.3s5M

N. Áy Dhionisios

Ák Gonia

New Port area

Tanks

To Préveza

⊕10 Igoumenitsa Channel (Outer buoys)
39°30'·10N 20°12'·06E WGS84

IGOUMENÍTSA OLD HARBOUR
⊕39°30'·1N 20°15'·7E

Inset labels:

Ferries

Park

2F.R (vert)5M

Ferry

Cargo

New harbour

Metres

Igoumenitsa looking out to the entrance channel from the south side of the bay

advised to enter the harbour to N or S of the buoyed channel where depths are adequate at least a boat's length outside the buoys.

Mooring Go stern or bows-to in the basin where convenient. The shelter here is reasonable from the prevailing northwesterlies, but it can get a bit bumpy – as much from the wash of craft in the harbour as from the wind. The new commercial quay in the SE of the bay appears to be complete, though curiously vacant, at least when I have visited. As yet the cargo and car ferries still use the old quay and harbour to the N of it.

A yacht can also anchor in the NW corner of the bay where the bottom shelves gently to the shore and this is really the best place to be. In calm weather there is a quite enchanting anchorage in the S corner of the bay, but the prevailing wind blows in here making it untenable in the summer. There is also reported to be a good lee under Nisis Ay Dhionisios in attractive surroundings, but I have no other details on the anchorage. The bottom around Igoumenitsa is mostly mud, good holding.

Facilities

Services Water on the quay and fuel in the town.
Provisions Good shopping for provisions.
Eating out Tavernas in the town although many of them are awful places catering for the itinerant population passing through.
Other Banks. ATMs. PO. Irregular buses to Preveza. Hire cars and motorbikes. Ferries to Italy, Patras, Corfu and Kavos.

General

Igoumenitsa was a small fishing village and sometime ferry harbour before the Second World War, rebuilt afterwards as a modern town and the ferry port for Corfu and Italy. It has the feel of a town where everyone is passing through, billboards point you to ticket agents, fast-food places let you grab a hamburger before you catch the ferry, and bars let you sit down to wait for the ferry. The town seems to have no purpose other than as a ferry port and it looks like it, though to be fair in recent years the waterfront has been tidied up and now has a pleasant seaside park.

Igoumenitsa is the place to make an excursion to Ioannina and to Dodona. Ioannina is one of the better preserved old Greek towns with the new quarter built next to the old quarter rather than on top of it. The old town next to the lake has an oriental feel to it with several mosques and minarets and a bazaar dating from the Turkish occupation. Ioannina was the stronghold of Ali Pasha, 'the lion of Ioannina', and he is buried on the island in the lake – boats run regular trips across in the summer.

Dodona is 21km from Ioannina along a good if winding road. The sanctuary of Dodona is one of the oldest in Greece, if not the oldest. Homer mentions 'wintry Dodona' and calls the servants of the oracle *selloi* or *helloi*, from where it is said, *Hellas*, the word for Greece and things Greek is derived. It was famous for its oracle long before Delphi arrived on the scene. It is likely that the sanctuary was established by Dorians moving down from the north and the oracle was said to come from the rustling of the leaves of a giant oak

Ali Pasha

At the end of the 18th century and beginning of the 19th Ali Pasha was a name feared by all in Ioannina and the surrounding district. Depending on what he could wring out of them, Ali allied himself with the Turkish Porte, the British, or the French to further his ambition and greed for power and wealth. He rose to power in the Ottoman war against the Austrians and was made Pasha of Trikala in 1788. In the same year he seized Ioannina and made it his base to control the Epirus.

Ali Pasha's rule was associated with cruelties of all kinds. He used ingenious methods of torture for his victims: roasting on a spit, crucifixion, flaying to death, grid-iron, drowning, any and every method was tested. In 1801 it is said that Kyra Phrosyne, the mistress of his oldest son, was drowned in the lake along with seventeen others. Kyra had refused his advances whereupon he raped her, had her bound live into a weighted sack and thrown into the lake. In 1803 sixty Souliot women, trapped in Zalongo Monastery by Ali's men, jumped to their death over a cliff rather than submit to the tyrant and his violent sexual practices. His harem was said to number over 500 and his lifestyle became a byword for luxury and hedonism.

In 1809 Lord Byron with Hobhouse visited Ali Pasha and marvelled at his luxurious lifestyle, something Byron was much accustomed to. In *Childe Harold's Pilgrimage* he describes Ali as a man under whose 'aged venerable face' are deeds that 'stain him with disgrace'. In a letter to his mother he goes further and calls Ali `. . . a remorseless tyrant, guilty of the most horrible cruelties. . . as barbarous as he is successful, roasting rebels, etc.' Ali Pasha met his end when the patience of the Sultan ran out and Turkish troops were sent to kill him. Ali escaped to the island in the middle of the lake where he was finally killed by a bullet fired up through the floor of the Monastery of Pantaleimon.

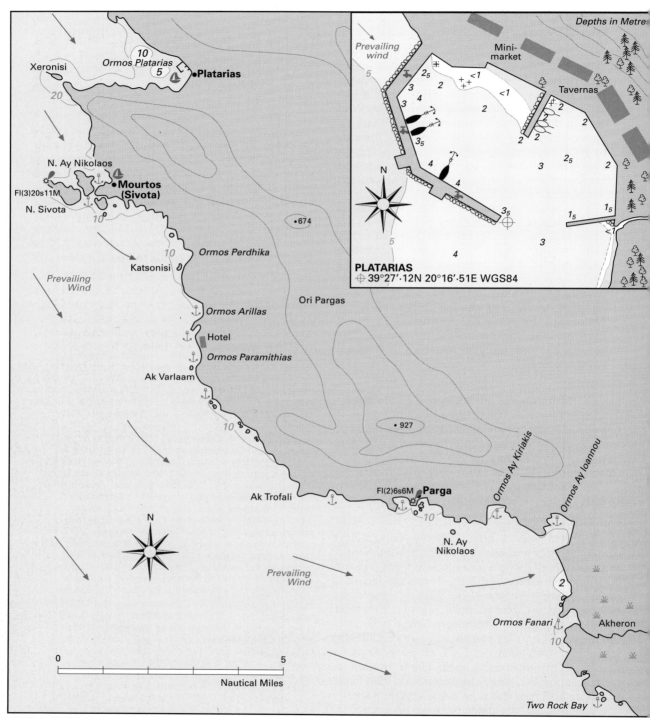

Xeronisi

Ormos Platarias
10
5
•**Platarias**

N. Ay Nikolaos
Fl(3)20s11M
N. Sivota
•**Mourtos
(Sivota)**

10

*Prevailing
Wind*

Katsonisi

10
Ormos Perdhika

•674

Ori Pargas

Ormos Arillas

Hotel
Ormos Paramithias

Ak Varlaam

10

•927

Ormos Ay Kiriakis

Ormos Ay Ioannou

Fl(2)6s6M •**Parga**
10

Ak Trofali

N. Ay
Nikolaos

N

*Prevailing
Wind*

2

Ormos Fanari
10
Akheron

0   5

Nautical Miles

Two Rock Bay

Depths in Metre

*Prevailing
wind*
5

Mini-
market

Tavernas

3   2₅   2
      + <1
3   +   +
3   4   <1
           2
3₅   2   2   2₅   2
       2

N   4   3   2₅   2

4

3₅
1₅   1₅

5   3

4   1₅   <1

3

PLATARIAS
⊕ 39°27'·12N 20°16'·51E WGS84

ORMOS PLATARIAS TO ORMOS FANARI

tree. One of the largest theatres in Greece was built here in the 3rd century BC, ten metres wider than Epidavros, and it is still largely intact today even if some of it has been stitched together with concrete. Other buildings have been excavated, but it is the theatre which is the star of the site and an annual theatre festival is held in August.

Platarias

A recently enlarged harbour inside Ormos Platarias, the large bay lying under Ak Kondramourto.

Pilotage

Approach Once into the bay the houses of the village are easily identified and the harbour will be seen in the NE corner.

Mooring Go stern or bows-to or alongside on the inside of the new breakwater extension. Good shelter from the prevailing wind.

Facilities

Water on the quay though you may have to find the waterman to unlock it. Petrol station up on the main coast road which can deliver by mini-tanker. Good shopping for provisions and tavernas and cafés on the waterfront.

General

Platarias is one of those places that seems to get largely passed by as visitors charge down to Sivota and Parga. This is its strength and the harbour and the small resort is a wonderful place with a good sandy beach and shallow water for swimming and just enough in the way of tourists for there to be some good tavernas and cafés.

Mourtos and nearby islands

Just over 5M S of Ak Kondramourto, the S entrance to Igoumenitsa, lie the Sivota Islands and, on the mainland shore opposite, the village of Mourtos. The high bold islands: Nisis Ay Nikolaos, Nisis Sivota, and Nisis Mavros Notos, are easily identified from the N or S.

Platarias   *Lu Michell*

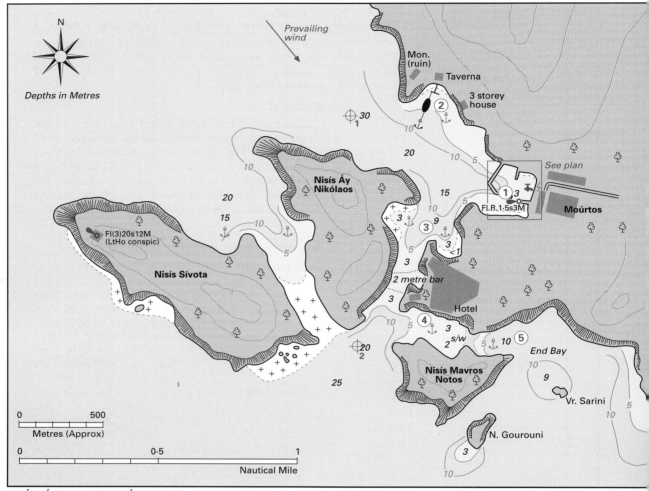

NISÍS SÍVOTA AND MOÚRTOS
⊕1 39°24'·66N 20°13'·82E WGS84
⊕2 39°23'·88N 20°13'·72E WGS84

Pilotage

Approach The lighthouse on the N end of Nisis Sivota is conspicuous and from the N a ruined three-storeyed house on the coast is easily identified. The entrance from the N or S is straightforward, but a yacht should not attempt to pass between Nisis Ay Nikolaos and Nisis Sivota where a reef obstructs the passage.

Mooring There are several anchorages around the mainland and islands.

1. ***Mourtos village*** The quayed area off Mourtos village is tenable in the prevailing winds although it is not always comfortable. Go stern or bows-to the village quay on the SE taking care of the depths. Work is in progress building a new, larger harbour to the north. The breakwaters are complete but there seems to be something of an impasse regarding completion of the harbour and yachts are not permitted to enter at the time of writing. The new breakwater does provide improved protection along the town quay and shelter inside the new harbour (when open) should be excellent. Ferry wash makes the town quay uncomfortable, but it is not usually dangerous.

2. ***Monastery Bay*** In the cove NW of Mourtos village off a restaurant. Anchor and take a line to the shore or to the short jetty if possible. There are mostly 1·5–2 metre depths off the outside of the jetty. Shelter here is better than it looks if you are tucked into the N corner.

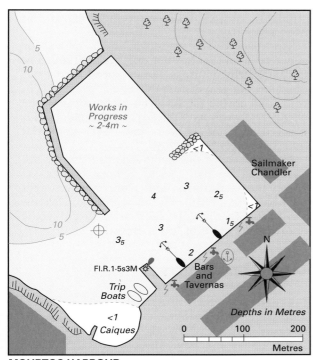

MOURTOS HARBOUR
⊕39°24′.47N 20°14′.27E WGS84

Unfortunately a garishly coloured water-park affair has been erected here which I guess will have its fans, though I am not one of them.

3. ***Middle Bay*** In the cove immediately S of Mourtos. This is one of the best places to be

The N entrance and anchorage in the channel at Nisís Sívota looking across to Nísos Áy Nikólaos   *Nigel Patten*

with good all-round shelter. Anchor where convenient and take a long line ashore or anchor in the channel, though it is quite deep. The bottom is mud and weed, generally good holding. In the summer there can be a strong S-going current, strong enough so that boats lie to the current rather than to moderate winds.

The small cove on the E side of Ay Nikolaos Island is mostly fairly shallow so most craft anchor just inside the entrance. Shallow draught craft can get further inside. Part of the bay is taken with permanently moored yachts. Care needs to be taken of a reef a short distance into the cove.

Note Depths in the channel between Nisis Ay Nikolaos and the mainland decrease abruptly to a 2m bar opposite the entrance to the next cove on the mainland. With care most craft drawing 1·8m or less can get through here, but it should be negotiated slowly. It is an eerie feeling coming up to 2m depths in crystal clear water from depths of 5–10m on either side.

4. ***Sand-bar Bay***. At the S end of the channel there is an enclosed cove sheltered by Nisis Mavros Notos with a sand bar blocking off the E end. Much of the bay is taken up with the moorings for dinghies of the hotel above, and there have been reports of notices forbidding anchoring. Booms have been reported, laid across the bay and restricting access. In any case the channel between Nisis Ay Nikolaos and the mainland south of the bar is the primary water-skiing area, so don't expect peace and tranquility here. Good shelter inside. If permitted anchor in 2–3m on sand.

5. ***End Bay*** or ***Fourth Bay***. If you circumnavigate Nisis Mavros Noros there is an attractive anchorage on the E side off the sand bar mentioned above. Good shelter in light to moderate northwesterlies, but strong westerlies send an uncomfortable swell in. Anchor in 4–10m with a long line ashore. The bottom is sand and weed, mostly good holding once the anchor is dug in. Care needed of dinghy moorings laid near the beach. Water-sports centre ashore.

6. In calm weather there are several attractive anchorages off the N end of the gap between Nisis Sivota and Nisis Ay Nikolaos. The bay on the N coast of Nisis Sivota has a buoyed swimming area, but there is room to anchor outside it. Once the prevailing wind gets up it

Mourtos town quay *Lu Michell*

strangely out-of-place water-slide feature in Monastery Bay.

Sand-bar Bay is overlooked by a monstrous concrete hotel that has not only claimed much of the bay with moorings for its speed boats and dinghies, but also disturbs this once tranquil spot with loud music far into the night. By day the channel between Ay Nikolaos and the mainland is plagued by water-ski boats and jet-skis going flat out. Swimmers beware.

Although called the Sivota Islands these are not thought to be the ancient Sybota Islands off which the Corinthians and Corcyraeans fought their battle in 433BC. The ancient Sybota Islands are probably the low hills around the creek immediately north of Igoumenitsa.

Ormos Paramithias

⊕ 39°20'·3N 20°17'·0E

Just under 5M SSE of Sivota Island, there is a long sandy beach around Ormos Paramithias. It is easily recognised by the large hotel on the slopes above the bay. Ormos Paramithias can only be used in calm weather as the prevailing wind blows straight into it.

Immediately N of the bay there is an inlet which offers good shelter in light to moderate westerlies and can be used overnight. The steep-to coast all the way along here has some wonderful isolated sandy beaches, notably Ormos Perdhika, Ormos Arillas, Ormos Paramithias, the bay under Ak Varlaam, and the bay above Ak Trofali.

Parga

Parga is the village tucked under the castle to the E of Ormos Valtou, the bay that is most used by yachts and sand and sea lovers. Parga harbour is not really for yachts and most make for Ormos Valtou and the small harbour on its W side.

Pilotage

Approach From the W the massive remains of Kastelli near the village of Ayia is easily identified. From the S the small islet of Ay Nikolaos with a white chapel and the houses of Parga village will be seen.

Mooring Yachts normally make for the small harbour on the W side of Ormos Valtou. In the approach to Ormos Valtou care needs to be taken of Voi Spiridhonia, a reef lying

blows straight into here so the anchorages must be vacated – until then they are enchanting places under the wild slopes of the islands. When you vacate the anchorage do not attempt to head south down between the islands as there is a reef and shoal water between them.

Facilities
Most facilities are in Mourtos village. For provisions or a meal you can walk from Monastery Bay (about 20 minutes) or from the anchorage in the channel. Better still take the dinghy around to the village. At Mourtos there is water and electricity on the quay. Fuel in the town. Most provisions can be found. Tavernas and bars on the waterfront or in the village proper. At Monastery Bay there is *Perri's Taverna* overlooking the bay.

General
The rugged islands close to the steep-to coast have always been a popular spot for yachties to hole up, but now there is a lot more competition from shore-based holidays. It remains an enchanting spot and Mourtos town quay has all been redeveloped in a sympathetic and convivial way that does not spoil the ambience of the place. The same cannot be said of Sand-bar Bay or the

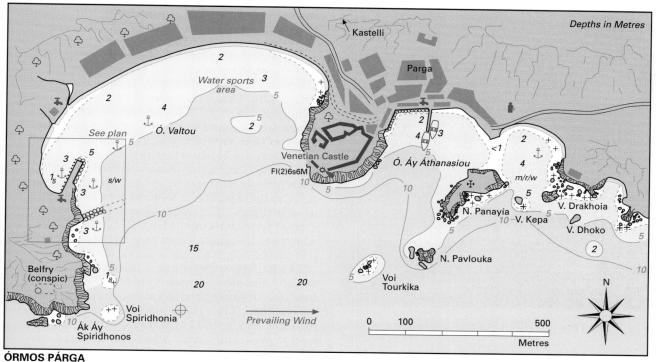

ÓRMOS PÁRGA
⊕39°16'·75N 20°23'·55E

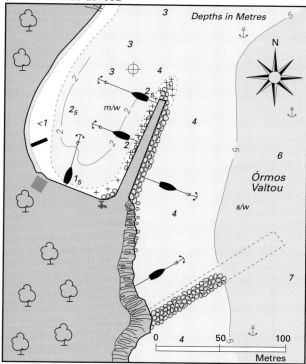

ÓRMOS VALTOU (PÁRGA)
⊕39°16'·9N 20°23·3E

approximately 100m off Ak Ay Spiridhonia. In calm weather it is easy to spot the reef, but with the whitecaps whipped up by the prevailing wind it can be difficult to see and it pays to round the cape a good distance off to avoid it. There is another rock with less than 2m over about 100m N of the reef.

Go bows-to where possible behind the mole. Care is needed as the rock ballasting projects some distance out in places.

The new mole being built to the S of the old one is not yet complete, but a yacht can anchor under it with a long line ashore or to the mole. Yachts can also anchor off to the S of the old mole though the ski and para-gliding boats operating off the beach don't like you anchoring anywhere too far E of the old mole. The bottom is sand and weed, good holding. Good shelter behind the old mole and reasonable shelter from the prevailing winds when anchored off in the bay.

A yacht can go stern or bows-to the jetty in Ormos Ay Athanasiou at Parga village itself, but there is usually little space amongst the tripper boats and the ferry.

Note Of late there have been numerous reports of

Ormos Valtou looking across the anchorage to the small
harbour *Nigel Patten*

theft from yachts here. Make sure you lock up
well and put any loose items away.

Facilities

In Ormos Valtou there are bars and tavernas on
the beach and minimarkets that open in the
summer, but little else. To really stock-up on
provisions you must walk into Parga village
around the beach and up around past the
Venetian castle – it is some distance but to
compensate the walk is a pleasant one. Water-
taxis also run to and from town. In Parga there is
good shopping for provisions and numerous
restaurants and bars. The *Castello Taverna* in
Parga village is much recommended and *Kosta's
Taverna* near the castle also has good food and
wonderful views out over the bay. PO. Bank.
Irregular buses to Igoumenitsa and Preveza. Ferry
and tripper boats to Paxos.

General

Parga is one of the most attractive places along
this coast with the old castle and the village
straggling up the hillside – it is sometimes called
the 'pine-cone' referring to its ellipsoid position
with the houses looking like the seeds of the cone
– and two picturesque bays on either side of the
fortified summit. Justifiably it attracts
considerable numbers of tourists in the summer

and consequently when you approach it from the
water you will find the beach on the W a sea of
bodies and umbrellas and the water churned up
by ski boats and paragliders and the occasional
tripper boat. Out of season it is more convivial.

The present village by the sea is actually new
Parga. Old Parga was inland to the N until
sometime in the 14th century when the
inhabitants decided to move to the present site.
Local folklore tells us that a shepherd discovered
an icon of the Virgin Mary in a cave by the sea
which was taken to old Parga. However the icon
miraculously returned of its own accord to the
cave, so the inhabitants took the hint and moved
to new Parga. The name Parga is said to be
derived from the Virgin Mary, *Panayia* in Greek,
which was bastardised over time to Parga, though
it is more likely the name is Slavic in origin.

The fort above the village is mentioned as early
as 1337 and would appear to have been Venetian
from the beginning though it may have Norman
antecedents. The Turks resented this Venetian
presence and in 1452 captured the town only to
lose it two years later when the townspeople
rebelled. It was the beginning of centuries of
battling against the Turks and ultimate betrayal
by the British. In 1537 Barbarossa, terror of the
Turkish navy, sacked the town and again the
Venetians helped the Pargiotes to rebuild and
further fortify the town. Most of the castle we see
now was built in this period as well as a fortified
wall around the town, though little now remains
of this. The Venetians regarded the castle as
pivotal for the protection of their trade route
bringing spices, silks, and precious metals and
stones back to Venice, and called Parga 'the eye
and ear of Corfu'.

When Napoleon ended Venetian rule in 1797
the Pargiotes were quite happy to come under the
protection of the French. However a new threat
hovered on the Pargiote horizon with the
ambitions of Ali Pasha who wanted to acquire the
fortress at Parga and the surrounding region. In
1800 Ali Pasha besieged the fortress and the
inhabitants cunningly hoisted the Russian flag, a
ruse they hoped would convince Ali Pasha they
were under the protection of a Russian fleet
patrolling the Ionian islands. Later in the same
year a treaty was signed between the Russians and
the Turks recognising Parga as an autonomous
town and region. In 1807 Ali Pasha again
attempted to take Parga and again failed – the
defensive position of the castle was well nigh

impregnable from the sea or land and contained large cisterns and a freshwater spring close by. In 1814 the Pargiotes rebelled against their French masters in favour of the British, at the instigation of British agents it is said, and briefly the Union Jack was hoisted over the fortress.

What subsequently happened is a shameful episode in British colonial history. After holding Parga for two years the British negotiated to sell it to Ali Pasha in return for a guarantee of non-aggression towards their possessions in the Ionian islands. So it was that Ali Pasha finally got the fortress at Parga and 4000 Pargiotes fled to Corfu on the 15th April 1816. It was not until 1913 that the town and region finally became a part of Greece.

Ormos Ay Athanasiou

In the bay off Parga village there are numerous islets and rocks peppering the approaches and the bay itself. These are all easily identified and with care present no problems to navigation.

In the W half of the bay there are no useful places to anchor without getting in the way of the ferry and tripper boats. In calm weather a yacht can anchor in the E half of the bay. Care is needed when entering between Vos Kepa and Vos Drakhoia, two above-water rocks surrounded by reefs. Anchor in 4m on mud, rock, and weed, not everywhere good holding. The anchorage is attractive and it is worth a row across to Nisis Panayia where there is a chapel and a few remains of a small Venetian fort.

Chapel on the islet off Parga town

Ormos Ay Kiriakis

⊕ 39°16'·6N 20°26'·5E

A large bay a mile E of Nisis Ay Nikolaos which is easily identified from the chapel on it. The distinctive red cliffs on the E side of the bay stand out clearly. A yacht can anchor in the NW corner where there is reasonable protection from the prevailing NW winds. Anchor in 3–10m on sand and weed, reasonable holding.

Ashore there is a hotel and villas around the beach. Several tavernas and bars open in the summer. The bay is thought to be the site of ancient Torine, a Greek and later Roman settlement, though little conclusive evidence has been unearthed and there are several other contenders for the site along the coast to the S.

Ormos Ay Ioannou

A large bay a mile E of Kiriakis. The approach and entrance are free of dangers and a yacht should head for the NW end of the bay and anchor in 4–10m on mud, rock, and weed, not everywhere good holding. The bay is subject to gusts off the hills with the prevailing winds so make sure your anchor is well in. The best place to be is in the inlet Agnali Skouliki in the NW corner, now the mussel beds have gone.

The bay is rather a bleak place without a decent beach and because of this is relatively little populated by visitors from the land or the sea making it a quiet if desolate spot. On the W side of the bay, off the inlet of Agnali Thoukidhikis, a freshwater spring wells up from the sea bottom creating a murky whirlpool where the freshwater mixes with the salt. There is a considerable volume of freshwater escaping here some 30m below sea level and if you taste the water it is brackish rather than salt – not quite the pure freshwater that local folklore says was skimmed from the surface by ships of old to replenish their stocks.

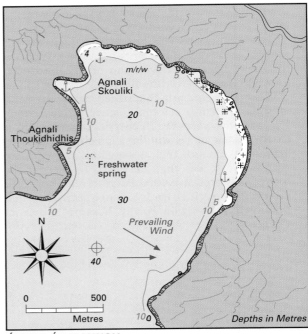

ÓRMOS ÁY IOANNOU
⊕39°16'·2N 20°28'·2E

Ormos Fanari

A bay 2M S of Ay Ioannou. Depths in the bay gradually shelve up towards the beach. Anchor under the north side of the bay in 2–2·5m on mud and sand. If the prevailing NW–W wind is blowing strongly the bay can be uncomfortable as a swell is pushed straight into it.

At the entrance on the south side is the Akheron River and it is possible to navigate up the river to a quay. The river is dredged periodically but is liable to silt to less than 1·5m, so it would pay to reconnoitre first in a dinghy. Tavernas near the quay on the river.

Potamos Akheron, the river that flows into the bay here is the ancient Acheron where the souls of the dead were thought to descend into the underworld. The spot must have been known as early as the 9th century BC when Homer has Odysseus descend into the Acheron to consult Teiresias on his return – here Circe gives Odysseus his instructions for the journey.

'You will come to a wild coast and to Persephone's grove, where the hill poplars grow and the willows that so quickly shed their seeds. Beach your boat there by Ocean's swirling stream and march on into Hades' Kingdom of Decay. There the River of Flaming Fire and the River of Lamentation, which is a branch of the Waters of the Styx, unite around a pinnacle of rock to pour their thundering streams into Acheron.'

Near the village of Mesopotamo on a rocky pinnacle is the Necromanteion of Ephyra, the sanctuary to Hades and Persephone and source of an oracle of considerable fame in the ancient world. The Necromanteion is well preserved and a fascinating site to visit. Pilgrims to the site were guided along a labyrinthine passage to the sanctuary where some sources say that hallucinogenic vapours stupefied them before a terrifying descent by windlass to a chamber where the priests relayed the answers to the questions put to the oracle. In former times the Necromanteion of Ephyra was surrounded by a large lake or possibly a gulf of the Ionian extended inland from the coast. Over millennia it has silted to become a swamp and has been partially reclaimed for farmland with the river Acheron meandering lazily through it. The remains of the site and its position still have an eerie feel to them, even in this monotheistic age.

Ormos Fanari is a spectacular setting hemmed in under cliffs to the north and the river valley opening out beyond the village to agricultural plains. The local fishing fleet quietly goes about its business suppling the nearby tavernas with fish for the visitors who come here in the summer. There are not a lot of them and this is a wonderful place to pull into, weather permitting, to get away from the beach umbrellas and ski-boats at Parga.

The canalised river at Ormos Fanari. Shallow draught yachts can get up to the boardwalk quay above the town *Lu Michell*

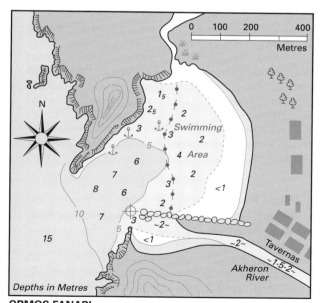

ORMOS FANARI
⊕39°14'·18N 20°28'·58E WGS84

Two Rock Bay

⊕ 39°12'·6N 20°29'·6E

A small bay lying just over 2M S of Fanari. It can be recognised from the two above-water rocks lying in the immediate approaches. It is fairly shallow in here with 2m depths in the entrance and 1·5m depths further in. There is good shelter from the prevailing winds and no sea enters. A quiet place that could be a million miles from Parga and usually you will be the only one swimming in the clear waters of the bay. There used to be a lot of sand dollar starfish on the bottom at one time, but people forget that even if everyone takes 'just one', it doesn't take long for them all to disappear.

Ligia

(Mitika)

A small rockbound harbour lying around 6 miles SSE of Two Rock Bay. The entrance is really very tricky and the approach should be made in calm

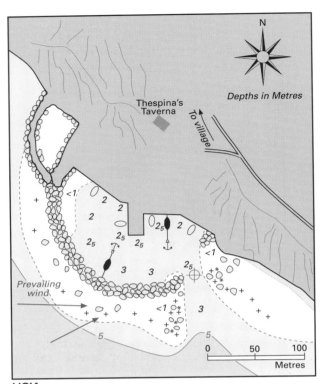

LIGIA
⊕39°09′·07N 20°34′·01E WGS84

Ligia looking over the harbour. Note the rocks on either side of the entrance   *Lu Michell*

weather only with someone up front conning the way in.

Pilotage

Approach The little cluster of houses above the harbour will be seen and closer in the rough stone breakwater can be made out against the steep slopes behind. The approach must be made from the SW heading between the two rock shelves either side of the entrance. Go very slowly and only make the approach in calm weather as the prevailing NW wind pushes a swell down onto the harbour and immediate approach. Once in the entrance you need to make a bit of a jink to starboard before turning into the harbour proper.

Mooring Berth stern or bows-to the outer rough stone breakwater with a long line ashore. Alternatively go stern or bows-to the quay if there is space. A number of local fishing boats use the quay so don't take any spaces allocated for them. Good shelter from the prevailing wind inside.

Facilities

The village is a short climb up the hill. Most provisions and several tavernas supply the bourgeoning tourist trade.

General

Once you have found your way into here between the rocks at the entrance, the harbour and village above are a wonderful low-key place to be. There is some shore-side tourist life but not too much and in the harbour you are well away from it anyway. Although Ligia is sometimes called Mitika, it is not to be confused with Ak Mitikas further south where Octavius marshalled his forces prior to his defeat of Antony and Cleopatra off Aktion.

Preveza

The town of Preveza sits just inside the entrance to Amvrakikos Kolpos and NE of the island of Levkas that shelters the 'inland sea'. It is entered along a buoyed channel and if you are approaching it in the late afternoon with the prevailing wind pushing you in, there may be some apprehension until you pick up the buoys marking the entrance to the channel.

Pilotage

Approach In the approach from the NW a low thickly-wooded knoll to the N of Preveza stands out on the otherwise flat plain. Closer in Fort Ay Yeoryios will be seen. In the summer planes taking off and landing at Aktion airport are a handy guide to where things are. The buoys marking the channel can be difficult to see until quite close-to although they are big enough.

Once identified the approach through the channel is straightforward. There is often a current flowing out of the channel from Amvrakikos Kolpos and with the onshore swell pushed into it there can be a choppy confused sea in the outer part of the channel. Once into the lee of the land the sea will flatten. Since the tunnel was completed in 2002 the ferry traffic across the channel has dwindled to a few a day, making it much simpler to proceed up the channel. Construction work continues on the north and east side of the commercial quay and yachts should keep well clear.

Mooring Go stern or bows-to the town quay wherever there is room. Good shelter from the prevailing winds but with southerlies it can be uncomfortable and may become untenable in a southerly gale. The primary construction work inside the marina is complete, but little else has been done. There will be laid moorings on the quay, but at present yachts berth wherever they can, usually alongside one of the piers. When the marina is up and running it is likely you will be directed to go stern or bows-to in a berth. Good shelter in the marina.

Facilities

Services Fuel in the town and water on the waterfront. When the marina is complete facilities should include water and electricity at berths and a shower and toilet block.

Provisions Good shopping for all provisions nearby in the town.

Eating out Tavernas and bars along the waterfront and in the town. The waterfront has now been pedestrianised and there are numerous new restaurants and bars.

Other Banks. PO. Hospital. Dentist. Hire motorbikes. International and domestic flights leave from Aktion airport just across the channel.

Preveza town quay   *Lu Michell*

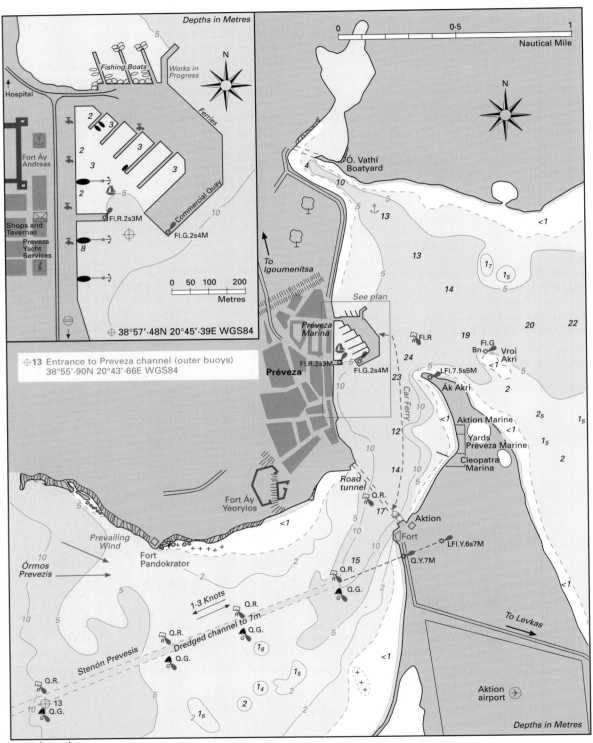

Depths in Metres

Fishing Boats

Works in Progress

N

Hospital

Ferries

Fort Áy Andreas

2 3
2 3 3
2 3 3
2
2 8

Fl.R.2s3M

Fl.G.2s4M

Commercial Quay

10

To Igoumenítsa

Shops and Tavernas

Preveza Yacht Services

0 50 100 200
Metres

⊕ 38°57'·48N 20°45'·39E WGS84

⊕ **13** Entrance to Preveza channel (outer buoys)
38°55'·90N 20°43'·66E WGS84

See plan

Préveza Marina

Fl.R.2s3M
Fl.G.2s4M

Préveza

Ó. Vathí Boatyard

4
10
5 5
13
13
<1
1₇ 1₅
14
5

20 22

19

Fl.G
Bn Vroi Akri
Fl.R
24 5 <1 5
23 LFl.7.5s5M
Ák Akri
2
2₅ 1₅
12
Aktion Marine
<1 <1
Yards Préveza Marine
1₅
Cleopatra Marina
2

14

Road tunnel
Q.R.
17
Aktion
Fort
LFl.Y.6s7M
Q.Y.7M

To Levkas

Fort Áy Yeoryios

<1

Prevailing Wind

Fort Pandokrator

Órmos Prevezis

10

5

10 5

1-3 Knots

Q.R.

Q.R.
Q.G.
Dredged channel to 7m

Stenón Prevesis

Q.R.
Q.G.

Q.G.
1₈

15

Q.R.
Q.G.

<1

5

2

2

1₅

1₄
2

2

Aktion airport

Q.R.
⊕ **13**
Q.G.
10

2 1₅

5

Depths in Metres

STENÓN PRÉVEZA

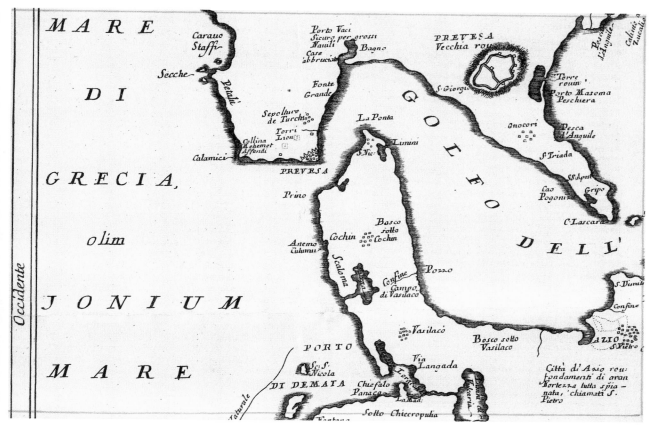

Preveza approaches from an 18th-century Venetian Chart

General

Preveza comes in for a lot of stick from the guidebooks which call it dull, dreary, drab, insignificant, somewhere to pass through as quickly as possible on the way to somewhere else. In an earlier guidebook I described it in much the same vein, but now it has been cleaned up I like the place and its back streets at least give a hint of what an everyday working Greek town looks like. It has one of the most helpful tourist offices around and the pedestrianised waterfront is popular for that evening institution, the *volta*, where you stroll at a pace at the opposite end of the spectrum to the strange American pastime of power-walking, stopping whenever you meet someone you know to say hello, exchange gossip, and have a drink if a café or bar is handy.

The town has an ancient pedigree dating from 290 BC when Pyrrhus, King of Epirus built a city here and named it Berenicia after his mother-in-law. Perhaps it did have disagreeable origins that

blighted everyones view of it for evermore. When Augustus built Nikopolis the population migrated to the new city and Berenicia declined. Preveza was not heard of again until the end of the 13th century when it was mentioned as the southernmost city in Epirus. By 1499 the Venetians had occupied it and begun building the massive fortifications around the town that can only partially be seen today.

It was ceded to the Turks by the Treaty of Carlowitz in 1699, but retaken by the Venetians in 1717 in an ongoing struggle between the two super-powers of the time to control the coastal seaboard of the Ionian. Venetian rule ended with Napoleon's conquest of the Republic and Preveza was suddenly under the tricolour, though not for long. While Napoleon was occupied with his campaign in Egypt the cunning Ali Pasha attacked and overwhelmed the French force.

The 'Destruction of Preveza' lasted two days as the Turks sacked the city and murdered the

Nikopolis

Around six kilometres N of Preveza lie the remains of Nikopolis, the city Octavius built after his victory over Antony off Aktion. This naval battle effectively resolved the civil war that had rent the Roman Empire and established Octavius as the one ruler, the legitimate Caesar of an Empire stretching from Spain to Egypt.

The story starts with the success of Julius Caesar during his campaigns in Gaul, against the Germans across the Rhine, and his triumphant return to Rome with Cleopatra on his arm. Although popular with his troops, he was not popular with the old aristocracy and it was they who arranged for his assignation in 44 BC, the `Et tu' Brute' scene in Shakespeare's Julius Caesar. Two figures emerged as successors: Octavius, Caesar's nephew, and Antony, Caesar's best general. The two came to terms with each other and quickly defeated the aristocrats in the Battle of Phillipi. The Empire was divided between Octavius and Antony, with Antony taking the east and Octavius the western provinces.

The difference between the two rulers could not have been more marked. Octavius was a sickly youth, given to stammering, a methodical man who wanted a sensible solution to problems and worked slowly and meticulously to that end. Antony was more in the mould of Julius Caesar, a brilliant general who was always in the thick of the fighting with his troops, a heavy drinker and notorious womaniser. Like Caesar he fell under the spell of Cleopatra whose powers of bewitching men seemed not to have dimmed. Anthony spent more and more time with his mistress, neglecting his men, the provinces, and his popularity in Rome. It was inevitable that a showdown with Octavius was in the offing. The two rulers marshalled their forces and met at Actium in the winter of 32/31 BC.

Antony lost the battle before it started. His army and navy were based at Actium and suffered from supply problems and lack of preparation for the campaign. The troops and rowers for the galleys were badly quartered, badly fed, and decimated by disease. One by one Antony's troops defected to Octavius and his rowers were replaced by farmers and shepherds from the local population. Octavius' fleet under the redoubtable Agrippa blockaded the supply routes to the S and cut off supplies to Antony's army.

Numerically Antony had the strongest and most experienced army, some 100,000 men against the 80,000 men of Octavius. Anthony's navy consisted of 500 ships including a large part of Cleopatra's Egyptian fleet, mostly heavy warships which had been covered in iron plate to withstand ramming, and appeared to be equipped for ferrying his numerically larger army to board the ships of Octavius. The opposing navy of Octavius was smaller, around 400 ships that were smaller and lighter and therefore more manoeuvrable. Antony desperately wanted a land battle, but Octavius refused to confront him on the land and kept up the blockade of supplies, finally hemming Antony in at Actium with a naval blockade right across the entrance to the narrow channel leading into Preveza.

Eventually Antony realised he had to take on the navy and prepared his fleet. His orders were bizarre. He told his rowers to put all the sails on board, they were normally removed for battle, in case of an offshore wind. Anyone who sails in these waters knows the prevailing winds are invariably onshore, even in late winter and spring. His oarsmen interpreted this as an order to flee, especially when they saw all movable valuables being loaded on the ships of the Egyptian squadron. Octavius divided his fleet into three and Antony was forced to do the same. The slow ships of Antony were surrounded and rammed by the smaller more manoeuvrable ships, but with his numerical advantage things were not going too badly until an entirely unexpected event. The Egyptian squadron suddenly appeared and sailed right through the naval battle and fled south. Antony promptly abandoned his men and with a fast ship pursued his mistress. Shakespeare catches the shame and despair of it all in this passage:

> She once being loofed
> The noble ruin of her magic, Antony,
> Claps on his sea wing, and like a doting mallard,
> Leaving the fight in height, flies after her.
> I never saw such an action of shame.
> Experience, manhood, honour, ne'Er before
> Did violate so itself.

The army could not believe their general had deserted them and not until a week later, when they heard he had arrived in Egypt with Cleopatra, did they finally surrender to Octavius. The conclusion is well known. Antony and Cleopatra committed suicide and Cleopatra's son by Caesar, a possible successor, was as one commentator put it, `tidied away into a small box'.

Octavius, now rechristened Augustus Caesar, built Nikopolis to commemorate his victory. It was a city on a vast scale encompassed by great walls. To populate this city built in the middle of nowhere Augustus forcibly moved the populations from towns throughout the region and even further afield. When you look at the remains of the city it should be remembered that this is the later contracted version built under the Byzantine Emperor Justinian, occupying about one fifth the area of the original city. The city was embellished with fine buildings, a large theatre and an odeum, a fine stadium, an aqueduct to carry water from the Louros, and boasted three harbours including one on the Ionian side.

Octavius had a memorial built to the battle on the site, it is said, where his tent was pitched to survey the battle. Part of it survives above the theatre and the end of an inscription . . . TUNO is guessed to be a dedication to Neptune, no doubt in thanks for the fortuitous naval battle. The city prospered and it is thought to be the `Nikopolis of Macedonia' where Paul spent a winter and wrote his Epistle to Titus. Towards the end of the 4th century AD it was attacked by Alaric the Goth and largely destroyed. Justinian rebuilt it, though the much smaller version that we see today. When the Slavs pushed south it was abandoned in favour of Navpaktos and it was never revived.

There is not really a lot to see at the site. The theatre, Augustus' monument, the baths, the odeum, and the walls built by Justinian remain in good condition. The old walls, the stadium, and the aqueduct can be found. There are some interesting Roman and Byzantine mosaics in the

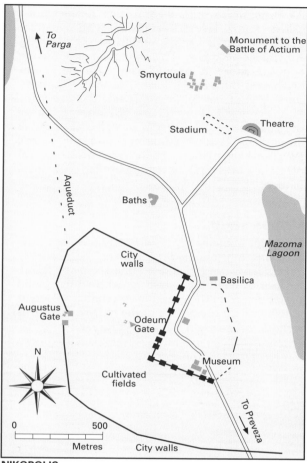

NIKOPOLIS

Nikopolis

Basilica. In recent years parts of Nikopolis have been restored and cleaned up and there is now a lot more to see. Beware of snakes around the ruins – they are said to be plentiful, though I have only ever seen one. Nikopolis is not somewhere that you have to go and see, but it is a pleasant place to wander aimlessly around and to dream on sultry summer days. The museum and the site are open 0900–1530 weekdays and 1000–1630 on Sunday.

inhabitants, French and Greek alike. Only one hundred Frenchmen were left alive, their compatriots were all beheaded, and local folk history tells us that these unfortunate hundred were forced to march to Constantinople carrying the heads of their comrades in sacks to present to the Sultan. The rape of Preveza was not complete. Ali Pasha then invited those who had fled the city to return, promising to restore their property and not to harm them further, indeed he swore on the Koran that none would be harmed, and dispatched ships to collect the scattered population. True to form Ali Pasha had the remainder of the duped population executed and it is said that on the tenth day the executioner died from his extensive labours. Like the rest of the region, Preveza only became Greek in 1912.

Much of the extensive fortifications erected by the Venetians around the city were dismantled in the 20th century, though the remains can still be identified. The city itself was enclosed by walls and a deep ditch with earthworks outside it. Two forts within the defensive ring, Ay Andreas in the N by the new mole and Ay Yeoryios in the S by the channel, formed a strategic inner defence. On

Ak Paliosarama there were further fortifications, called 'Punta' by the Venetians, with a battery that prevented ships entering or leaving Amvrakikos Kolpos. The triangular fort on the opposite shore at Aktion, where the car ferries berth, was built by Ali Pasha. At the entrance to the Preveza Channel on the N side there remains Fort Pandokrator protecting the approaches to the channel. For walkers it is a pleasant ramble around to Fort Pandokrator and on to Ak Parginoskala, where there are also several pleasant coves and beaches popular with local bathers.

Ormos Vathi

The inlet immediately N of Preveza. At one time this was a prohibited anchorage, but recently yachts have used it and no-one seems to mind. Anchor in 6–10m on mud, good holding. Good protection from the prevailing westerlies. There is a boatyard on the N side of the narrow inlet. It is a short and pleasant walk into Preveza.

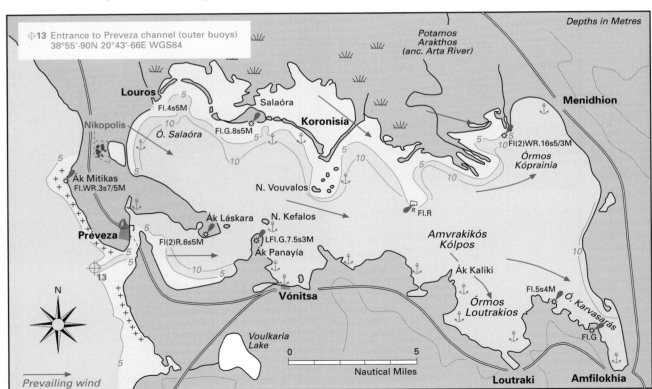

AMVRAKIKÓS KÓLPOS (Gulf of Amvrakia)

Amvrakikos Kolpos

(Gulf of Amvrakia)

The landlocked gulf entered from Preveza. The channel into the gulf is well marked by buoys and beacons. The gulf itself has a number of harbours and anchorages and is a pleasant spot to get away from it all – few yachts make the excursion into it. The N side of the gulf is largely low-lying marshy land with shoal water bordering it for some distance off. This is a breeding ground for water-birds of all types and also for estuary type fish such as sole and eels – some of the restaurants have good fresh flat-fish seldom seen elsewhere in the Ionian.

It is a strange experience to anchor off the N shore surrounded by water with little land nearby. At the beginning of this century H M Denham recorded that underwater volcanic activity at the E end of the gulf at Amfilokhia killed all the fish, which floated to the surface and were collected by the locals. The gulf also attracts numbers of dolphins which feed on the rich fish stocks and mercifully, despite the decline in numbers of dolphins in the Mediterranean generally, there

are still good numbers in the gulf according to the reports of friends sailing here recently.

Nisis Kefalos

The islet directly off Ak Panayia. In settled weather a yacht can anchor off here in the shallow water fringing the islet, though it is really only suitable as a lunch stop and not an overnight anchorage.

Vonitsa

Pilotage

Approach Once into Ormos Vonitsa the town and the castle on the slopes immediately W will be seen.

Mooring Work is in progress extending the town quay westwards in front of the fort. The blocks are in place but the quay is unfinished, although much of it is already occupied with local craft. Yachts can go stern or bows-to on the stubby quay but care is needed of

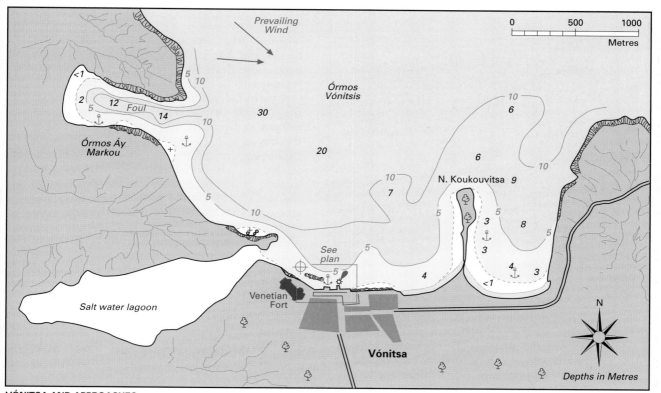

VÓNITSA AND APPROACHES
⊕38°55'·39N 20°53'·14E WGS84

Vonitsa looking over the harbour to Nisis Koukovitsa   *Lu Michell*

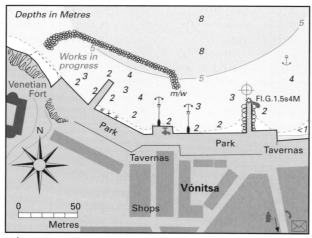

VÓNITSA
⊕38°55'·27N 20°53'·31E WGS84

underwater ballasting. Mooring bollards and rings are scarce here and a jury rigged mooring rope along the quay may be necessary. In most places it pays to go bows-to as ballasting extends out underwater and there are bits of rock and rubble that could damage the rudder

when going stern-to. Now the outer breakwater has been extended there is good protection from the prevailing wind on the town quay.

A yacht can anchor in Ormos Ay Markou on the W side of the bay where there is good protection from the prevailing wind. Much of the bay is quite deep so it is probably worth anchoring with a long line ashore to the N side of the bay. Otherwise potter around for a bit looking at depths. Care is also needed here of the remains of the old mussel farm moorings and stakes on the bottom which can foul your anchor.

An alternative anchorage is off the E side of Nisis Koukouvitsa, the wooded islet on the E side of Ormos Vonitsa, tucked as close as possible into the lee of the island. It is a wonderful place, covered in pine, with a small church on the S end.

Facilities

Water on the quay. Fuel in the town. Most provisions can be found and there are good local tavernas. *John and Angy's Taverna* is the first one along the beach, and despite the name is recommended for good Greek food. PO. OTE. Bank. ATM.

General

Vonitsa is a pleasant sleepy sort of place that gets a few tourists in the summer, enough unfortunately for a disco, but not enough to overrun the place. The castle prominent W of the town is largely Venetian, constructed in the 17th century, but incorporating part of an earlier Byzantine fortress. It is an interesting place to ramble around with good views out over the gulf from the ramparts.

Vonitsa is said to be the place where the Norman adventurer Robert of Guiscard died of fever, probably malaria, along with 10,000 of his troops. As often seems to happen in accounts of these things, he is also supposed to have died in Fiskardho on Cephalonia where the remains of a Norman church commemorates his death and the name of the place, Fiskardo, is a corruption of his name.

Ormos Rougas

⊕ 38°55'·5N 21°00'·0E

On the W side of the bay are a number of coves and bights which offer surprisingly good shelter from the prevailing westerly winds. Anchor in convenient depths in mud and weed, good holding. Pleasant pastoral landscape ashore.

Loutraki

⊕ 38°53'·5N 21°04'·5E

An inlet at the bottom of the large bay immediately W of Ormos Karvasaras. The anchorage in the inlet here and in Ormos Palaeomylos on the W side are now mostly obstructed by fish farms, but there is usually somewhere that a yacht can find shelter.

Amfilokhia

A village with a small harbour at the head of Ormos Karvasaras. A yacht will normally go alongside the N end of the quay with an anchor laid out to the NE to hold off. It is very deep in the bay, 12–15m, so ensure you have plenty of scope. With the prevailing wind blowing straight down into the bay a considerable swell is kicked up making it uncomfortable and at times possibly dangerous.

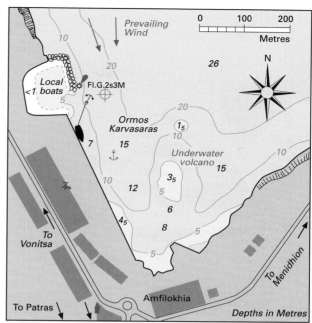

AMFILOKHIA (Ormos Karvasaras)
⊕38°52'·0N 21°09'·8E

Fuel and water in the town. Most provisions can be found and there are tavernas. PO. OTE. Bank. ATM.

The Admiralty Pilot states that the shoal patches in the harbour are the results of two eruptions of an active underwater volcano during the 19th century. The eruptions reputedly killed all the fish in the gulf and covered the water in a layer of sulphur as far as Preveza.

On a hill behind the town are the remains of ancient Limnaia, a city of some importance mentioned by Thucydides. Little remains today to be seen. The town of Amfilokhia, formerly Karvasaras like the bay, was founded by Ali Pasha as a military garrison. The name Karvasaras is said to be a corruption of *caravanserai*. Today the village is a likeable enough place, but not somewhere you will want to stay for long because of the uncomfortable harbour.

Menidhion

A small village and harbour in Ormos Kopraina in the NE corner of the gulf. A yacht can go bows-to on the end of the mole or anchor off. The bottom is mud, good holding. Reasonable shelter from the prevailing wind except if it really blows from the W. There is a long fetch across Ormos

Fishing boat with reed net. Menidhion

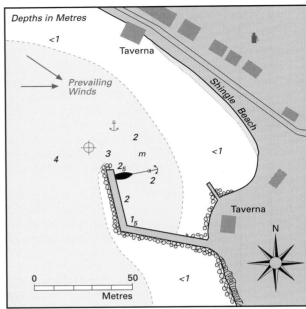

MENIDHION
⊕39°02'·5N 21°07'·1E

Kopraina which sends a fair amount of swell into the anchorage off Menidhion. If it does blow up you really need to anchor off Ak Kopraina.

Fuel from the petrol station up on the main road. Water from one of the tavernas. Most provisions can be found and there are numerous tavernas ashore. The small village attracts a few, mostly local, tourists and is a popular place for an evening out at one of the many tavernas. You will often find fresh flat-fish caught in the river estuaries flowing into the gulf near here.

Menidhion is the best place to organise a trip to Arta about 20km away – buses pass by on the main road above or you can order a taxi at one of the tavernas. Arta is a pleasant town built on a loop of Potamos Arakthos, the large river that flows into the gulf just W of Menidhion. At one time it was said that you could cross the river bar by dinghy and get up to Arta that way, but as hydro-electric barrages hold back the water and then release it to drive the turbines, this makes a trip impossible because there will either be no

Arta

Arta is built on the site of ancient Ambracia, the capital of Epirus under King Pyrrhus, though only bits and pieces of the ancient city remain. The population was transported to Nikopolis in 30BC and it soon declined to become a small provincial town. Its difficult to think of this small provincial town being the most wealthy and powerful ancient city in the region.

It also has interesting remains from the Middle Ages including the quirky church of Panayia Paragoritissa with a dangerous-looking dome supported by antique columns on a primitive cantilever principle.

Still straddling the river is an old Turkish bridge, though it is said to be built on the foundations of a bridge from Alexander the Great's time, which according to legend has the overseer's wife walled up inside it. Poems, songs, a play and even an opera have been written about the bridge and the unfortunate wife. The sacrifice of a human victim to ensure the solidity of the bridge is a common theme in Greece and there are reputed to be other such bridges with victims walled up inside them, notably on the island of Kos and near Thermopylae. According to Lawson quoted in Richard Stoneman's anthology, it was considered propitious in Zakinthos to wall up a Moslem or a Jew in any new bridge right up into the 19th century.

Menidhion

water or it will be dangerous because of the turbulence from large amounts of water suddenly released.

Nisoi Vouvalo

A group of islands on the N side of the gulf opposite Ak Yelada. The islands are joined by shingle bars with a lagoon in the middle and here a yacht can find excellent shelter from the prevailing wind. Anchor in 2–3m off the beach on the E side of the 'island'. Wonderful deserted surroundings totally away from the hubbub of the resorts.

Koronisia

⊕ 39°00'·8N 20°54'·7E

A new harbour lying approximately 2½M E of Salaora. The entrance to the harbour has silted so only small yachts can use it and even then with some care for the depths. Make the approach from due S and keep very close to the extremity of the W breakwater where there are 1·5m depths – reconnoitre first in the tender if in doubt. Go bows-to the W quay. Good shelter from the prevailing winds. Three tavernas ashore.

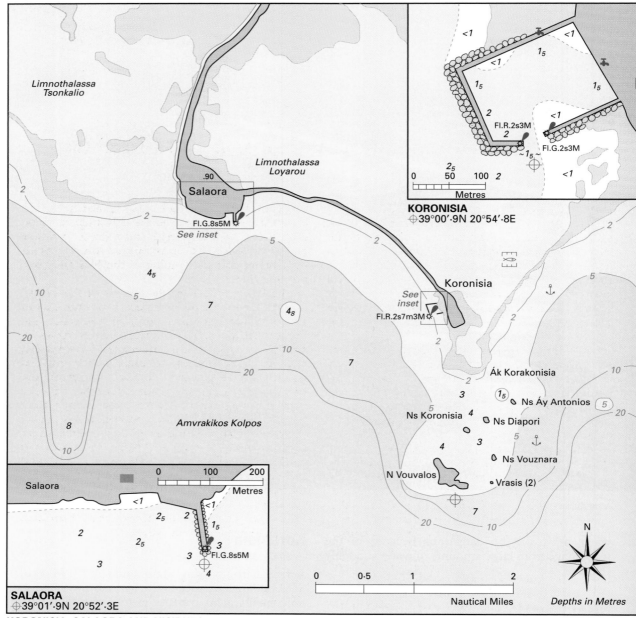

Limnothalassa
Tsonkalio

Limnothalassa
Loyarou

.90

Salaora

Fl.G.8s5M

See inset

Amvrakikos Kolpos

KORONISIA
⊕ 39°00'·9N 20°54'·8E

Fl.R.2s3M

Fl.G.2s3M

0   50   100
Metres

See
inset

Fl.R.2s7m3M

Koronisia

Ák Korakonisia

Ns Koronisia

Ns Áy Antonios

Ns Diapori

Ns Vouznara

N Vouvalos

Vrasis (2)

Salaora

0   100   200
Metres

Fl.G.8s5M

SALAORA
⊕ 39°01'·9N 20°52'·3E

KORONISIA, SALAORA AND NISIDHES VOUVALOS
⊕ 38°59'·0N 20°55'·0E

0   0.5   1   2
Nautical Miles

N

Depths in Metres

Salaora

⊕ 39°01'·9N 20°52'·3E

There is a short rough mole off Salaora where limited shelter can be found. Anchor in 2·5m on the E side of the mole and take a line ashore. A cluster of dilapidated shacks ashore.

A yacht can also anchor off on the W side of Ormos Salaora within what looks like walking distance from Nikopolis.

3. The Inland sea.
Levkas, Meganisi, Ithaca, Cephalonia and Zakinthos

The Inland sea is the area of water enclosed by the islands of Levkas, Cephalonia and Zakinthos on the W and the mainland on the E. Other islands are dotted around the Inland sea and to some extent it resembles a huge lake with land on three sides, or so it seems. It is a wonderful cruising area, one of the best in Greece, and it should be no surprise that it is a popular cruising area for yachts. The area is tailor-made for charter and flotilla sailing and dinghy sailing schools are well established, indeed I spent two seasons as a flotilla skipper in this area many moons ago. Despite the numbers of charter boats here there are so many harbours and anchorages all around the Inland sea that it is possible to get away from it all should you feel claustrophobic during the high season.

Until quite recently there was little tourism apart from yachts and a few determined land travellers. Transport between the islands was not well developed and except for Zakinthos, the area was pretty much off the beaten track. Now that new ferry routes have been opened up and regular flights to Aktion, Cephalonia and Zakinthos introduced, the area is better known than it used to be, though no-one could say it was 'touristy' apart from a few patches here and there.

The history of the area is a mixture of influences that broadly follows the history of the rest of the Ionian. Within the group of islands lies the thin hour-glass outline of Ithaca, an island forever haunted by the words of Homer. The ramifications, extrapolations, and metaphorical geography that have been wrung out of Homer's words runs to volumes of commentaries and interpretation, popular and academic, some of which I look at in the introduction to this book. The Greeks and Romans barely bothered with the islands, with the exception of Cephalonia, and though they were all duly colonised and incorporated into the Greek and Roman empires, they were much neglected and subject to piracy and privateering. Under Byzantine rule they fared little better and the coming of the Normans was not unwelcome.

The lasting effect on the islands of the Inland sea was undoubtedly Venetian. From the castles and forts the Venetians built, the churches, the old gnarled olives they encouraged the locals to plant, the architectural influences incorporated into the local houses, to more subtle cultural imports, the Venetians put their stamp on the islands. It is important to remember that with the singular exception of Levkas, the islands were never really under Turkish occupation, a matter of decades rather than the centuries the mainland opposite had to endure. British influence was confined largely to constructing roads and buildings on Cephalonia and Zakinthos and then the islands were left pretty much to themselves, to some extent forgotten on the western periphery of Greece, at least until tourism touched them here and there in the last few years.

Nisos Levkas
(Nisos Lefkas, Levkadha, Leucas)

Levkas is only an island by virtue of the canal running through the salt marsh between it and the mainland. The present canal is of recent origin, built by the Greeks with British help in 1905, but a canal has existed here since the 7th century BC if we are to believe Thucydides. He also tells us it had silted by 427 BC when the Peloponnesians had to drag their ships over the Levkas isthmus. The Romans repaired the canal, probably under Augustus around the time Nikopolis was built,

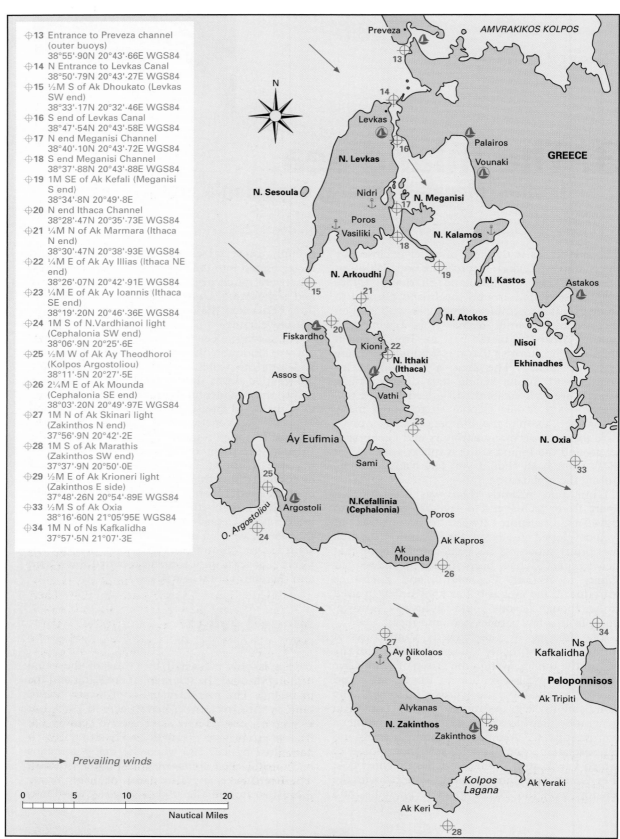

13 Entrance to Preveza channel
(outer buoys)
38°55'·90N 20°43'·66E WGS84
14 N Entrance to Levkas Canal
38°50'·79N 20°43'·27E WGS84
15 ½M S of Ak Dhoukato (Levkas
SW end)
38°33'·17N 20°32'·46E WGS84
16 S end of Levkas Canal
38°47'·54N 20°43'·58E WGS84
17 N end Meganisi Channel
38°40'·10N 20°43'·72E WGS84
18 S end Meganisi Channel
38°37'·88N 20°43'·88E WGS84
19 1M SE of Ak Kefali (Meganisi
S end)
38°34'·8N 20°49'·8E
20 N end Ithaca Channel
38°28'·47N 20°35'·73E WGS84
21 ¼M N of Ak Marmara (Ithaca
N end)
38°30'·47N 20°38'·93E WGS84
22 ¼M E of Ak Ay Illias (Ithaca NE
end)
38°26'·07N 20°42'·91E WGS84
23 ¼M E of Ak Ay Ioannis (Ithaca
SE end)
38°19'·20N 20°46'·36E WGS84
24 1M S of N.Vardhianoi light
(Cephalonia SW end)
38°06'·9N 20°25'·6E
25 ½M W of Ak Ay Theodhoroi
(Kolpos Argostoliou)
38°11'·5N 20°27'·5E
26 2¼M E of Ak Mounda
(Cephalonia SE end)
38°03'·20N 20°49'·97E WGS84
27 1M N of Ak Skinari light
(Zakinthos N end)
37°56'·9N 20°42'·2E
28 1M S of Ak Marathis
(Zakinthos SW end)
37°37'·9N 20°50'·0E
29 ½M E of Ak Krioneri light
(Zakinthos E side)
37°48'·26N 20°54'·89E WGS84
33 ½M S of Ak Oxia
38°16'·60N 21°05'95E WGS84
34 1M N of Ns Kafkalidha
37°57'·5N 21°07'·3E

Preveza

AMVRAKIKOS KOLPOS

N

Levkas

Palairos

Vounaki

GREECE

N. Levkas

N. Sesoula

Nidri

N. Meganisi

Poros
Vasiliki

N. Kalamos

N. Arkoudhi

N. Kastos

Astakos

N. Atokos

Fiskardho

Kioni

Nisoi

Ekhinadhes

Assos

**N. Ithaki
(Ithaca)**

Vathi

N. Oxia

Áy Eufimia

Sami

**N.Kefallinia
(Cephalonia)**

Poros

Argostoli

O. Argostoliou

Ak Kapros

Ak
Mounda

Ay Nikolaos

Ns
Kafkalidha

Peloponnisos

Alykanas

Ak Tripiti

N. Zakinthos

Zakinthos

*Kolpos
Lagana*

Ak Yeraki

Ak Keri

→ *Prevailing winds*

0   5   10   20
Nautical Miles

NISOS LEVKAS, NISOS ITHACA, NISOS CEPHALONIA AND NISOS ZAKINTHOS

Quick reference guide

	Shelter	Mooring	Fuel	Water	Provisions	Tavernas	Plans
Levkas							
Levkas Town	A	A	A	A	A	A	•
Levkas Marina	A	A	A	A	A	A	•
Ligia	B	AC	B	A	C	B	•
Nikiana	B	A	B	A	B	B	•
Nisis Sparti	O	C	O	O	O	O	
Nisis Khelona	C	C	O	O	O	O	
Periyiali	B	AB	B	B	C	C	•
Nisis Madhouri	O	C	O	O	O	O	•
Nidri	B	AC	B	A	B	A	•
Tranquil Bay	A	C	O	B	O	O	•
Ormos Vlikho	A	AC	B	A	C	C	•
Ormos Dessimou	C	C	O	B	O	C	•
Stenon Meganisou (Meganisi Channel)	C	C	O	O	O	O	•
Ormos Rouda	C	C	O	B	C	C	•
Ormos Sivota	A	AC	O	A	C	B	•
Ormos Ammousa	O	C	O	O	O	C	
Vasiliki	B	AC	B	A	B	B	•
Skorpios and Skorpidhi							
Skorpios	C	C	O	O	O	O	
Meganisi							
Spartakhori	B	AC	O	A	C	B	•
Vathi	A	AC	O	B	C	C	•
Ormos Kapali and Abelike	A	C	O	O	O	O	•
Port Atheni	B	AC	O	B	C	C	•
Meganisi E coast	O	C	O	O	O	O	
Nisis Thilia	C	C	O	O	O	O	•
Ithaca							
Frikes	B	AB	O	B	C	C	•
Ormos Frikon	C	C	O	O	O	O	•
Kioni	B	AC	O	O	C	C	•
Kolpos Aetou	C	C	O	O	O	O	•
Vathi	A	AC	B	AB	B	B	•
Ormos Sarakiniko	C	C	O	O	O	O	
Pera Pigadhi	C	C	O	O	O	O	•
Ormos Ay Andreou	C	C	O	O	O	O	•
Ormos Pis'aitou	O	C	O	O	O	O	•
Ormos Polis	C	C	O	O	O	C	•
Cephalonia (Kefallinia)							
Fiskardho	A	AC	B	A	B	A	•
Kalo Limini	C	C	O	O	O	O	•
Ay Eufimia	B	AC	B	A	C	B	•
Limin Sami	B	AB	B	A	B	C	•
Poros	B	AC	B	A	B	B	•
Ormos Kateleios	O	C	O	O	C	C	•
Pessades	C	AC	O	O	O	C	•
Argostoli	A	A	A	A	A	A	•
Argostoli Marina	A	A	O	O	A	C	•
Maistratos Harbour	A	A	A	B	B	B	•
Lixouri	B	A	B	B	B	C	•
Ay Kiriakis	O	A	O	O	O	C	•
Assos	O	AC	O	B	C	B	•
Zakinthos							
Limin Zakinthos	B	A	B	A	A	A	•
Ormos Ay Nikolaos	B	A	B	B	C	C	•
Zakinthos Marina	B	A	B	A	A	A	•
Alykanas	B	AC	O	O	C	C	•
Kavos	B	AC	O	B	C	C	•
Porto Roma	O	C	O	O	O	C	
Ay Yerakas	C	C	O	O	O	C	
Ormos Lagana	O	C	O	B	B	B	•
Lithakia	C	A	O	B	C	C	•
Ormos Keri	C	AC	O	B	C	B	•
Ormos Vroma	C	C	O	O	O	C	•

and after that it is likely it was used under Byzantine and Norman rule, though I can find no concrete references.

Under the Venetians the canal, or at least the deeper parts of the lagoon, were used to allow ships to pass on the E side of the island. It is likely the Turks used it as well during their occupation. The Russians are known to have dredged a route through the lagoon and built the two small forts, Fort Constantine and Fort Alexander, to guard the 'canal'. The canal we see today is thought not to be anywhere near the original Corinthian canal nor to bear much resemblance to the channel used by the Venetians. Ships then drew much less than they do today and the canal is unlikely to have been more than 1½–2½m deep.

Recently the canal has been widened and dredged though for what purpose no-one is quite sure. There is talk of cruise ships entering the canal and tying up to the quay at Levkas town, but this is more than likely wishful thinking by local entrepreneurs. Tourists are far more likely to arrive overland than over-the-water and to this effect a new floating bridge was installed at the N end of the canal to replace the chain ferries. Not that the town council can countenance the new contraption as a bridge: it is the ferry boat *Ag Maura*, the name boldly painted on the side of the bridge in case anyone should mistake it for anything else, a little island subterfuge designed to keep the special grants and tax concessions that islands in Greece get from the government in Athens.

Though there may be technical quibbles about whether Levkas is an island or not, (some guidebooks on the Greek islands do omit it), the

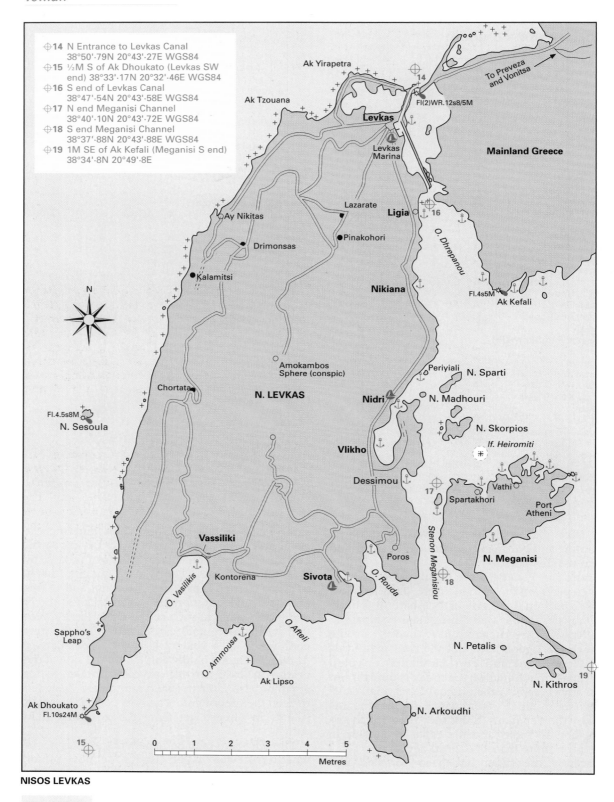

⊕**14** N Entrance to Levkas Canal
38°50'·79N 20°43'·27E WGS84
⊕**15** ½M S of Ak Dhoukato (Levkas SW
end) 38°33'·17N 20°32'·46E WGS84
⊕**16** S end of Levkas Canal
38°47'·54N 20°43'·58E WGS84
⊕**17** N end Meganisi Channel
38°40'·10N 20°43'·72E WGS84
⊕**18** S end Meganisi Channel
38°37'·88N 20°43'·88E WGS84
⊕**19** 1M SE of Ak Kefali (Meganisi S end)
38°34'·8N 20°49'·8E

Ak Yirapetra

To Preveza
and Vonitsa

Ak Tzouana

14

Fl(2)WR.12s8/5M

Levkas

Mainland Greece

Levkas
Marina

Lazarate

Ligia

16

O. Dhrepanou

Ay Nikitas

Drimonsas

Pinakohori

Kalamitsi

Nikiana

Fl.4s5M

Ak Kefali

N

Amokambos
Sphere (conspic)

Periyiali

N. Sparti

Chortata

N. LEVKAS

Nidri

N. Madhouri

Fl.4.5s8M

N. Sesoula

N. Skorpios

If. Heiromiti

Vlikho

Vathi

Dessimou

17

Spartakhori

Port
Atheni

Vassiliki

Stenon Meganisiou

N. Meganisi

Kontorena

Poros

Sivota

O. Rouda

18

O. Vasilikis

Sappho's
Leap

O. Afteli

N. Petalis

O. Ammousa

19

Ak Lipso

N. Kithros

Ak Dhoukato
Fl.10s24M

N. Arkoudhi

15

0   1   2   3   4   5

Metres

NISOS LEVKAS

place has the feel and look of an island once you are across the causeway and from anywhere other than Levkas town you don't ever ask the question. Even from the canal you can see it is a high island with the main mountain range running down the middle from N to S. Around much of the coast the mountains drop precipitously down to the sea, an impressive coast made beautiful in places by abundant olive groves pierced by tall cypress.

In the SW the steep limestone cliffs give the island its name. Originally it was called Nirikos after the colony established by the Corinthians, near present day Levkas town, but was changed to Leucas or Lefkos meaning 'white' referring to the white cliffs or possibly to the white (limestone) mountains of which the island is composed. It may be that this was to honour Sappho's lovelorn leap over the cliffs (sometime in the 6th century? BC) or it may be just a piece of straight description. This name, variously bastardized to Lefkas, Levkas, and often the diminuitive, Levkadha, continued to be used except under Venetian occupation when the name of the fort guarding the land and sea approaches in the N, Santa Maura, was more commonly used. It reverted to Levkas when it became Greek.

For many years Levkas was considered the poor cousin of the islands in the Inland sea, locked into a poverty that was partially historical and partially the result of its geography. Compared to the other islands Levkas has large areas of flat fertile land suited to agriculture and consequently it has been self-sufficient for many of its needs. It is still the largest wine producer of all the Ionian islands, Zakinthos and Corfu included. This restricted emigration, the lads were needed to work the fields, unlike the other islands where emigration was and still is a part of island life. But whereas the other islands received money sent back by the emigrants once they had established themselves in America or Australia or South Africa, Levkas did not and remained a truly insular place.

The geography aided this history. The island has no deep water port and until recently had only poor road communications with the mainland. Until the F/B *Ag Maura* made getting across the canal easier, the old chain ferries would have traffic backed up for miles at busy times. It was forgotten until the recent incursion of tourism bounced it into the 20th century, though this has been gentle enough and fortunately dispersed around the island.

Getting around

On the whole the bus service around the island is patchy. The main bus terminal in Levkas is on the SE quay. A circular route runs around the island several times a day and there are more regular services to Nidri and some other villages. The best way to get around is on a hire motorbike available from several agencies in Levkas and Nidri. Hire cars or jeeps are comparatively expensive and really only worth it if there are four of you.

Roads are good for the main routes, but deteriorate rapidly for secondary routes. It is well worth visiting the villages inland. The countryside is green and wooded in places and there is some magnificent mountain scenery as well. Do not trust the local maps entirely for minor roads which may exist only as tracks or sometimes not at all.

Levkas

Levkas town sits in a corner of the salt marsh where the land starts to rise up to the hills. After midday the sea breeze starts to blow in from the NW and a yacht reaching Levkas in the late afternoon is faced with the terrifying prospect, at least for the first time, of heading for a lee shore with breakers heaping up in the shallowing water, until the entrance to the canal is spotted and negotiated.

Pilotage

Levkas Canal

From the N the location of the entrance to the canal is difficult to identify. A long sandy spit extends to the W and NE of the canal entrance. Often a haze obscures the island and the mountains cannot be seen until you are five or so miles off. The wine factory and warehouse on the W of the canal and Santa Maura fort on the E can be distinguished. The buildings of Levkas town will also be seen inland. Closer in the breakwater sheltering the entrance will be identified. From the W two windmills stand out on Yera spit.

A yacht should get all sail off before entering the canal. Rounding the breakwater keep a prudent distance off the end as a sand bank builds up here – it is periodically dredged. On the S side of the entrance off Santa Maura fort there are underwater rocks and debris which are sometimes marked by two 44-gallon drum 'buoys', but not always!

A yacht must normally wait before the floating bridge (the F/B *Ag Maura*) opens, which it does on the hour, every hour. Between 2100 and 0600 you will need to call up the bridge operator on

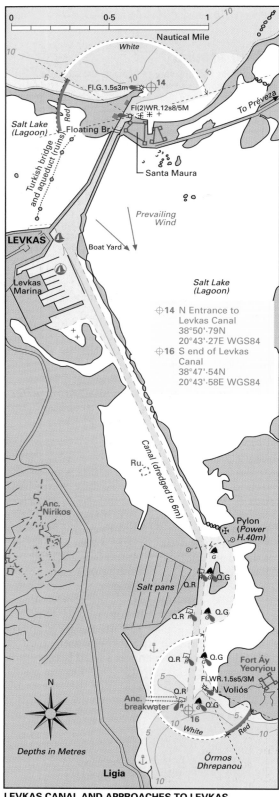

LEVKAS CANAL AND APPROACHES TO LEVKAS

VHF Ch 12. For most yachts a section of the bridge at the island end is raised, for very large yachts the bridge is swivelled to lie parallel to the mainland bank. Contrary to conventional IMO regulations, traffic heading southwards has right of way according to a special regulation. In practice though yachts proceeding N go first and yachts going to Levkas town and S go afterwards. You may find the bridge operator waves either north or southbound traffic through first and then there is chaos as yachts charge all over the place. Keep an eye on the operator and play it by ear. There is often a current in the canal, sometimes as much as 1½–2kt, so manoeuvring can be difficult and a yacht is recommended to go alongside the W quay under the breakwater until the bridge opens. The current also makes it difficult to get through the gap left when the bridge section is raised and care is needed. A sense of timing is critical so that you are not too near the yacht in front to get into trouble and not so tardy that the bridge operator throws a tantrum and flusters you as he jumps up and down urging you through.

From the S the entrance to the canal is

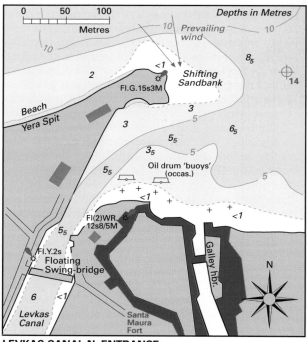

LEVKAS CANAL N. ENTRANCE

⊕ **14** N Entrance to Levkas Canal
38°50'·79N 20°43'·27E WGS84

The lifting/swinging bridge at the northern end of the Levkas Canal   *Lu Michell*

Looking out from the coast over the shoal water east of the entrance to the Levkas Canal.

comparatively easy to spot. In Ormos Dhrepanou aim for Fort Ay Yeoryios conspicuous on a summit on the E side of the canal entrance. Closer in you will see Nisis Volios with a light structure on it and the two conical buoys marking the entrance to the channel. Do not cut outside the two buoys: there is a reef on the E and the remains of an old breakwater on the W. Once into the channel the way is clearly shown by buoys and beacons marking the channel. The channel through the salt marsh is straightforward and clearly marked by poles with cones and baskets. The direction of buoyage is from either end of the canal until Levkas town.

Levkas Town
Pilotage
Approach The buildings of the town are readily identified whether coming from the N or S.
See separate entry for Levkas Marina.

Mooring Go stern-to the NE quay or bows-to the E or SE quay. On the latter quays the ballasting extends underwater so it is best not to go stern-to. Protection is best on the E quays where the wind blows you off, but which are often crowded in the summer. On the NE quay the wind is blowing side-on to a yacht so lay the anchor well out – the bottom is mud and excellent holding. A yacht can also go stern or bows-to the causeway above the bridge where again the wind blows you off.

Shelter is generally good although strong southerlies, especially gales from the SE, can make it uncomfortable and even dangerous at times.

Facilities
Services Water on the quay. Fuel on the E quay or by mini-tanker.
Provisions Good shopping for all provisions in the town. *Marina market* at the western end of the town quay is very helpful. Several supermarkets around the town.
Eating out Numerous restaurants in the town. *Chicken shack* or properly *Regantos* in the alley running W from the town square is a long time

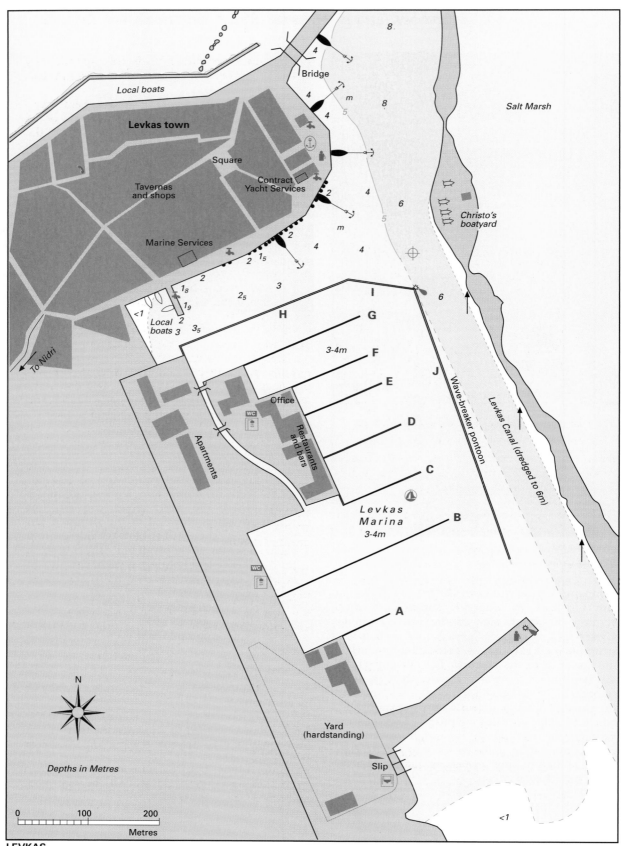

Local boats

Bridge

4

4

4

2

2

2

2

1.5

2

1.8

1.9

2

3

3.5

8

m

8

5

m

5

6

4

4

4

4

4

2.5

3

<1

Salt Marsh

Christo's boatyard

6

6

Levkas town

Square

Contract
Yacht Services

Marine Services

Tavernas
and shops

To Nidri

Local
boats

I

H

G

3-4m

F

E

D

C

B

A

J

Wave-breaker pontoon

Levkas Canal (dredged to 6m)

Office

Restaurants
and bars

Apartments

WC

WC

*Levkas
Marina*
3-4m

Yard
(hardstanding)

Slip

<1

N

Depths in Metres

0	100	200

Metres

LEVKAS
⊕38°49′·98N 20°42′·78E WGS84

The distinctive 'earthquake-proof' town clock in Levkas

favourite. *Molos* near the library serves excellent modern European cuisine. *Karabulias* is a good fish restaurant on the south quay.

Other PO. OTE. Banks and ATMs. Hire motorbikes and cars. Buses to Athens (usually six a day). European flights to and from Aktion nearby.

General

It is a strange town, unlike any others in the area, looking like a Greek town that has taken on board Third World architecture from somewhere like downtown Rio di Janero. In recent years it has been tarted up somewhat, but it still retains a distinctive architecture that is remembered if not always admired. The earthquakes that afflict this region have spawned all sorts of earthquake-proof buildings and the ones in Levkas are one variation on a theme. The ground floors of the houses look much like the architecture found throughout the Ionian, but the first and in some cases second storeys are usually constructed of corrugated iron or sheet iron over a wooden sub-structure. The roofs too are more often than not corrugated iron. This eccentric architecture is designed to be flexible in the event of an earthquake so it literally sways rather than falling down as stone and bricks do.

The locals are sceptical about reinforced concrete and while there are a few new reinforced concrete apartment blocks on the outskirts of the town, no-one really wants to live there. They may have a point, after all the new reinforced concrete buildings now scattered around the Ionian have yet to be tested by the sort of earthquake that hit the area in 1948 and 1953. Whatever the theory, the town has largely been saved from the soulless architecture that blights some Greek towns and the brightly painted distinctive houses of Levkas give it a special character that people either love or hate.

For what was a forgotten part of the Ionian, Levkas has a remarkable tradition in the arts and literature. Two of Greece's national poets were born here. Aristoteles Valaoritis (1824–79), a poet who wrote in a rather pompous manner attempting to emulate the epics, is becoming popular again after a period of decline. He was involved with the intricacies of Greek political life until he retired in 1868 to the island of Madhouri off Nidri. Angelos Sikelianos (1884–51) was also born here and is remembered as much for his attempts to rebuild Greek literary and cultural life as for his poetry.

Every year in August the town sponsors a Festival of Arts and Literature which includes music, dance and theatre from all over the world. For a little over two weeks the town is a riot of events. The festival attracts concert and dance groups from all over the world – in different years I have seen groups from most of the Eastern European countries, from Russia, Thailand, Malaysia, Indonesia, China, India, Scandinavia, France, Italy, Spain, and Germany, in fact from most of the countries in the world. Every night there is a different group performing and at times you will have to pinch yourself if you are to believe this is a small town in the Ionian. In Santa Maura castle concerts are held – one year I saw Hadzidakis perform a selection of his works, in mine and others opinions his music will be remembered long after the more popular Theodrakis. In other years ballet companies, opera companies, and well known orchestras and conductors have performed here in the spooky shadows of the fort with the last of afternoon wind tugging at the flags around the perimeter and the sound of the sea in the background.

Santa Maura

The fort of Santa Maura at the N end of the canal is well worth exploring. It is not always open at the main gates, but there is always a way in around the walls if you are remotely athletic. The fort has not been restored, but you can easily sort out the different parts of it. One of the most picturesque parts is the old galley port on the E side.

It was originally built in the 13th century by a Latin prince, probably John I. It commands the obvious entry point to Levkas Island along the spit of land from the mainland with the sea on one side and salt marsh on the other. A causeway of some sort connected it to Levkas town at most times. It was enlarged by Charles I Tocco for Spain and the moats and galley port constructed.

The fort takes its name from a chapel erected by an Empress of Byzantium. With variations the story goes something like this. Sometime after the fall of Constantinople to the Turks in 1453, the former empress Helen Palaeologus and mother of the last

emperor, Constantine XI, who died defending the city, was caught in a storm off Corfu. She was probably en route to Venice or Genoa to escape the omnipotent Turk. Her ship was pushed down to Levkas where she was saved on the feast day of Saint Maura. In gratitude she built a monastery inside the fort and, so the story goes, spent the rest of her life here until she died.

The saint could not save the fort from the Turks who captured it in 1479. Under Beyazid II a causeway and aqueduct were built. A story, probably apocryphal, relates that Beyazid ordered a causeway that was wide enough for a carriage to pass over it. The costs were enormous: the causeway was over a kilometre long and was reported to have 366 arches. However when finished the causeway was found to be exactly the width of a carriage and therefore impractical for a carriage to pass over. The contractor was duly beheaded.

The fort changed hands again in the early 16th century when it was captured by the Spanish. It was returned to the Turks a year later when a treaty was signed and

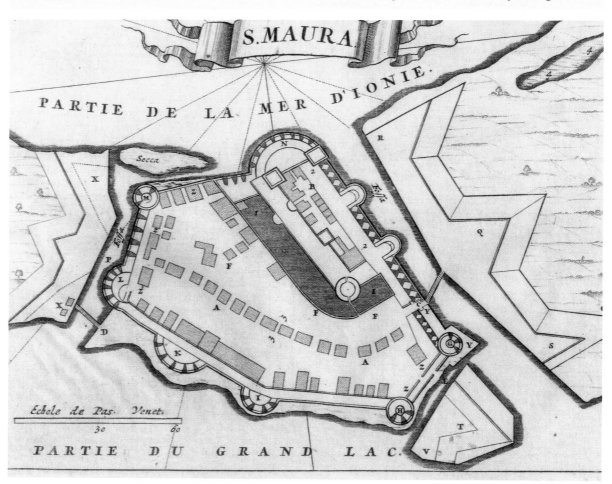

French plan of Santa Maura from the 19th century

The old galley harbour at Santa Maura looking out to the northern entrance of the Levkas Canal

was to remain Turkish until 1684 when Morosini captured it for the Venetians. Santa Maura and Levkas formally became Venetian in 1698 with the Treaty of Carlowitz and it was to remain thus until Napoleon brought the Venetians to their knees in 1797. During the Venetian occupation the fort was further strengthened and Fort Ay Yeoryios was built at the S end of the canal on the mainland summit overlooking Ormos Dhrepanou. This was to be the last major work carried out on the fort and what we see today is largely Venetian enlarging on the earlier Spanish and Turkish works.

It is a pleasant spot to wander around when the festival is not on. Large cannon lie scattered around the defensive walls and a chapel to Santa Maura still sits in the middle of the fort. There is nothing of exceptional historical interest to see, just a quiet place with picturesque views out over the sea and salt marsh, a place to sit and dream in the sun.

Remember to take insect repellent – it is feeding time for the mosquitoes at concert hour.

While Levkas town may not seem the sort of place you would travel a long way to see, in fact those who come here for even a short time often end up staying. I have many good friends here and you can get the sort of insight into Greek life, warts and all, that is often difficult to find in larger places that hide it and smaller places where local life has been submerged under western influences. Numerous eccentric foreign travellers have succumbed to the discreet charm of the place and settled down in Levkas.

At one time it used to be a base for the cigarette smuggling boats. Fast speedboats like *Channel Breeze*, a forty foot aluminium planing boat with very little superstructure for her size and turbo-charged 1300hp diesels, were based here for maintenance between smuggling runs. In Christo's boatyard on the other side of the canal there used to be an assorted selection of speedboats that for one reason or another, too slow or not reliable enough, were left to rot and no-one but no-one would touch them or even tell you who owned them. On the NE quay it was common to see several small tramp steamers that were used to pick up the cigarettes in Albania and ferry them across to just outside Italian territorial waters. When trade died down in the early 80's the port police eventually had them moved to the S end of the canal where they were run up on the mud to rot.

Levkas Marina

The planned north pontoon was not in place at the time of writing, though there are still plans to install it at a later date.

Pilotage

Approach The marina is easily identified from either direction.

Mooring Levkas marina may be contacted on VHF Ch 69. Berth where directed in the marina where you may be assisted by marina staff. There are laid moorings tailed to the quay. A charge is made.

Shelter in the marina is generally good although some berths may be affected by southerlies.

Facilities

Services Water and electricity at all berths. Shower and toilet block. 100-ton travel-hoist.
Provisions Minimarket in the marina.
Eating out Restaurants and bars in the marina.

General

This new marina was opened in July 2002 and is now virtually complete, although some of the landscaping has yet to mature. There are restaurants and bars dotted around the waterfront and some shops and boutiques as well. In the future it is likely more shops will open, but don't forget it is a pleasant walk around to Levkas town on the other side.

Levkas Canal: south end

At the S end of the canal it is possible to anchor off the W shore. With care a small yacht should head W from between the last and second-to-last set of buoys. The depths here are variable, between 2–4m, with less closer to the shore. Anchor where convenient on mud. The prevailing wind blows from the N to NW off the land.

Note Care must be taken of the old submerged mole running across from the coast to the last set of buoys. A yacht should not attempt to pass between the last buoys and the coast. This submerged mole most likely enclosed a harbour for the ancient city of Nirikos on the slopes above, although it may have been reconstructed and enlarged in a later age.

Ligia

A small fishing harbour on the W side of Ormos Dhrepanou. From the end of the canal the village and breakwater are easily identified. Many of the deep water berths along the breakwater are occupied by a fleet of *gri-gri* fishing boats but there is usually space on the end to go stern or bows-to and there may also be space further along. The locals will tell you if you occupy a fishing boat berth. Depths off the village quay are mostly shallow though there may be a space where a small yacht can go bows-to. Good shelter inside from the prevailing wind.

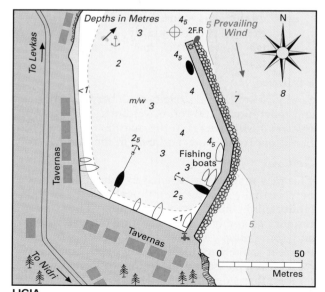

LIGIA
⊕38°47′·34N 20°43′·32E WGS84

Yachts anchor off the shore in 3–7m on mud and thick weed. Shelter here is not the best with the afternoon breeze, but it is tenable and gets more comfortable when the breeze dies at night. Make sure you do not obstruct the entrance as the *gri-gri* boats tend to return in the early morning hours.

Ashore some provisions can be found and there are several tavernas including *Yiannis* taverna on the waterfront which has excellent fresh fish straight off the boats.

Nikiana

A small harbour in Ormos Episkopi, the bay lying just under 2M S of the end of the Levkas canal. There are 2–4m depths along the outer end of the mole where a yacht can berth stern or bows-to. The bottom is mud and weed, good holding. Care needed of old mooring chains fouling the bottom about 25m off the quay at the outer end of the mole. The harbour is often crowded with charter boats, but there are usually a few berths free. Good shelter behind the mole. A yacht can also anchor off in the bay in 4–10m where there is reasonable shelter from the prevailing wind.

Ashore in the village of Nikiana most provisions can be found and there are several tavernas.

Ancient Nirikos

On the slopes above Kariotes are the remains of ancient Nirikos. There is little to see, a section of wall and other large blocks of *ashlar* masonry distributed about the olive groves. No doubt much of the ancient city was incorporated into the various forts built nearby to guard the canal. From the remaining foundations and masonry it can be seen that this was a large city surrounded by substantial walls and fortified towers.

Little is known about the city except that it was established by the Corinthians in the 7th century BC. At this time it may be that the island was joined to the mainland across Paliokhalia. At an early date the name of the city and the island was changed to Leucas. The Leucadians had three ships at the Battle of Salamis. In the Spartan Wars the island sided with Sparta and suffered for it. In 436 BC it was sacked by the Corcyreans and in 446 BC by Athens. It recovered and came under Roman occupation.

At sometime a bridge was probably built from Nirikos to the mainland and it has been suggested that parts of the old bridge can still be seen – though I have never seen anything resembling bridge supports here. The city declined at the end of the Roman era and never recovered with the new settlement built where present-day Levkas town is sited.

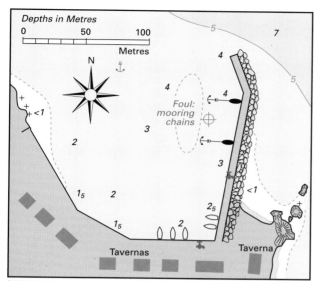

NIKIANA
⊕38°45'·6N 20°43'·25E

Nisis Khelona

(Nisis Socava)

A small islet lying close off the coast of Levkas. A yacht can pass between the islet and the coast though care is needed of shoal water off the coast of Levkas and at the S end of Nisis Khelona. In light to moderate NW winds a yacht can anchor off the coast of Levkas to the N and S of Khelona.

Periyiali

A long straight quay in the northern approaches to Nidri, partially obscured by Nisis Sparti. The quay is reasonably well sheltered from the prevailing northwesterly, but should a northeasterly blow overnight off the mountains on the mainland, which is not uncommon, it will

Those around the harbour are as good as any. The original village has grown considerably to cope with its tourist trade and there are numerous new villas and small hotels along the beach, but it remains a pleasant enough place with a wonderful long beach around the bay and a wooded hinterland.

About 1½M S of Nikiana a number of hotels are conspicuous on Ak Mayemenos. On the S side of the cape there is a small cove that a yacht can use in calm weather, though care is needed of above and below-water rocks off the coast. A hotel ashore.

Nisis Sparti

A steep-to island lying about ¾M off the coast of Levkas. It is covered in *maquis* and has the framework of a reinforced concrete building on it. The passage between Sparti and Levkas is deep and free of dangers except for a rocky shoal patch (see below) off the S end of Sparti. In calm weather a yacht can anchor in the bight on the NW side of the island although it is quite deep here. The anchorage is exposed to the prevailing wind and is untenable in a brisk NW breeze.

Deep draught yachts need to be careful of the shoal (least depth 2·7m) lying about ¼M W of the S end of Sparti. It is not always the easiest to spot even in calm weather so if you draw 2 metres or more care is needed in the vicinity.

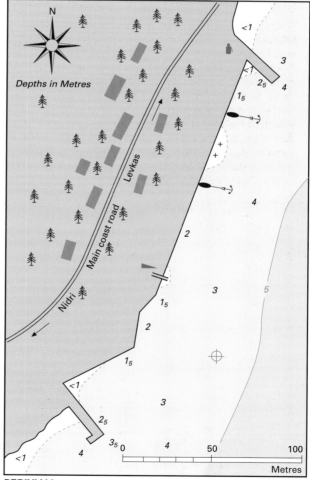

PERIYIALI
⊕38°43'·1N 20°43'·4E

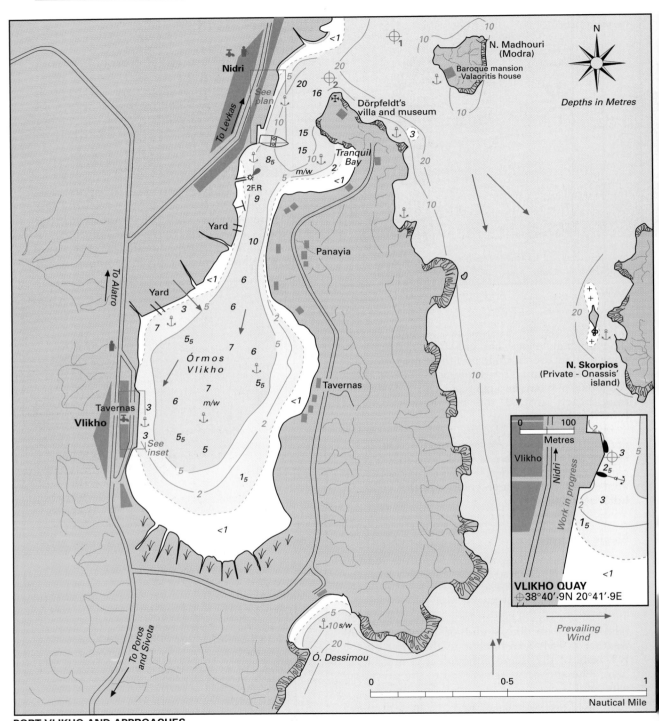

PORT VLIKHO AND APPROACHES
⊕₁ 38°42'·61N 20°43'·24E WGS84
⊕₂ 38°42'·38N 20°42'·87E WGS84

Nidri

To Levkas

See plan

2F.R
9

Yard

Yard

Yard

To Alatro

Tavernas

Vlikho

To Poros and Sivota

Órmos Vlikho

Panayia

Tavernas

Dörpfeldt's villa and museum

Tranquil Bay

N. Madhouri (Modra)

Baroque mansion - Valaoritis house

Depths in Metres

N

N. Skorpios
(Private - Onassis' island)

Ó. Dessimou

m/w

10 s/w

VLIKHO QUAY
⊕ 38°40'·9N 20°41'·9E

0   100
Metres

Vlikho

Nidri

Work in progress

Prevailing Wind

0   0.5   1
Nautical Mile

The Valaoritis villa on Nisis Madhouri

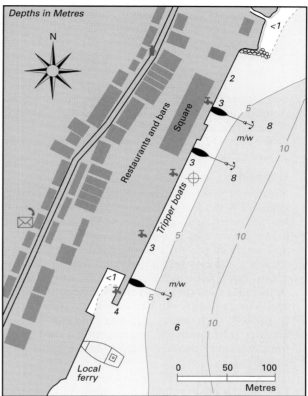

NIDRI
⊕38°42′·5N 20°42′·8E

blow straight onto the quay here and it can be uncomfortable and may become untenable. Go stern or bows-to where convenient. Ashore the main road runs adjacent to the quay and it can be quite noisy when berthed here.

Nisis Madhouri

(Nisis Modra)

The small island lying S of Sparti and immediately E of Nidri. Madhouri is a wooded island easily identified from the S by the Baroque villa on the SW. This is the family home of the Valaoritis family. The villa was originally built by Greece's national poet and composer of the national hymn, Aristoteles Valaoritis. There is reasonable shelter from the prevailing winds in the anchorage off the SW coast of the island.

Nidri

At the entrance to Ormos Vlikho is the village of Nidri. It is easily recognised by the cluster of buildings ashore and the cluster of boats berthed off the town quay.

Pilotage

Approach The approach is straightforward though care needs to be taken of tripper boats, ferries, sailing dinghies, water-bikes, sailboards, and yachts in the immediate approaches. Nidri is something of a Clapham Junction for anything that floats and the water around is constantly churned up by the wake of passing boats in the summer.

Mooring Berth stern or bows-to where possible on the town quay, leaving the area for the ferries and tripper boats free. The depths drop off quickly from the quay so you will be dropping your anchor in 8–10m depths. The bottom is mud and weed, reasonable holding. Reasonable shelter from the prevailing wind which does not blow home, but does send in a chop. The wake from the tripper boats and ferries also affects the quay.

The quay is crowded in the summer, but you can anchor off to the S in 3–7m. The pier running out from the shore S of the quay at Nidri is the home base of *Neilson* flotilla boats, but you may be able to find a space for a while if no boats are expected back. Do enquire in advance. A little further S there is another T-pier where you may find a berth.

Facilities

Services Water on the quay. Fuel can be delivered by mini-tanker.

Provisions Good shopping for all provisions in the main street.

Eating out Numerous restaurants and bars. When I first came to Nidri in 1977 there were only two tavernas here, *Nick the Greek* and *Panorama*, both of which still exist. There are now said to be well over twenty at the last count. Take your pick of where to go, local allegiances change along with the quality of the food from year to year, but you cannot complain about lack of choice.

Other PO. OTE. ATM. Bank. Hire motorbikes and cars.

General

Nidri was once a little fishing and agricultural village. I hesitate to call it a village today, which it was some ten or so years ago, as like many resorts it has grown out of the sleepiness of village life and acquired the fittings and fixtures of a resort, to wit a main street lined with bars, souvenir shops, fast-food counters, ice-cream shops, travel agents and surrounded on the perimeter by hotels and 'village rooms'. In the season the main street is packed with weary tourists looking for yet another recommended taverna or bar and given the choice the process can go on for most of a holiday.

Yet despite its rapid transition from olive oil to sun-tan oil, Nidri retains, just, some of its former character and friendliness. The old widows dressed all in black look on bemused at scantily clad nymphs, shake their heads, and go back to their crochet and embroidery. Nick the Greek, known to the Onassis' before they deserted Skorpios, still runs his taverna and casts a lecherous eye over the girls while Voula toils in the kitchen. On the waterfront there must be one of the most picturesque nautical views around across to the islands and to the wooded slopes of Tranquil Bay – and there is always plenty of activity in the harbour.

On the outskirts of the village there are pleasant walks and one of the best known is up to the spring and waterfall that supplies Nidri with its water. From Nidri walk along the main road towards Levkas to the sign to Rahi village, turn left and walk to Rahi. At Rahi the road forks, take the right-hand road and walk on past the football pitch and old water mill to Nidri Reservoir. Carry on along the track beside the creek until you have to take to the creek-bed itself. Continue walking up the gorge which gradually gets narrower until you get to the waterfall and pool, a cool shaded place in the summer. In the spring you may find a lot of snakes in the creek-bed dining on the local frog population.

If you want to hike to the top of the waterfall go back to the Nidri Reservoir and take the track off to the left. For a bit of variation on the way back

Wilhelm Dörpfeld

On the far slopes of the headland above Tranquil Bay sits Dörpfeld's villa, now a museum housing some of his collection of artefacts. Wilhelm Dörpfeld assisted the great Heinrich Schliemann to excavate Troy and along with Schliemann believed that Homer should be interpreted literally rather than metaphorically as the academics of Britain and Germany insisted. Schliemann found Troy this way and Dörpfeld set off to look for Odysseus' city state using Homer as his guide.

He was disappointed not to find anything of consequence on Ithaca and for some reason turned his attention to Levkas. His later rationalisation was that Homer's description of Ithaca as an island with estates on the mainland and sheep ferried from the island to the mainland, identified the island as Levkas. Dörpfeld pointed out that Homer's description of Ithaca as 'the farthest out to sea' and 'slanting to the west' did not apply to Ithaca as Cephalonia was the westernmost of the Ionian islands. He hypothesised that the ancients' idea of geography positioned the Ionian islands in a line stretching away from the entrance of the Gulf of Patras and therefore Levkas was the furthest and in the ancient Greeks' mental geography the westernmost island. Remember that there was no compass or points of the compass at this time, so the idea of 'westernmost' has to be an anachronistic translation of something like furthermost or outlying which Levkas was in a northwesterly sort of way.

He identified a site near Nidri as the capital of this Ithaca, Sivota as the bay where Odysseus was put ashore and met Eumaeus the swineherd, and a cave near Evgiros as the sacred cave of the Nymphs. He unearthed various artefacts dating back to the Mycenean period, though there is some doubt about whether they correspond to the time of the Trojan Wars.

So why is Levkas called Levkas and Ithaca called Ithaca? Dörpfeld's answer was that Levkas was originally called Ithaca. The migration of the Dorians from the north in 1200–1100 BC pushed mainland tribes into Levkas forcing the Leucadians south where they settled on the island they now called Ithaca. Few historians put much credence in Dörpfeld's theory today, but then there are few viable alternatives. Nidri took Dörpfeld to its heart and he was by all accounts a much loved man in the village. He is buried by the monument, the Mnimion Dörpfeld, on the slopes by the museum. It is a pleasant walk around to the monument with wonderful views over the sea and islands, perhaps to contemplate the geography and compare notes with Homer's brief description of the Ithaca of the *Odyssey*.

The museum in Levkas also holds some of Dörpfeld's finds.

take the left fork from Rahi until you get to a track on the left leading to Neochori and Paliokatouna from where there is a road back down to Nidri. This waterfall walk is popular in the summer and at the height of the season a walk around the slopes of Tranquil Bay is a good alternative.

Tranquil Bay

Opposite Nidri there is a bay much frequented by yachts. The entrance is deep and free of dangers, but care is needed of a shallow muddy shelf extending for some distance from the head of the bay and around the S side. It can be difficult to see unless it is flat calm. Anchor in 8–12m on soft mud and weed. Because it gets so crowded in here it is not a bad idea to anchor on the N side of the bay and take a long line ashore. You can pull the boat quite close to the coast as depths come up quickly from 8–10 metres here. The bottom is good holding once your anchor is properly dug in, but it may take several attempts before it is holding to your satisfaction. Good all-round shelter.

There is a well at the head of the bay though it is not drinking water – take care not to let soap suds run down into it if you do washing here. It is a longish row over to Nidri if you don't have an outboard.

In earlier times when it was a quiet little-visited place, H M Denham christened it 'Tranquil Bay' in his *The Ionian Islands to Rhodes*. With the increased number of yachts it can no longer be called tranquil, but it remains a wonderful place and at times it has a certain peace and quiet to it that even those with loud sound systems on their boats feel disinclined to pollute. The slopes around are covered in olives with pencil-thin cypress everywhere and there are wonderful walks around the slopes.

Ormos Vlikho

(Port Vliho, Vlihou)

From Nidri the bay of Vlikho extends down through the bottleneck entrance and opens up into a landlocked oval bay with the village of Vlikho on the W side.

Pilotage

A yacht can anchor anywhere where there are sufficient depths. A shallow shelf extends a short distance out around parts of the W and E sides and a considerable distance out at the S end. Depths in Ormos Vlikho are mostly 5–10m in the middle and shelving to less at the edges. There are several favoured anchorages:

1. On the NE side of the bay. Anchor in 5–6m. Good shelter from the prevailing wind which tends to gust down from the north. Good tavernas nearby on the east side.
2. On the NW side off the boatyard. Anchor in

Tranquil Bay opposite Nidri

Ormos Vlikho looking towards Nidri

5–6m taking care of the shallow ledge off the NW corner. Good shelter.

3. Off Vlikho village. Anchor in 5–6m on mud and weed. Good holding. The wind tends to gust into here but the holding is good and there is no fetch for any chop to build up.

4. On the quay at Vlikho. Where the quay projects there are 1·5–2·5m depths and you can go stern or bows-to here if you can find room. There are a number of yachts which seem to berth permanently alongside taking up most of the quay space. It can be quite uncomfortable on the quay as the prevailing wind tends to push a chop onto the quay. Make sure your anchor is well dug in.

The prevailing wind blows in from the NW to N, but usually does not blow home with any great strength, though it will blow at 20 knots on occasion. Care is only really needed when you are on the quay at Vlikho where a bit of chop is pushed onto it by the wind. The bottom is mud and weed, good holding once through the weed.

Facilities

Water on the quay at Vlikho. Most provisions and several good tavernas in the village. Also several tavernas on the E side and in Nidri. Other facilities in Nidri.

General

Vlikho has been little touched by tourism though now it is being tarted up in readiness to latch onto the success of Nidri. The quay has been cleaned up, trees planted, and a water sports base set up. For the time being it remains a quiet relaxed place compared to the bustle and noise of Nidri. There are pleasant walks around the head of the bay – take the main road going S then turn off to the left and follow the road. Alternatively take a wander up to the boatyard.

Ormos Dessimou

⊕ 38°40'·0N 20°43'·0E

A large bay about a mile S of Nisis Madhouri. It offers good shelter from the prevailing wind, but is quite deep. Anchor in the N corner in 5–10m. The bottom drops off very quickly to 20–30m. Ashore there is a camping ground with a small shop and taverna.

Stenon Meganisiou

(Meganisi Channel)

Between Levkas and Nisos Meganisi, Stenon Meganisiou or the Meganisi channel gives one of the most beautiful vistas to be seen from the deck of a boat in the Ionian. The channel, ½M wide at the narrowest point, passes between the high slopes and cliffs of Levkas with a number of ravines cutting down to the sea; and on the other side, the lower slopes of Meganisi with a long sandy beach fringing much of it. Cypress and *maquis* grows where it can get a hold on the Levkas side and covers much of the slopes of Meganisi. Towards the N end of the channel Nisis Thilia, a small wooded islet, lies just off the coast of Meganisi.

The wind in this channel is fickle. What usually happens is that it blows from the N to NW at the N end of the channel and from the S to SW at the S end. In the middle there is often a flat spot with no wind or light winds from either direction. It can be disconcerting to be running down the channel with the wind aft of the beam and to see a yacht coming in the opposite direction also with the wind aft of the beam.

There are several pleasant anchorages on the Meganisi side of the channel – the Levkas side is mostly too deep. See notes on Nisis Thilia.

At the S end of the channel there are several caves on the Levkas side including the one that features in Hammond Innes' thriller *Levkas Man*. It is worth getting hold of a copy of this book to read while you cruise around as all of the locations can be identified from the descriptions in the book and it is still a good holiday read.

Ormos Rouda

A large bay on the SE corner of Levkas, just around the corner from Stenon Meganisiou. A swimming area is cordoned off with small buoys at the head of the bay and you need to anchor outside this area in 12–15m. The prevailing wind gusts out of here, but a swell may still work its way in from the breeze blowing around the bottom of Levkas. A number of tavernas ashore.

In the NE corner is Mikro Yialis and a short quay. The quay has mostly 1·5–2m depths off it and if there is room you could go stern-to. Most of the quay is the preserve of the local fishing boats so if you do berth here, enquire whether or not you are occupying someone's place.

Ashore there are two camping grounds and small holiday bungalows. Most provisions can be obtained from a shop at the camping ground and there are several tavernas.

The bay has historically served the village of Poros on the slopes to the east of the bay, but as with many seaside places it is gaining a life of its own beyond that of the hill village.

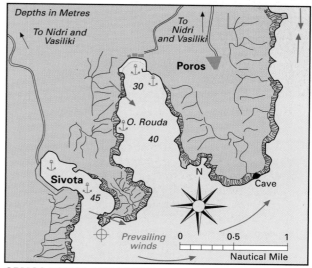

ORMOS ROUDA AND SIVOTA
⊕38°36'·87N 20°41'·52E WGS84

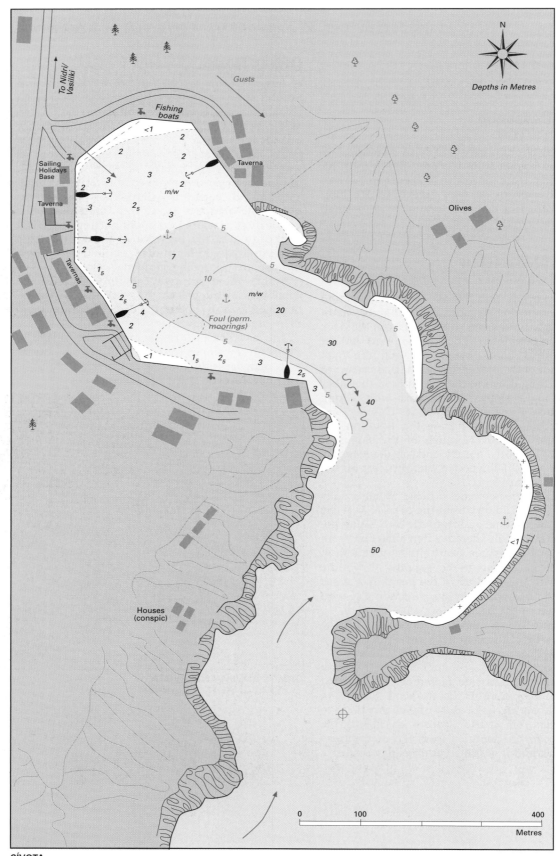

Depths in Metres

To Nidri/
Vasiliki

Gusts

Fishing
boats

Sailing
Holidays
Base

Taverna

Taverna

Tavernas

Olives

<1
2
2
2
2
2
3
3
3
2
2
m/w
3
2₅
3
1₅
5
5
5
7
10
m/w
20
2₅
4
Foul (perm.
moorings)
5
30
2
5
<1
1₅
2₅
3
2₅
3
5
40
5

50

Houses
(conspic)

0   100   400

Metres

SÍVOTA
⊕38°36′·87N 20°41′·52E WGS84

Ormos Sivota

A landlocked bay immediately W of Ormos Rouda.

Pilotage

Approach The entrance is difficult to see from any direction although in the summer yachts will be seen disappearing or appearing as if from the very cliffs along the coast. A cluster of small bungalows on the W side of the entrance and a villa on the summit between Rouda and Sivota will be seen. Closer in a few red roofs will be glimpsed across the isthmus on the E side of the entrance. Once into the entrance the hamlet will still not be seen until you round the dogleg and enter the anchorage proper.

Mooring Sivota is very popular and gets crowded in the summer so you will have to berth wherever possible. Much of the bay now has a concrete quay around it and the bottom nearby has been dredged, though unevenly in places. Berth stern or bows-to anywhere around the

Sivota

Sivota   *Peter Sewell*

quay in the bay, though larger yachts drawing 2 metres or more should take care of the depths off some of the quay. The deepest area is on the S quay. Yachts can also anchor off although depths drop off quickly in the outer part of the bay and you may be anchoring in 15–20 metres here.

The bottom is mud and weed, good holding once through the weed, though this can take some doing at times and will test your anchoring skills. The shelter in here is excellent, fleets of flotilla and charter boats are wintered afloat, but with the prevailing wind there are gusts off the high land around the bay which can be bothersome.

Facilities

Water at a number of points around the quay. The taps have a coin operated meter. Some provisions available from a couple of minimarkets. A surprisingly large number of tavernas fuelled by the charter fleets which pull in here. I used to recommend some tavernas here, but now I suggest you wander around and make

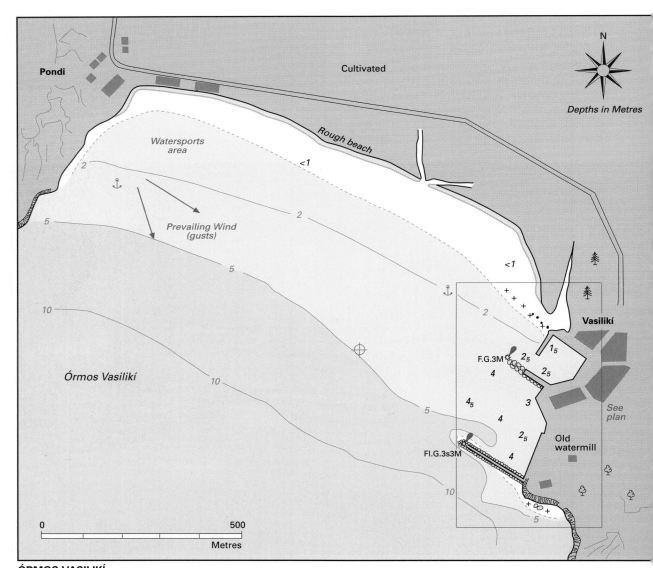

ÓRMOS VASILIKÍ
⊕38°37'·7N 20°36'·15E

your own choice. Most of the food is pretty much of a muchness in all of them.

General

Sivota relies for much of its income on the passing trade from waterborne traffic. It is a wonderful spot, the slopes around are planted with olive trees and the old houses of the hamlet are clustered around the water. But the ubiquitous reinforced concrete is encroaching on the village with several new buildings around the perimeter rising out of earth scars on the slopes. It is so popular in the summer and can get so crowded that its ambience is shattered by the noise and numbers of people. A sad consequence is that the numbers generate lots of sewage which goes into the bay and it can get smelly in the summer heat.

Sivota was Dörpfeld's choice for the landing place of Odysseus and he identified Evgiros to the W of Sivota as the cave of the nymphs.

Ormos Afteli

A large bay W of Sivota. In calm weather a yacht can anchor at the head although it is very deep. With the prevailing wind a swell is pushed into here.

Ormos Ammousa

A bay immediately W of Ak Lipso. A yacht can anchor in wonderful surroundings at the N end of the bay in a small cove under a large villa. It is quite deep. When the prevailing wind sets in it blows into here so you will probably have to get out. You get a good slant across to Fiskardho from here or you can run back to Sivota or plug around to Vassiliki.

Ormos Vasiliki

The large bay formed by Ak Dhoukato on the W side. The prevailing wind tends to gust out of here with some force so care is needed in the approaches.

Pilotage

Approach The white lighthouse on Ak Dhoukato is easily identified and once into the entrance the buildings at Pondi in the NW corner will be seen. From the E the village of Vasiliki cannot be seen until you are right into the bay. In the summer there are sailboards everywhere

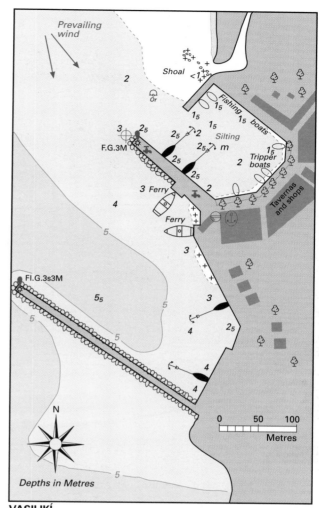

VASILIKÍ
⊕38°37'·7N 20°36'·4E

operating off the beach at the head of the bay.

Mooring It is possible to anchor at the head of the bay in 2–5m on sand and weed, suitable with moderate winds blowing off the land, but uncomfortable with strong gusts. You are better off going into the harbour at Vassiliki village and going stern or bows-to the W or S quay. Care is needed in the inner harbour which is silting and there are a number of shallow patches forming in the harbour – if you draw 2m or more care is needed. Alternatively if the inner harbour is full you can go on the east quay in the outer harbour. If you do go here make sure your anchor is well in and lay a second anchor just to be sure as the prevailing

Vasiliki looking into the harbour

wind blows straight into here. There are gusts into the harbour, but shelter is good tucked inside and the gusts usually die down at night. In unsettled weather the harbour is uncomfortable and some berths untenable.

Facilities

Services Water on the quay. Fuel on the outskirts of the village.

Provisions Most provisions can be found. Good baker in the village.

Eating out Numerous tavernas around the waterfront.

Other PO. Metered telephone. Exchange facilities. Ferry to Fiskardho.

General

Vasiliki is a pleasant relaxed little place with a wonderful waterfront shaded by trees and festooned with drying nets. In recent years it has played host to packaged watersports holidays, almost exclusively windsurfers who come here for the brisk afternoon wind off the hills. According to the pros Vasiliki ranks in the top ten places for board-sailing in the Mediterranean. Most of the accommodation for the holidays is at the W end of the beach at Pondi or in hotels behind the beach.

The village is a well-watered place with abundant springs and it is odd to hear water running away into the sea when a short distance away, on the island of Ithaca and parts of Cephalonia, it is a precious commodity. If you walk around the coast to the S of the harbour there is an old water mill (converted to a bar) and

Sapp...

Off Ak D... ...imestone cliffs that
give Levk... ...ho is supposed to
have leap... ...spurned by her
lover. For ... ...n known by the
name Sapp... ...ared thus in poems
and prose do... ...d is even marked
on the old Ad... ...Byron's Childe
Harold sailed ... ...s he saw `...
Leucadia's far p... ...d hail'd the
last resort of fruitless love`. Despite all the labels there
is no conclusive proof that Sappho jumped to her
death here or that she even visited Levkas. Nonetheless
underneath the myth there is a fascinating trail of
animism and human sacrifice attached to the cape and
the Temple of Apollo that stood here in ancient times.

In antiquity a leap was performed from the cliff-top to
the sea below (known as katapontismos), though
whether this was punishment for crime, sacrifice to
Apollo, a trial (much like bungee-jumping or high
diving I suppose), or some other pursuit, is unknown.
We do know that in the Roman era the jumpers had
either feathers or the branches of trees tied to them
depending on the commentator.

In *Pausanias, Volume I, Book X*, there is a short account
of a similar cult in Magnesia. `The Magnesians on the
river Lethaios have a place called the Tunnels, where
Apollo has a grotto, not very marvellous for size, but
the statue of Apollo is extremely ancient and gives you
physical powers of every kind; men consecrated to this
statue leap from precipitous cliffs and high rocks, they
pull up giant trees by the roots, and travel with loads
on the narrowest footpaths.' In a footnote Peter Levi
who translated this edition of *Pausanias* adds: `Leaping
into the sea from a cliff was a feature of Apollo's
festival on the island of Leukas; a shaggy man carrying
an uprooted tree of about his own size appears on the
imperial coinage of Magnesia. Nilsson believed that
leaping into the sea at Leukas was some kind of bird
cult . . .'

Little is written or generally known about this
shamanistic cult though there is endless speculation.
Criminals were believed to be pardoned if they made
the leap and survived. Those jumping at the Festival of
Apollo were believed to be picked up by boats in the
sea below if they survived. Perhaps forsaken lovers did
jump here though all the references point to an
exclusively male pursuit. If for no other reason Sappho
should have the last word.

. . . I know I must die. . .
yet I love the tenderness of life
and this and desire keep me here in
the brightness and beauty of the sun

further around an old public wash-house where
ice-cold spring water flows through large tubs and
out again into the sea. If you do your washing
here tidy up afterwards. On the valley plain
behind the beach the river is used to irrigate the
rich soil for crops.

Nisis Skorpios and Skorpidhi

Lying close E of Ormos Vlikho and S of Nisis
Sparti are the twin islands of Skorpios and
Skorpidhi, the island retreat of the Onassis family
or those few who are left. Aristotle the patriarch,
his son Alexander and daughter Christina are all
buried here, in a simple church under the shade
of an old plane tree, a last resting place surprising
for its simplicity given the former opulence of the
Onassis lifestyle.

Aristotle Onassis bought Skorpios sometime in
the 1960's for what the Nidri locals say was a
'song'. Gradually he landscaped the island, built
a road right around it, installed security systems
that no-one really knows anything about except
that they work, installed a small farm on the SW
corner to keep horses for riding and cows to
supply fresh milk, and built the harbour facilities
in the bay on the N for his beloved yacht (read
'ship') *Christina*. Aristotle never slept on the
island but stayed on *Christina* at night although
there are living quarters ashore for guests. In the
late 1970s and early 1980s it was usual to see the
Christina moored off in the N bay, but after
Aristotle's death the yacht went to the Greek
government; apparently his will stated that if his
daughter did not want it then the state got it – and
Christina didn't want her father's toy.
(Alexander, the only son, died in 1973 in a plane
accident which Aristotle was convinced had been
a CIA plot.)

The late Jackie O's chic beach hut on the south side of
Skorpios

After her father's death Christina flew into Skorpios on odd occasions though she didn't use it as often as Aristotle had. Since Christina's death, like Alexander's shrouded in some mystery though drink and drugs appear to have played a part, the island has been little used though it is still tended by the island staff. It is very much a parkland, carefully planted and pruned, with dazzling green lawns and shaded tennis courts. Staff buildings are on the NE corner with guest buildings further W. The small chapel and the graves of the three Onassis' are on the NW corner. On the edge of a tiny beach, in an idyllic setting, is a small Cyclades-style house Jackie had built so she could get away from it all and swim in the beautifully clear water of the cove. The future of the island is uncertain, but for the meantime the lawns are kept green through the summer and the punters are kept off the beaches.

There are few permanent staff on Skorpios, probably around ten or fifteen, but every day a ferry runs additional staff over from Nidri. Aristotle had a soft spot for Nidri and in *Nick the Greeks* there are faded newspaper accounts of the Onassis' goings-on in and around Nidri, including photos of Nick himself – looking somewhat younger but no less licentious.

You can sail around Skorpios and Skorpidhi though you cannot land. Greek law states that though you can buy an island, you cannot own anything below the high water mark. This means you can anchor off and swim off the beaches, that you can set foot on the beach below the high water mark, but you cannot wander around it. In the summer there are regular patrols by land and sea keeping an eye on yachtsmen anchored off and on the tripper boats running out of Nidri. I don't know what detection systems are used on the island but they work. A friend coming back from Meganisi one night put a piston through the top of his outboard and the nearest land was Skorpios. He paddled over to the beach on the S side and within fifteen minutes was explaining his predicament to staff who had detected him. They were friendly enough and towed him over to Nidri, but have been known to rough up paparazzi who attempted to sneak ashore at night when Jackie was on the island.

There are several anchorages around the island, but only one really good one. The cove on the SW where Jackie had her 'beach-hut' built is sheltered from the prevailing wind, but is quite deep to anchor in. Further W it is possible to anchor off the W side of a sandy isthmus, though again it is quite deep. The best place is on the E side of the isthmus off the beach where there are more convenient depths and good shelter from the prevailing wind. You will probably be observed by a staff member in one of the island's mini-mokes, so don't try to wander around ashore.

Vos Heiromiti

Between Skorpios and Meganisi there is a shoal patch and a reef just under the water. The reef lies approximately ½M SE of the midway point of Skorpios. The Heiromiti reef is sometimes marked in the summer, but this cannot be relied upon. The reef is easily spotted in calm weather, but can be difficult to see when there is a chop with the prevailing wind.

If the reef cannot be seen a yacht should hug either Skorpios or Meganisi. If you keep S of a transit between the SW corner of Skorpios and Ak Makripounda on Meganisi, you will pass S of the reef. Have someone keep a lookout from the bows just to be on the safe side.

Nisos Meganisi

Meganisi is the Rorschach blob of an island lying close off the E coast of Levkas. Its much indented N coast is riddled with sheltered bays and coves next to each other, all of them wonderfully situated in beautiful surroundings. From ancient times right up to the 20th century it has been a pirate haunt. In 1610 William Lithgow of Lanark, (known as Cut-lugged Willie because the relatives of a young woman he had, let us say offended, cut off his ears), was on a ship attacked by Turkish pirates between Levkas and Meganisi in 1610. His account gives a real insight into the dangers of travel and piracy in times past.

'During the course of our passage, the captain of the vessel espied a sail coming from sea; he presently being moved therewith, sent a mariner to the top, who certified him she was a Turkish galley of Biserta, prosecuting a straight course to invade our back: which sudden affrighting news overwhelmed us almost in despair.'

Lithgow rallied the crew and passengers who, he said, were willing at first to give up without a fight, and urged captain, crew, and passengers to fight the Turk.

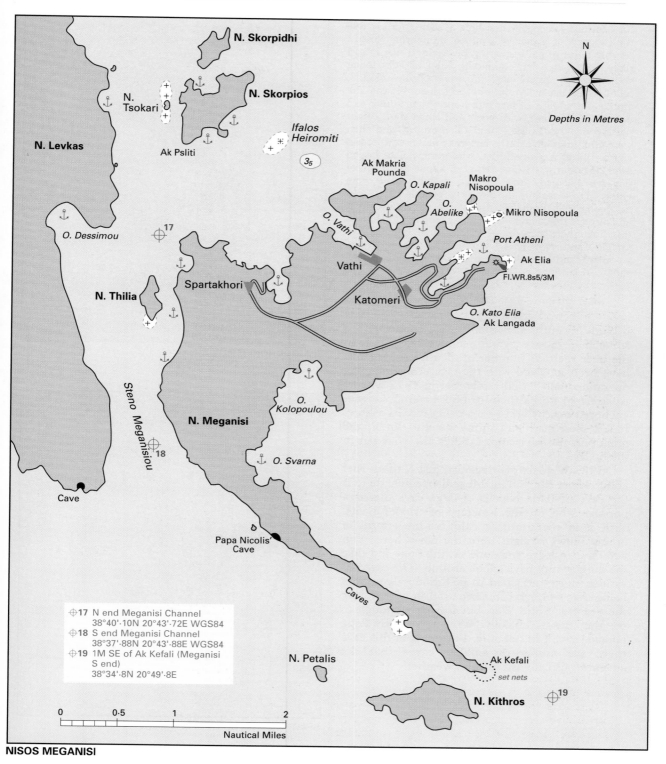

N. Skorpidhi

N.
Tsokari

N. Skorpios

Ifalos
Heiromiti

Ak Psliti

N. Levkas

3_5

Ak Makria
Pounda

O. Kapali

Makro
Nisopoula

O.
Abelike

Mikro Nisopoula

N

Depths in Metres

O. Dessimou

17

O. Vathi

Port Atheni

Ak Elia

Vathi

Fl.WR.8s5/3M

N. Thilia

Spartakhori

Katomeri

O. Kato Elia
Ak Langada

Steno Meganisiou

N. Meganisi

O.
Kolopoulou

18

O. Svarna

Cave

Papa Nicolis'
Cave

Caves

17 N end Meganisi Channel
   38°40'·10N 20°43'·72E WGS84
18 S end Meganisi Channel
   38°37'·88N 20°43'·88E WGS84
19 1M SE of Ak Kefali (Meganisi
   S end)
   38°34'·8N 20°49'·8E

N. Petalis

Ak Kefali

set nets

19

N. Kithros

0	0·5	1		2

Nautical Miles

NISOS MEGANISI

125

'In a furious spleen, the first hola of their courtesy was the progress of a martial conflict, thundering forth a terrible noise of galley-roaring pieces; and we, in sad reply, sent out a back-sounding echo of fiery flying shots, which made an equivox to the clouds, rebounding backward in out perturbed breasts the ambiguous sounds of fear and hope. After a long and doubtful fight, both with great and small shot, (night parting us) the Turks retired till morning, and then were mindful to give us the new rencounter of a second alarm. But as it pleased him, who never faileth his, to send down an irresistible tempest, about the break of day we escaped their furious designs; and were enforced to seeke into the bay of Largostolo (Argostoli) in Cephalonia; both because of the violent weather, and also for that a great hole was sprung in our ship. In this fight there were of us killed, three Italians, two Greeks, and two Jews, with eleven others deadly wounded, and I also hurt in the right arm with a small shot.'

William Lithgow
Totall Discourse of the Rare Adventures and Painefull Peregrinations 1632

Until recently the island was connected to smuggling, mostly cigarette smuggling to Italy in the later years. A number of men from Meganisi have been involved with the cigarette smuggling operations and I well remember in 1977 when I woke up in Port Atheni to find a tramp steamer anchored nearby and boxes being ferried ashore. It left soon after and didn't go into Vathi, the main port for the island. I didn't ask what was in the boxes.

On the W coast of Meganisi, just S of an islet about where the 'tail' of Meganisi begins, there is the cave of Papa Nicolis, a large cave that is a popular stop on the itinerary of tripper boats. Visit it in the morning calm as the afternoon breeze blows straight onto the coast here. You will have to leave someone on the boat and take the dinghy in to have a look around. The cave has various stories attached to it, the most common being that a Greek submarine hid in here during the Second World War, but it is easy enough to see that this is unlikely. Why it is called Papa Nicolis' cave I'm not sure. Further S of this cave there are numerous smaller caves that the adventurous can visit in calm weather.

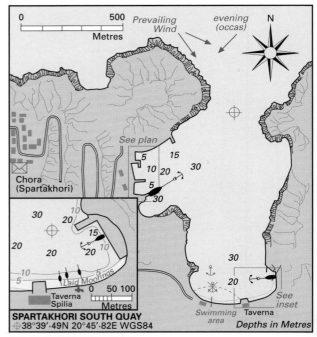

SPARTAKHORI SOUTH QUAY
⊕38°39′·49N 20°45′·82E WGS84

SPARTAKHORI (SPIGLIA)
⊕38°40′·10N 20°45′·82E WGS84

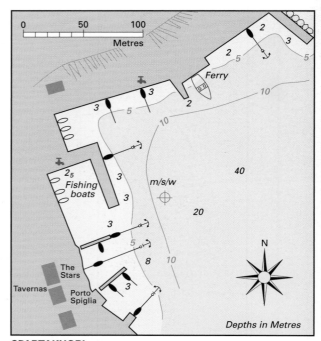

SPARTAKHORI
⊕38°39′·75N 20°45′·6E

Spartakhori

(Port Spiglia, Ormos Spiliou)

A large bay on the NW of Meganisi with a small harbour on the W.

Pilotage

Approach The village of Spartakhori perched on a summit on the W side of the bay will be seen and closer in the entrance to the bay.

Mooring Go stern or bows-to the quay where shown. The harbour is popular in the summer and often full. Take care not to obstruct the ferry berth. The depths drop off very quickly from the quay and you will be dropping your anchor in 12–20m, so make sure you have plenty of scope ready. The north quay and the south pontoon have laid moorings for you to pick up.

At the head of the bay is a taverna with a small quay and laid moorings. In the SE corner a new quay and stubby breakwater has been built where there may be room to go stern-to. Good shelter from the prevailing winds, although the evening NE breeze can make some berths on the west side of the harbour uncomfortable. Alternatively anchor outside the buoyed swimming area off the beach at the head of the bay in 5–10m.

Facilities

Services Metered water tap on the quay. There are only limited garbage disposal facilities so preferably take it elsewhere.

Provisions Most provisions available in the village.

Eating out Two tavernas by the harbour and one at the head of the bay. The *Porto Spiglia* and *The Stars* are favourites with flotillas and their food is good. Tavernas in the village also – *Lakki's* is worth a visit.

Spartakhori

Graham Sewell

General

The bay is an enchanting spot: deep cobalt blue water, steep slopes planted with olives or covered in *maquis*, and the winding road shaded by cypress and pine leading to the village. Even on the hottest day you should climb up to the village, or better still go up in the evening for a drink or dinner. The view is wonderful out over Nidri, Madhouri, Skorpios, and right across to the mountains of the mainland on the E. The village is a fascinating warren of alleys and lanes, most too small to get a car through as the village was never designed for motorised transport, but for four-legged transport.

Vathi

(Port Vathy)

The main port of the island immediately E of Spartakhori.

Pilotage

Approach The entrance to the bay is difficult to make out and the houses of the village will not be seen until you are into the entrance, but following the N coast of Meganisi the approach is straightforward. Once into the entrance a windmill behind the village will be seen.

Mooring Go stern or bows-to in the harbour where convenient. Alternatively anchor to the W of the mole or in one of the coves on the W or E side. Depths are mostly considerable,

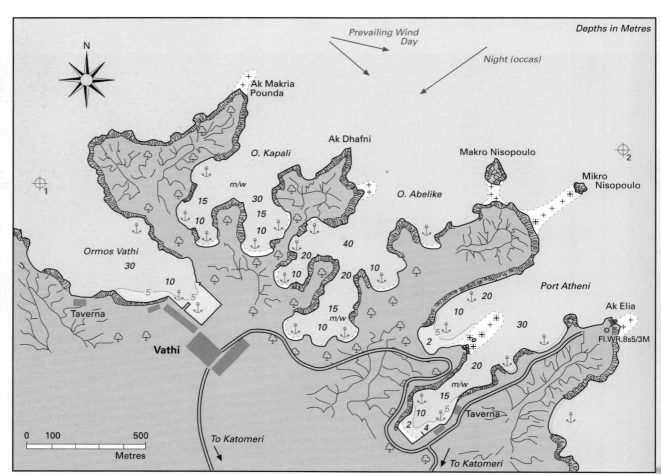

NISOS MEGANISI: PORT VATHI TO PORT ATHENI
⊕₁ 38°40´·60N 20°48´·70E WGS84
⊕₂ 38°40´·26N 20°46´·60E WGS84

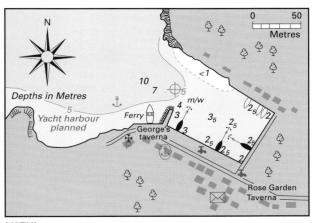

VATHI
⊕38°39'·8N 20°47'·0E

usually 10m or more. Shelter from the day breeze is good, but in the evening a katabatic breeze may blow in from the NE making the W side of the bay uncomfortable and sometimes untenable.

Note A yacht harbour is planned for here but work has not yet started.

Facilities

Services Water on the quay although it is often turned off in the summer.

Provisions Some provisions can be found.

Eating out Several tavernas in the village. Y*eorgiou's* (George's) behind the mole often has fresh fish and the *Rose Garden* further into the village has good food in pleasant surroundings.

Other PO. Metered telephone. Ferry to Nidri.

Vathi on Meganisi

General

The small village is the main port and capital of the island, though it would be hard to envisage a more sleepy capital in the Ionian. It is a pleasant relaxed place with some fine walks through the olive groves to the bays to the E.

Ormos Kapali and Abelike

Between Vathi and Port Atheni there are two large bays with small coves dotted around the edges. A glance at the plan shows the much indented bays and the different places a yacht can anchor. The heads of these bays are now buoyed off as swimming areas so you will need to anchor clear of the buoys in rather deeper water than in the past.

The coves in the two bays can get crowded in the summer, but these are peaceful places for all that. There are no facilities nor should there be. It is about a 10-minute walk from Kapali over the saddle to Vathi.

Note
1. In Abelike part of the bay is now buoyed off for swimmers. A road has been cut around the coast from Vathi, some villas are under construction and it is likely that there will be more land-based tourism in the future. In some of the bays laid moorings have been put down, but there is no authority for this so ignore them or anyone who tells you not to anchor there.
2. There have been reports of bold rats here attracted by the rubbish left by yachts on the shore. Since I and a lot of skippers expended some energy in keeping the place clean in years gone by, I'd suggest that anyone visiting here do likewise. It is not a place to dump or bury rubbish.

There are considerable depths in the bays, mostly 8–12m rising abruptly to the shore. The best policy is to anchor and take a long line ashore to a tree or rock. The bottom is mud and weed, good holding once through the weed. Shelter from the prevailing day breeze is good, but in the evening a katabatic wind from the NE can be uncomfortable in some of the coves, though it normally dies down after a couple of hours.

There are no facilities here and nor should there be. The coves are peaceful places surrounded by olive groves and clear water. They are popular places for barbecues and anyone

using the bays for this purpose must ensure the fire is built well away from the trees and that a bucket of water is handy. The fire should be damped down before you leave and take any rubbish away with you – there is no point in burying it on the island as olive trees don't exactly thrive on tinfoil and plastic.

Port Atheni

(Ormos Atherinou)
The large bay on the NE of Meganisi.

Pilotage

Approach The two islets of Megalo Nisopoulo and Mikro Nisopoulo can be identified from the W and the light structure on Ak Elia will be seen from the E. A yacht should keep outside Makro and Mikro Nisopoulo as they are connected by a reef to Meganisi. Care is also needed of the reef extending off Ak Elia.

Once into the bay care is needed of the reef running out into the middle of the bay. It appears to be a bit of a blind spot for sailors if the numbers of yachts running aground on it are anything to go by.

Mooring Anchor in the cove on the W where there are considerable depths, 10–20m, though if you can get near the head of the cove there are 3–8m depths. Take a long line ashore to the W side.

Alternatively anchor in one of the coves on the SE side. Here it is also deep, coming up quickly from 10–15m to 2m and less near the head. Again take a long line line ashore. If there is room a yacht can go stern or bows-to the quay running around the head of the bay. The south end is crowded with local boats, but in any case is mostly shallow, with less than 1m depths off the quay. Depths of 2–4m can be found along the north end of the quay. You can also go bows-to off the taverna here though some care is needed of underwater rocks and rubble near the rough quay.

The bottom is sand and rock in the W cove and mud and weed in the E cove. Shelter from the prevailing wind is generally good although there can be strong gusts from the W. In the evening a katabatic wind may blow in from the NE.

Port Atheni on Meganisi

Facilities

A metred water tap on the quay. Mini-market.

Niagas Taverna is situated in the south creek and you can park your yacht right outside bows-to.

It is about a 30-minute walk to the village of Katomeri inland from Port Atheni. Here some provisions can be found and there are several tavernas. Remember to take a torch for the walk back.

General

The bay is a pleasant spot, like the others surrounded by olive groves and *maquis*. The W cove is the more pleasant as here the water is translucent over the sand and rock bottom, whereas the E cove is murky when the fine silt is stirred up though it is no less clean than the W cove. The bay is popular by day but quieter at night. Inevitably the character of these places is changing though Port Atheni is really only crowded in July and August.

Meganisi East Coast

On the E of Meganisi there are several bays suitable in settled weather. The afternoon wind tends to curl around the bottom of Meganisi and blow from the SW to S making them uncomfortable and sometimes untenable once the morning calm has gone.

In the morning or with light afternoon winds a yacht can anchor in Ormos Langada just above

Ak Langada, Ormos Kolopoulou and Ormos Svarna just above the 'tail' of Meganisi. Depths in these bays are considerable and it may pay to take a line ashore.

Off the tail of Meganisi some care is needed as there are set nets here and even when the nets are not in place there have been reports that poles and other obstructions may remain.

Nisis Thilia

This teardrop-shaped island has a narrow channel running between it and the west coast of Meganisi which offers several calm weather anchorages. Care should be taken of reefs extending off both the northwest and southern ends of the island.

A yacht can anchor in convenient depths on either side of the channel on patches of sand. It is a peaceful spot and is somewhere that the

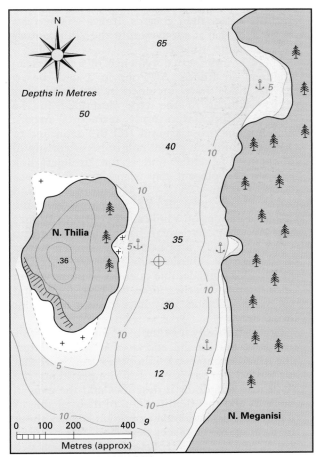

NISIS THILIA ANCHORAGES
⊕ 38°39′.03N 20°44′.02E

famously persistent Meganisi wasps don't frequent in numbers. The bight on the east side of Nisis Thilia is suitable for an overnight stay in settled weather, although care is needed of rocks and shoal water close to the island. Before the afternoon wind gets up it is possible to anchor off the beach on Meganisi south of Nisis Thilia though it is mostly deep here apart from a few sandy patches off the beach.

Nisos Ithaca

Within the Inland sea no other name carries such a burden of myth and historical association with it as Ithaca. I have already talked about the connections with the *Odyssey* and there is really nothing more to say. The places in the *Odyssey* have all been located and signposted on Ithaca, but there can be no certainty that these are the places that Homer described and in the end they are little better than guesses. Ithaca's fame rests on the fact that it survived into the 20th century with the name 'Ithaca'.

There is little actual evidence of a Mycenean kingdom on Ithaca. At Polis in a cave below Stavros finds have included twelve geometric tripods similar to the type described in the *Odyssey*. More importantly terracotta masks, including one from around 100 BC dedicated to Odysseus, indicate a later cult of hero-worship of the man. The latter find is the strongest link between the present day island and the Ithaca described in the *Odyssey*. A Mycenean house and pottery shards were also found nearby. Near the village of Stavros on a hill called Pelikata a Bronze Age Mycenean settlement has been found, but it is too small to be a principal city. On Mt Aetos, on the narrow isthmus joining the two halves of the island, a considerable quantity of pottery from Corinthian and earlier times has been found and it is surmised there may have been a temple or shrine here.

That is basically it in terms of ancient artefacts and sites, and in the end does it really matter? The island occupies a mythopoeic geography that has lasted for a good deal longer than the Mycenean kingdoms it describes and the gaps in the finds and the identification of them enable us to play detective and make our own guesses about the location of the places described. When Byron visited Ithaca from Cephalonia it was suggested by the local dignitaries he visit some of the local

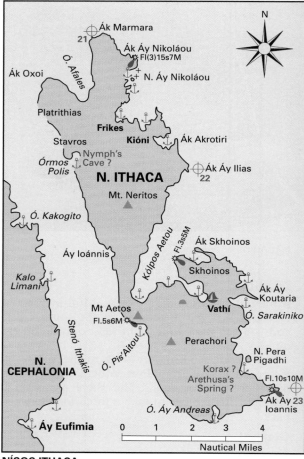

NÍSOS ITHACA

⊕21 ¼M N of Ak Marmara (Ithaca N end)
38°30'·47N 20°38'·93E WGS84
⊕22 ¼M E of Ak Ay Illias (Ithaca NE end)
38°26'·07N 20°42'·91E WGS84
⊕23 ¼M E of Ak Ay Ioannis (Ithaca SE end)
38°19'·20N 20°46'·36E WGS84

sites associated with the *Odyssey*. Trelawny, who accompanied him recorded that Byron turned to him, and muttered as an aside: 'Do I look like one of those emasculated fogies? Let's have a swim. I detest antiquarian twaddle. Do people think I have no lucid intervals, that I came to Greece to scribble more nonsense?' The bard had good advice to give sometimes.

The island is a delightful place to sail around, if a bit windy in the summer. It is mostly a barren place with just a sprinkling of *maquis* on the slopes and the only wooded places are a few valleys where underground springs enable the vegetation to survive through the hot summer months. The

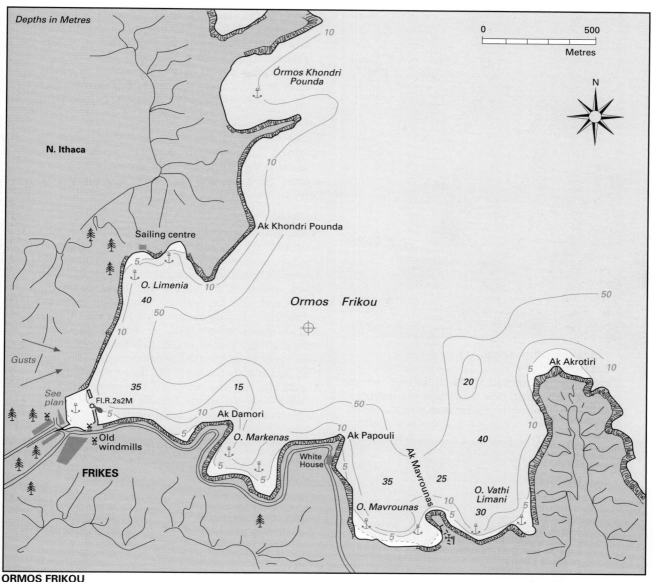

Depths in Metres

Órmos Khondri
Pounda

N. Ithaca

0   500

Metres

N

Ak Khondri Pounda

Sailing centre

10

Ormos   Frikou

50

O. Limenia

40

50

10

Gusts

35   15

See
plan

Fl.R.2s2M

5   10   Ak Damori

5   *O. Markenas*

Old
windmills

White
House

FRIKES

5   5

Ak Papouli

10

Ak Akrotiri

10

20

50

10

40

25

*O. Vathi
Limani*

Ak Mavrounas

35

O. Mavrounas

30

10

5

ORMOS FRIKOU
⊕ 38°28′·00N 20°40′·02E

local authorities have declared many of the villages and houses to be of special historical interest and it is prohibited to build large hotels that do not fit into the scheme of things. It's a pity the authorities did not apply the same criteria to the ugly reverse osmosis plant at Sarakiniko, but overall they have succeeded in retaining an architectural cohesion in harmony with the island's history.

Frikes

A small harbour and hamlet tucked into the westernmost corner of Ormos Frikes, the large bay on the NE of Ithaca.

Pilotage

Approach Except for the islets and reefs under Ak Ay Nikolaou, the approaches are free of dangers. However with the prevailing westerlies there can be severe gusts off the land

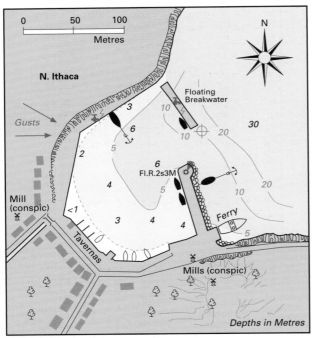

FRIKES
⊕ 38°27'·60N 20°39'·91E WGS84

Mooring Berth alongside the short mole or on the detached pontoon. There is not a lot of room and it gets crowded in the summer. Large yachts can go stern-to the outside of the mole with a long line to it keeping well clear of the ferry berth. In light westerlies or calm weather the anchorages around Frikes can be used.

Facilities

Water on the quay. Most provisions can be obtained and several tavernas open in the summer. One of the tavernas serves homegrown organic produce and has been recommended. Ferry to Vassiliki.

General

Frikes is a delightful place set at the bottom of a steep and wooded valley, the old houses clustered around the small harbour, and several old windmills standing sentinel on a rocky bluff above, proof of the winds that howl down the valley and off the slopes. The once isolated hamlet has recently seen a little tourism, though not so much as to spoil it. The village is of comparatively recent origin as villages were not commonly built by the sea prior to the 18th and 19th centuries because of the risk of pirate attacks. In fact the name of the village may be derived from the pirate Frikon who used it as a base according to some local sources.

and care is needed. The buildings of the hamlet including two windmills on the rocky bluff immediately E will be seen when close-to.

Frikes

Anchorages in Ormos Frikon

There are numerous anchorages in the bay that can be used according to the wind direction and sea state. In most of them the depths are considerable unless you can get in close and if necessary take a long line ashore. From the N these are as follows.

Port Ay Nikolaos A bay directly under Ak Ay Nikolaos. Care is needed of the reef around Nisis Ay Nikolaos. Good protection from the prevailing winds although there are gusts.

Ormos Khondri Pounda A bay just above Ak Khondri Pounda. Good shelter from the prevailing wind, though some swell works its way in during the afternoon.

Ormos Limenia A two-headed bay under Ak Khondri Pounda. In the W cove there is a watersports centre. Anchor in either cove on shingle, sand and weed. Reasonable shelter from the prevailing winds although there are gusts.

Ormos Markenas The bay immediately E of Frikes. Shelter is not as good as it looks on the plan as the prevailing winds send a chop in. In calm weather or light westerlies anchor in the SW corner on sand, shingle and weed.

Ormos Mavrounas The next bay along from Ormos Damori. Like Damori shelter is not as good as it looks. In calm weather anchor on sand, shingle and weed.

Ormos Vathi Limani The bay next to Mavrounas on the E side of the rocky headland. In calm weather anchor where convenient. Ashore there are the ruins of the monastery of Ay Nikolaos which was destroyed in the 1953 earthquake, though the church still stands.

Kioni

A village and harbour in Ormos Kioni just S of Ormos Frikes.

Pilotage

Approach From the N and E the three windmill towers on the end of Ak Psigadhi, the S entrance point of the bay, show up well. From the S they will not be seen until close-to if you are hugging the coast. The entrance into the bay is straightforward and free of dangers although there are severe gusts out of the bay with the prevailing westerlies.

Mooring Go stern or bows-to the quay or anchor

Kioni

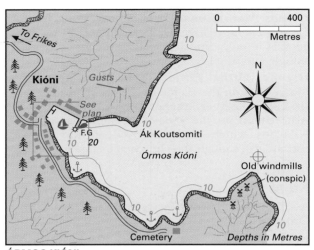

ÓRMOS KIÓNI
⊕38°26'·84N 20°42'·17E WGS84

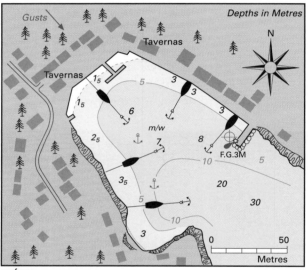

KIÓNI
⊕38°27'·0N 20°41'·5E

off. There are considerable depths off the quay and you will probably be dropping your anchor in 10m or so. If you are anchoring towards the outer part of the bay it is very deep, 20m in line with the breakwater, so put out plenty of scope. The best thing to do in the restricted room available is anchor with a long line ashore to the SW side or to the outside of the stubby mole.

The bottom is mud and weed, not everywhere the best holding. Shelter is good although the gusts can be bothersome. In calm weather or light westerlies a yacht can also anchor in the cove on the S off the cemetery although again depths are considerable. The wash from ferries can also be bothersome here.

Facilities

Most provisions can be obtained ashore and there are several tavernas on the waterfront. Caique ferry to Vathi.

General

The village is a gem: an amphitheatre of houses built around the steep slopes of the bay, the slopes and the valley behind planted in olive groves with the odd tall cypress poking through, and the deep blue waters of the bay itself.

In the 19th century the village was a prosperous place, as can be seen from the houses, with a population of over a thousand, but today the population is less than 200. Like many of the villages in the islands the population started drifting away to the cities or emigrated overseas to America and Australia in the 20th century. The earthquake of 1953 further reduced the population when many decided not to move back after being evacuated from the village. Today you will often come across an American drawl or an Aussie twang from a former inhabitant or one of their sons or daughters feeling totally out of place in this little Greek village miles from a metropolis.

Kolpos Aetou

(Aito, Gulf of Molo)

The large gulf on the E side of the isthmus joining the two halves of Ithaca. The capital and main harbour, Vathi, lies in a large bottleneck bay on the SE side of the gulf.

Pilotage

In the summer the gulf is a very windy place, one of the windiest in the Ionian. The prevailing wind creeps up over the waist of Ithaca and then tumbles down into Kolpos Aetou. It tends to follow the land and blows from the SW on the W side of the gulf and from the NW down into Port Vathi. Off Kolpos Aetou it tends to blow from the W to NW, but curves around Ak Skhoinos and Ak Sarakiniko to blow from the N to NW.

There are few good anchorages around the gulf suitable with the winds gusting off the hills, but in calm weather or light westerlies a number of anchorages can be used.

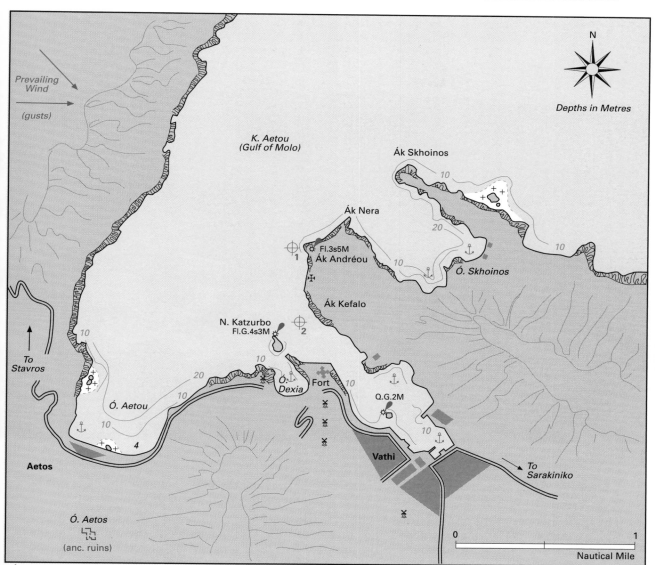

KÓLPOS AETOU (GULF OF MOLO)
⊕₁ 38°23'·14N 20°42'·01E WGS84
⊕₂ 38°22'·66N 20°42'·06E WGS84

Ormos Aetou The bay in the SW corner of the gulf. Anchor in 5–10m on the W. Care is needed of the reef around the rock off the shore about half way along. The bottom is sand and weed.

Ormos Dexia The bay lying under Nisis Katzurbo. Anchor in 5–12m on mud and weed, not the best holding. The protection from the prevailing wind is not as good as it looks on the plan as it blows straight in here, so the anchorage can become untenable at times.

Ormos Skhoinos The large bay lying immediately under Ak Skhoinos, the E entrance to Kolpos Aetou. Anchor in 8–15m in the SW corner or in 5–12m in the SE corner. The bottom is sand or mud and weed, not the best holding. In light to moderate westerlies some yachts stay in the SW corner, though it is not the most comfortable and if the wind increases you may have to get out.

Vathi looking north from near Palaiochora

Nigel Patten

Vathi

(Port Vathi)

The main harbour of the island on the E side of Kolpos Aetou. Vathi means 'deep' and the approaches and most of the harbour are just this – deep.

Pilotage

Approach The town of Vathi cannot be seen until you are right into the bay. A chapel and light tower on Ak Andreou are easily identified and likewise the light structure and the island of Nisis Katzurbo. Once into Port Vathi the houses of the town will be seen at the head of the bay.

Care is needed in the approaches and in Port Vathi itself as the prevailing wind gusts in from the NW making berthing and anchoring difficult at times. Care also needs to be taken of the large ferries using Vathi, normally they will let you know if you are in the way with a blast from the ship's horn and the basic rule of the road is keep out of the way.

Mooring Near Vathi yachts can go stern or bows-to the short mole, along the quay SE of the ferry berth, or on the projecting quay at the head of the bay. The quay E of the ferry berth is usually the best place to be although it is quite deep off here – you will be dropping your anchor in 10–15m. The small basin has been largely filled in and what is left is crammed full of local boats. The prevailing wind blows into the bay on all of these berths and you should ensure you put out plenty of scope and that the anchor is holding. The bottom is mud and thick weed, poor holding.

You can anchor off in the SE of the bay, but make sure your anchor is in and holding. It takes a bit to get through the weed, but once in the holding is better than in the NE corner of the bay.

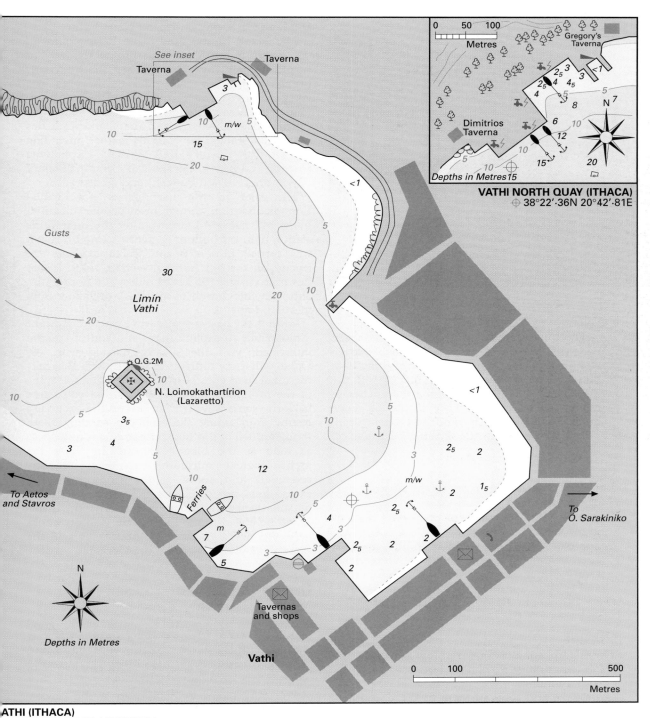

VATHI NORTH QUAY (ITHACA)
⊕ 38°22′·36N 20°42′·81E

Gregory's Taverna

Dimitrios Taverna

Depths in Metres

Taverna

See inset

Taverna

Gusts

Limín Vathi

Q.G.2M

N. Loimokathartírion
(Lazaretto)

m/w

Ferries

To Aetos
and Stavros

m

Tavernas
and shops

Vathi

N

Depths in Metres

To
Ó. Sarakiniko

0   100   500

Metres

ATHI (ITHACA)
⊕ 38°21′·95N 20°43′·14E WGS84

The new quay in the northeast corner of Vathi on Ithaca
Lu Michell

The quay in the northeast corner has been widened, making it possible for yachts to go stern or bows-to, keeping clear of fishing boat berths. The depths increase quickly off the quay and you will be dropping the anchor in depths of 10–15m so have plenty of scope ready. The bottom is mud and thick weed, poor holding, but shelter is better here than off the town.

Facilities

Services Water and electricity on the N quay. Fuel can be delivered by mini-taker.

Provisions Good shopping for provisions close by in the town. Ice available.

Eating out Numerous tavernas in the town. A good taverna (*Gregorys*) with lots of interesting Greek dishes on the E side of the NE corner, and another a little further around to the W.

Other PO. OTE. Bank. ATM. Hire motorbikes and cars.

General

The island capital is a relaxed low-key place that only seems to bustle when the ferries arrive. Many of the buildings were destroyed in the 1953 earthquake and some of them to the E and S of the centre have been left as ruins. Many others have been repaired and despite the new buildings, mostly in the centre, Vathi retains a pleasing aspect to it. The proper name of the town is actually Ithaca, but most people refer to the town and harbour as one under the name Vathi.

The island capital used to be Palaeochora on the slopes above Vathi and out of the way of surprise attacks by pirates. When the Venetians brought some law and order to the area, the villagers moved down to Vathi and to Perachori. Under the Venetians the area around Vathi was called Val di Compare and the island itself has also been known by various names including Nerikii (7th century BC), Piccola Cephalonia (Middle Ages), Thrakoniso and Thiakou (Byzantine), Fiaki (Turkish) and Thiaki.

The islet in the harbour is now called Loimokathatirion, though most people still call it by its old name, Lazaretto, after the quarantine station that was built on it. During English rule it was turned into a prison which explains the legend on the old Admiralty chart 1620. It was destroyed in the 1953 earthquake and not rebuilt, although the church of 'Sotiros', originally built in 1668, remains.

Vathi is the best place to leave a yacht and take a motorbike to explore the island and, if you are interested, visit the sites associated with the *Odyssey* that are difficult to visit by sea. Basically the main road goes N from Vathi along the spine of the mountain range to Frikes and you come back the same way. It is an interesting excursion testing your riding skills on the winding road, though much of it is now tarmac so it is quite easy as long as the bike holds up. In Vathi the archaeological museum has been recently reopened and some of the finds from the excavations are displayed here. An inscription outside displays a quotation from Byron: 'If this island belonged to me I would bury all my books here and never go away'. I thought he said the same thing about Naxos in the Cyclades.

Ormos Sarakiniko

⊕ 38°21'·7N 20°45'·0E

A large bay under Ak Koutaria where good shelter can be found with the prevailing wind. A large building is conspicuous on the coast just S of the bay. There is also a pleasant bay just N of Ak Koutaria that can be used.

The only blight at Sarakiniko is the reverse osmosis water plant that supplies Ithaca with fresh water. There are also several fish farms in the vicinity.

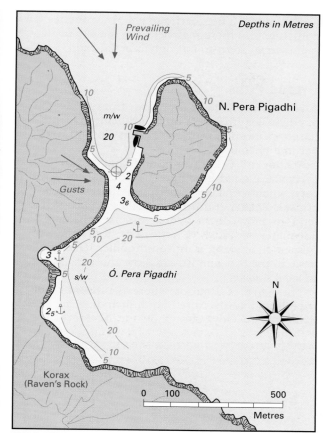

PERA PIGADHI
⊕38°20'·15N 20°44'·80E

Pera Pigadhi

Between Ak Sarakiniko and Ak Ioannou at the SE tip of Ithaca, the islet of Nisis Pera Pigadhi lies close to the coast. From the distance it is difficult to distinguish from the coast itself and not until you are close to it will you be able to pick it out.

On the W side of the islet and in Ormos Pera Pigadhi, the bay on Ithaca immediately S of the islet, there is reasonable shelter from light to moderate westerly winds. The prevailing northwesterly does not reach here until late in the afternoon and although it gusts down onto the islet and the bay, there is something of a lee here. However in the summer proper there can be exceptionally strong gusts and it can become untenable. In the morning and early afternoon it makes a wonderful lunch stop with crystal clear water over a sand and rock bottom ideal for swimming and snorkelling.

Either go stern or bows-to the quay or alongside on Nisis Pera Pigadhi or anchor where

convenient just S of the channel or in Ormos Pera Pigadhi. There are 4m least depths through the middle of the channel though the clarity of the water makes it look much less. Out of the channel the depths drop off very quickly and you will usually be dropping the anchor in 10–20m. The bottom is sand, rock and weed, mostly good holding. Anyone staying the night on the quay on the islet should know there have been reports of very big and bold rats living here, so take adequate precautions to prevent them getting on board.

The situation here is wonderful with turquoise water and the steep cliffs of Ithaca rising sheer from the sea. The high rock slope is called Koraka, corresponding to the Korax of the *Odyssey*, the 'Ravens Rock', where the Fountain of Arethusa flowed, and indeed there is a spring here. This is where Eumaeus the swineherd lived and kept his pigs, at least it has been identified as such by those dabbling in mythic geography. In fact there are several other places that could be so identified, Ay Andreou around the corner is one, but the fact that the name Koraka has stuck to the present day in this lonely place is pertinent – the power of old place-names should not be underestimated.

Ormos Ay Andreou

A steep-sided inlet on the S of Ithaca. The exact location can be difficult to identify until close-to. Anchor at the head of the inlet in 8–15m or in the cove on the W side with a long line ashore. There is room for only three or four yachts in here, late-comers will have to anchor in considerable depths further out. The bottom is sand, shingle and weed, not everywhere good holding. Shelter from the prevailing wind is good though a reflected swell will often rebound in making it uncomfortable and there are strong gusts off the slopes. However the savage beauty of the place and its complete isolation will make the discomfort worthwhile for some.

Ormos Pis'aitou

A bight on the waist of the W coast of Ithaca. It is suitable only in calm weather as the prevailing wind funnelled down the Ithaca Channe sends a considerable swell in. Anchor in 5–20m on mud and weed. This is an age-old port for ferrying goods and people across the channel to

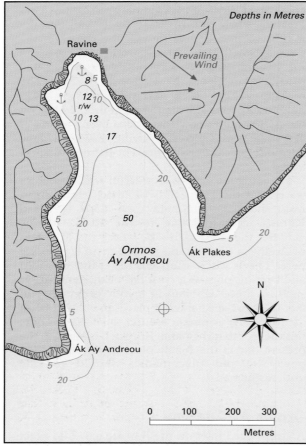

ORMOS AY ANDREOU
⊕38°18′·2N 20°43′·6E

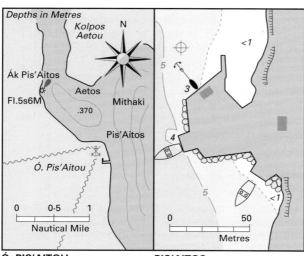

Ó. PIS'AITOU

PIS'AITOS
⊕ 38°21′·0N 20°41′·1E

Cephalonia. The harbour in the bight is miniature and there may be room for one or two yachts to go stern-to but only in a flat calm.

Ormos Polis

A bay on the W coast just down from the N end of Dhiavolos Ithakis. It can be difficult to identify the exact location from the N, but close-to it will become obvious.

Anchor in 5–20m on sand and weed, not everywhere good holding. The bottom drops off very quickly making choosing a spot to anchor critical. Shelter from the prevailing winds which tend to blow down and across the channel is adequate, although a reflected swell may be pushed in making it uncomfortable. The small mole in the bay is mostly shallow and usually full of local *caiques*.

The Cave of Louizos where the Bronze Age tripods and masks were found, including the one dedicated to Odysseus, is on the N side of the

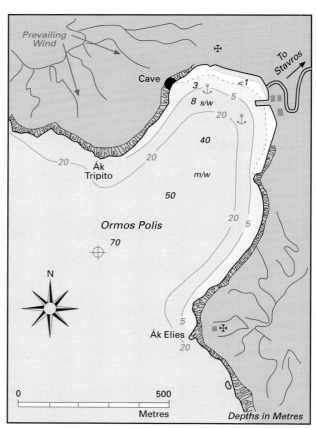

ORMOS POLIS
⊕ 37°26′·15N 20°38′·2E

Ormos Ay Andreou

bay. It is said that in the bay there are the remains of a Byzantine town called Ierousalem, destroyed in an earthquake around AD 967, though I can find few details on it and I have never seen any evidence of it underwater.

Nisos Cephalonia

(Kefallinia, Kefallonia)

Cephalonia is the largest island in the Ionian, around twice the size of nearby Zakinthos and about 30% bigger than Corfu. Yet it never seems that big, partially because those on the water seldom cruise right around it and even land travellers are put off by the mountainous interior and tend to stick to a few areas. It is not as green as some of the other Ionian islands because the winter rain is not trapped beneath the rock and tends to run straight off down ravines and gullies to the sea. Consequentially there are no major rivers. Some of the slopes are covered in pine and cypress, including a species of pine named after the island, *Abies cephalonica*, that grows above 750m to 1700m, though it is not unique to the island and in fact is found all over Greece.

The main mountain ridge runs in an L-shape down the middle of the island, approximately from N to S, with another high mountain ridge in the far W and the SE. These mountains drop straight down into the sea everywhere except for a few small valleys, so you will usually be sailing right at the foot of impressive mountain scenery. This can create a few problems with strong gusts

off the high land, especially on the S and E sides of the island, though nothing that cannot be coped with if you take care.

Cephalonia has a number of ancient associations, though there are few substantial remains to be seen. Homer mentions Same and Dulichium as neighbours of Ithaca: 'For neighbours we have many peopled isles with no great space between them, Dulichium and Same and wooded Zacynthus'. It is likely that Same is the ancient city of Sami near the present day ferry port of Sami tucked into the bay on the E side of Cephalonia. It has been suggested that Dulichium was one of the other ancient city states on Cephalonia at Pale (Lixuri), Kranoi (Argostoli) or Pronoi (Poros). Then again some authorities believe Dulichium was present-day Levkas.

The four city states were separated by mountainous terrain and largely operated as separate kingdoms with their own coinage and trade agreements. The cities slowly declined in later periods. Cephalonia duly passed to the Romans and in fact the whole island was the private estate of a certain C Antonius at one time according to Strabo. The Normans under Robert Guiscard, the Pisans, various Latin princes including Orsini and the Tocchi, the Turks, the Venetians, the French, and the English, in that order, ruled the island until union with Greece in 1864.

It is an odd mix of an island. It has a definite Italianate feel to parts of it and therein lies an interesting tale. In the Second World War it was

Getting around inland

During the English administration a number of paved roads were built and these formed the basis for the present road system. For the size of the island the road network is poorly developed – smaller islands like Corfu and Zakinthos are much better served than Cephalonia. To get around the island you really need to hire a motorbike or car, for the rougher roads you will need a four-wheel drive jeep, as the bus service is not comprehensive or frequent.

Motorbikes and cars and jeeps can be hired at Argostoli, Lixuri, Poros, and Fiskardho. In Ay Eufimia there is a car and motorbike agent although he seldom seems to have very much to actually hire! An excursion inland is well worthwhile. The mountain scenery so spectacular from seawards is every bit as spectacular in amongst it, wonderful wooded valleys, steep terraced slopes, bare rocky peaks above the tree-line, and small villages tucked away in the interior.

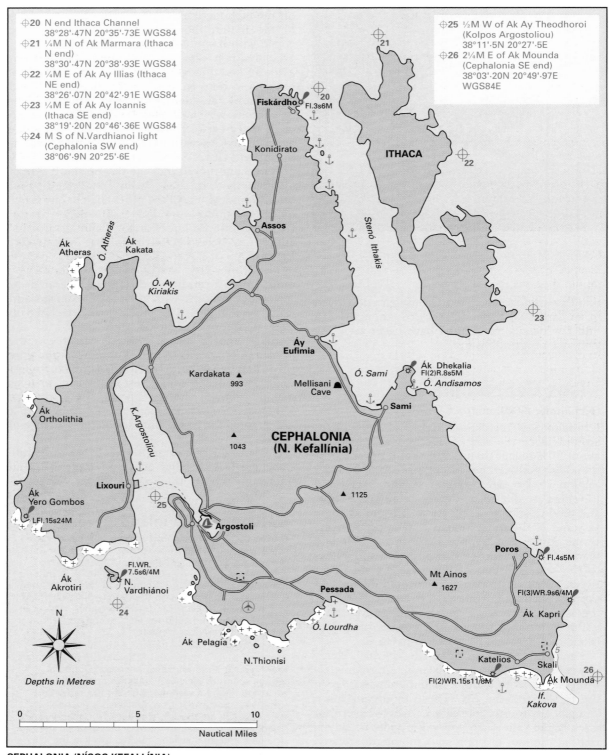

⊕**20** N end Ithaca Channel
38°28'·47N 20°35'·73E WGS84
⊕**21** ¼M N of Ak Marmara (Ithaca
N end)
38°30'·47N 20°38'·93E WGS84
⊕**22** ¼M E of Ak Ay Illias (Ithaca
NE end)
38°26'·07N 20°42'·91E WGS84
⊕**23** ¼M E of Ak Ay Ioannis
(Ithaca SE end)
38°19'·20N 20°46'·36E WGS84
⊕**24** M S of N.Vardhianoi light
(Cephalonia SW end)
38°06'·9N 20°25'·6E

⊕**25** ½M W of Ak Ay Theodhoroi
(Kolpos Argostoliou)
38°11'·5N 20°27'·5E
⊕**26** 2¼M E of Ak Mounda
(Cephalonia SE end)
38°03'·20N 20°49'·97E
WGS84E

Fiskárdho
Fl.3s6M
Konidirato

ITHACA

Ák
Atheras
Ó. Atheras
Ák
Kakata

Assos

Ó. Ay
Kiriakis

Stenó Ithakis

Áy
Eufimia

Ák
Ortholithia

Kardakata ▲
993

Mellisani
Cave

Ó. Sami

Ák Dhekalia
Fl(2)R.8s5M
Ó. Andisamos

Sami

K. Argostoliou

▲
1043

**CEPHALONIA
(N. Kefallínia)**

Ák
Yero Gombos
LFl.15s24M

Lixouri

⊕
25

▲ 1125

Poros
Fl.4s5M

Fl.WR.
7.5s6/4M

Ák
Akrotiri

N.
Vardhiánoi

⊕
24

Argostoli

Mt Ainos
▲ 1627

Fl(3)WR.9s6/4M

Ák Kapri

N

Pessada

Ó. Lourdha

Ák Pelagia

N.Thionisi

Katelios
Skali

Ák Mounda
26

Depths in Metres

Fl(2)WR.15s11/8M

If.
Kakova

0   5   10

Nautical Miles

CEPHALONIA (NÍSOS KEFALLÍNIA)

occupied in 1943 by 9,000 crack Alpine Acqui soldiers. When the Germans arrived the Italian troops refused to co-operate and then refused to hand the island over to the Germans. For seven days the Italians fought the Germans until eventually the remaining soldiers of the Acqui division, around 3,000 men, surrendered and were executed, it is said on Hitler's personal order. Few survived, but one of those who did, and who was smuggled off the island by the Greek resistance, later became the captain of one of the large ferries operating between Italy and Patras – every time he passed Cephalonia he would salute the island with three long blasts on the ship's horn.

Cephalonia was recently put on the literary map with a novel by Louis de Bernières. *Captain Corelli's Mandolin* was one of those wonderful escapees from the publishers list which by word of mouth became a best-seller. It deals with the Italian quasi-occupation of Cephalonia mentioned above and the love affair between Captain Corelli and a young Greek girl Pelagia. Intertwined through it all is the history of the Italian occupation, the arrival of the Germans, the Communist resistance and things just generally Greek. If you haven't read it go out and buy it now, if you have read it take it along to read again. The 2001 film shot on the island was subject to curious censorship by the governor of Cephalonia concerning material on the role of the communists during the war. Sadly the movie didn't come close to the book.

The island produces some of the best wines in the Ionian, though the impetus for this comes not from nearby Italy, but mostly from local initiative with some help from the French and later an Englishman who developed wine-making here. The Cephalonians themselves, thwarted by their island and its lack of water and flat fertile ground for cultivation, have always been ready to emigrate. Many of the men have worked in the merchant navy and many others have emigrated to America, Australia and South Africa over the years. The big earthquake of 1953 prompted massive emigration and today the island is only thinly populated for its size. Some of these prodigal sons and daughters have returned in recent years, so there is a smattering of colonial accented English spoken in the villages dotted around the island.

Fiskardho

(Phiscardo)

An enclosed bay and harbour on the NE tip of Cephalonia. The harbour is a gem, offers good all-round shelter, and consequently is popular in the summer, though you can't always find somewhere to moor.

The old Venetian lighthouse under the new(-ish) lighthouse on the northern entrance of Fiskardho

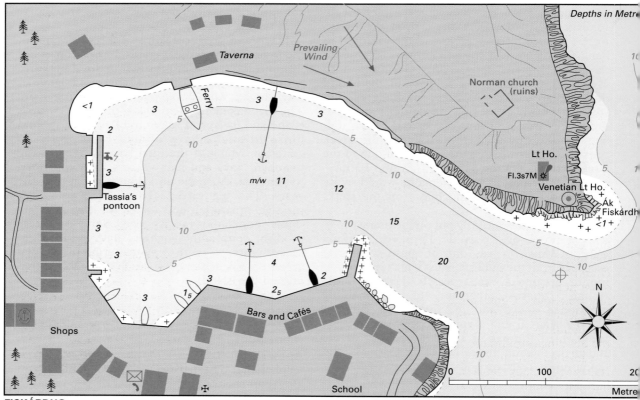

Depths in Metre

Taverna

Prevailing Wind

Norman church (ruins)

Ferry

Lt Ho.

Fl.3s7M

Venetian Lt Ho.

Ák Fiskárdh

Tassia's pontoon

m/w 11

12

15

20

Bars and Cafés

Shops

School

N

0   100   20

Metre

FISKÁRDHO
38°27'·53N 20°34'·94E WGS84

Pilotage

Approach It can be difficult to work out exactly where the bay is although it is easy enough to work out the general location at the N end of the Ithaca Channel. A cluster of villas in the bay N of Fiskardho are conspicuous and closer in the new lighthouse, the ruined tower, and the old Venetian lighthouse on the N side of the entrance will be seen – although it can be difficult when coming from the NE looking into the setting sun. The villas and hotel on the S side of the entrance will also be seen.

Mooring Berth stern or bows-to where possible on the town quay leaving the SW corner for local *caiques*. Care is needed at the E end of the quay where the ballasting extends underwater a short distance. A pontoon has been installed on the W side and is run by *Tassia's Taverna*. When the quay is full, anchor and take a long line to the shore on the N side keeping well clear of the ferry berth. The bottom is sand, mud and weed with a few rocks scattered around for good measure, mostly good holding once through the weed. Good all-round shelter in the bay.

Facilities

Services Water and electricity on the yacht pontoon. You may be able to get water on the quay from other sources. Fuel can be delivered.

Provisions Good shopping for provisions nearby.

Eating out Numerous restaurants some of which are excellent. A number of bars offer snacks and drinks with a ringside seat to watch the goings-on in the harbour. Yachties often meet up at *Captains Cabin* for early evening drinks. *Herodotus* on the road out of the village has a good selection of interesting dishes and repays a visit as does the *Garden Taverna*.

Other PO. OTE. Exchange facilities in the PO. Hire cars and motorbikes. Ferry to Frikes on Ithaca and Vassiliki on Levkas.

General

Fiskardho is a picture-postcard spot, one of the most photogenic places on Cephalonia and a favourite haunt of yachties who generally end up staying longer than intended. It has become a rather smart 'place-to-be-seen-in,' a sort of 'Kensington by the sea' and is consequently hugely busy in the summer. Fine if you have a good spot, but expect crossed anchors and worse at times. I prefer to visit by ferry in summer. In spring and autumn it is a lot quieter. In winter it is a ghost town and buildings apart, strangely like it was when I first visited in 1977 with just a single café open on the front and no-one around except a few locals.

It is said that Aristotle Onassis once wanted to buy the N side of Fiskardho, but was thwarted by the multiplicity of owners including an obdurate church, so turned to Skorpios instead. One of the attractions of Fiskardho is that it was one of the few places on Cephalonia to escape wholesale destruction in the 1953 earthquake, (over 90% of the buildings on the island were destroyed), so the buildings around the harbour are all typical of a vanished architecture, mostly 19th-century Italianate-looking houses. Add to this the safe harbour, nearby coves with crystal clear water (there are not what you could call good beaches in the area), pleasant walks around the pine-clad coast, the friendly intimate atmosphere of the place and it is no wonder that Fiskardho is a popular spot and gets more than a little crowded at the height of summer.

It takes its name from Robert Guiscard, the Norman adventurer who challenged Byzantium for its territory in Italy and western Greece and by and large succeeded in taking it. Byzantine rule was harsh in many areas with excessive taxes levied and little given in return. With a few of his companion knights Guiscard stormed through Italy and western Greece. In Fiskardho he succumbed along with many of his men to fever, possibly typhoid or malaria, and died here. The ruins of the Norman church on the N side of the bay are said to have been built to commemorate the man. There is a slight problem here in that he is also said to have died at Vonitsa in the Gulf of Amvrakia. Guiscard or Guiscardo became corrupted over time to Fiskardho, so perhaps the place takes precedence over Vonitsa's claim to the man. On the N entrance point there is an excellent example of a Venetian lighthouse: a round tower with a sheltered top with gaps in it so the oil fire could be seen.

In the disastrous 1953 earthquake over 90% of the buildings on Cephalonia were destroyed. Fiskardho was spared, it is said, because it sits on a bed of clay that absorbed the shockwaves

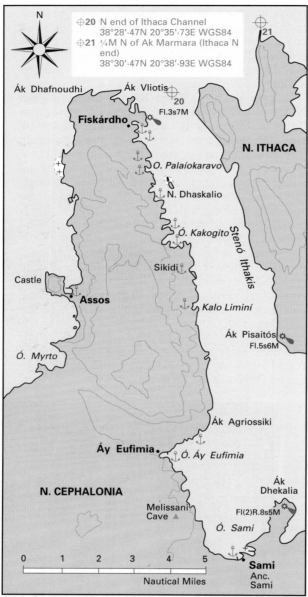

20 N end of Ithaca Channel
38°28'·47N 20°35'·73E WGS84
21 ¼M N of Ak Marmara (Ithaca N end)
38°30'·47N 20°38'·93E WGS84

Ák Dhafnoudhi
Ák Vliotis
21
20
Fl.3s7M
Fiskárdho
O. Palaíokaravo
N. ITHACA
N. Dhaskalio
Ó. Kakogito
Stenó Ithakís
Sikidi
Kalo Limini
Castle
Ák Pisaitós
Assos
Fl.5s6M
Ó. Myrto
Ák Agriossiki
Áy Eufimia
Ó. Áy Eufimia
Ák Dhekalia
N. CEPHALONIA
Melissani Cave
Fl(2)R.8s5M
Ó. Sami
0 1 2 3 4 5
Sami
Anc. Sami
Nautical Miles

STENÓN ITHAKIS (ITHACA CHANNEL)

Dhiavlos Ithakis

The channel between Cephalonia and Ithaca is hemmed in by high mountains on either side which funnel the prevailing wind down the channel. There are also gusts, sometimes severe, off the high land and down the valleys on the W side of the channel. Although the wind strength is increased over that on the open sea and the gusts off Cephalonia can be unnerving, there are no

real problems that a little prudence cannot cope with; for which read reef well down first and then shake the reefs out if you have been overly cautious.

Anchorages between Fiskardho and Ay Eufimia

Along the coast of Cephalonia on the W side of Dhiavlos Ithakis there are numerous attractive anchorages in bays and coves which can be used according to the wind and sea. The slopes around many of the bays are covered in pine and cypress and offer wonderful solitude and crystal clear water. Many of them cannot be reached by land although a new road has made some of them more accessible for landlubbers.

Boats visiting this stretch of coastline should do everything in their power not to disturb things too much. The Mediterranean monk seal, *Monachus monachus*, inhabits the waters around here, some of the last remaining members of a species that is very nearly extinct. It is a shy animal, easily disturbed, and if you see one do not chase it to get a better look at it, but discretely and quietly leave it alone.

Most of the bays along the coast are very deep, usually you will have to anchor in 10m plus of water. The bottom is mostly sand, shingle and weed, poor holding if you strike thick weed or a lot of shingle, so select the spot you anchor in with care. The water is normally very clear so you can pick out a good spot on the bottom to drop the anchor onto. With the prevailing NW wind there are gusts off the land in most of these anchorages so if possible take a long line ashore. While there are gusts off the land, the wind blowing from the N down the channel sends a swell into some of the bays. From the N the anchorages are as follows:

Ormos Fiskardho In the S of the bay there is an inlet with an old gravel-loading plant on the N side. It is very deep in here so take a long line ashore to counter any gusts off the land. Good shelter.

Palaiokaravo Just under a mile S of the inlet above there is an attractive bay suitable in calm weather or light westerlies.

Nisis Dhaskalio A small islet lying close off the coast. A chapel is conspicuous on it. Above and below-water rocks fringe the islet. On the coast opposite are several attractive coves suitable in

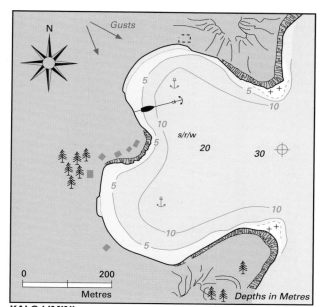

KALO LIMINI
⊕ 38°22′·4N 20°37′·0E

Ay Eufimia

(Ayias Euphemias, Ag Evfimia, Pilaros Cove)
The large bay and harbour lying on the same parallel as the S end of Ithaca.

Pilotage

Approach Coming down Dhiavlos Ithakis from the N you will not see the village and harbour until you round Ak Agriossiki. From the E and SE the village is easily identified. Closer in the breakwater will be seen. With the prevailing wind there are strong gusts out of the bay, though the sea is usually flat.

Mooring Berth stern or bows-to the quay on the N. The prevailing wind gusts down onto the harbour so make sure your anchor is well in and if in doubt lay a second anchor. Much of the quay has been extended so that underwater rubble is not the problem it once was. Alternatively anchor off clear of the anchors of yachts berthed on the quay. The bottom is mud and weed with some rocks, not everywhere good holding, so with the gusts make sure the anchor is well in. With the prevailing wind there are gusts down the valley and into the harbour, mostly bothersome and rarely dangerous.

Facilities

Services Water and electricity on the N quay. Fuel can be delivered.
Provisions Most provisions can be found.

calm weather or light westerlies.

Ormos Kaminus A bay about a mile S of Nisis Dhaskalio. Suitable in calm weather.

Ormos Kakogito A large bay about ½M S of Kaminus. The shelter in here is not as good as it looks on the chart as the prevailing wind sends a swell in.

Ormos Sikidi A small bay about ½M S of Kakogito. Reasonable shelter. There are several other similar coves down the coast to Kalo Limini.

Kalo Limini A twin-headed bay just over a mile S of Sikidi. It is easily recognised by the few houses on the shore. Anchor in 10–15m with a long line ashore. The N cove offers the best shelter. Although there are gusts off the land and some swell enters, it is a suitable overnight anchorage in settled weather.

Ormos Sarakiniko An inlet about 1½M S of Kalo Limini. Suitable in calm weather.

Ak Agriossiki Immediately SW of the cape there is a narrow inlet offering some shelter from the prevailing wind. There is usually something of a lee around the cape until you encounter the wind gusting out of Ay Eufimia. Room for a few yachts to anchor in pleasant surroundings.

Ay Eufemia
Nigel Patten

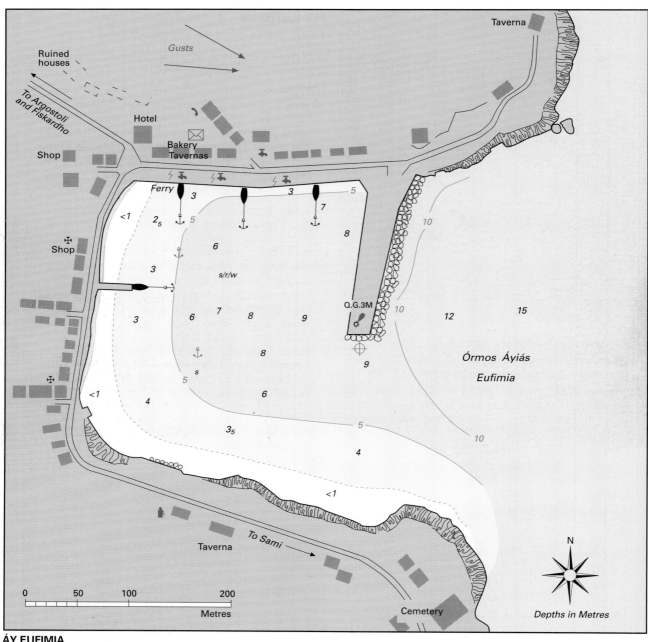

ÁY EUFIMIA
⊕38°18′·2N 20°36′·1E

Eating out Several tavernas including an excellent one situated at the end of the track running along the coast from the harbour breakwater – here you sit with a view over to Ithaca and the food is good (Kefallonian pie served).

Other PO. Telephone. Hire cars although there may not be one available!

General

Ay Eufimia used to be the main ferry port for Cephalonia until the 1953 earthquake destroyed

Mellisani Cave near Ay Eufemia

that the roof of the cave did not fall in courtesy of the 1953 earthquake as is often stated, but several thousand years ago. The water of the cave is slightly brackish and is in fact seawater that enters at the water mill on Ak Ay Theodoroi at Argostoli and travels through underground passages to the Mellisani lake, bubbling up into the sea nearby. Apparently the exact source of the water flowing through Mellisani was not determined until the 1950's when a French team used red dye to trace it from Ak Ay Theodoroi. Also nearby is the Cave of Drogarati.

Limin Sami

(Samis)

The main ferry port for Cephalonia in the large bay at the S end of Dhiavlos Ithakis.

Pilotage

Approach Once into Ormos Sami the buildings of the town are easily identified. The approach is straightforward and free of dangers.

Mooring Berth stern or bows-to or alongside the new pier inside the basin. The prevailing wind blows straight down Dhiavlos Ithakis into the harbour making it uncomfortable at times. Although the wind does not blow home, (it tends to lift over the high hills behind), a surge can develop as the sea gets pushed through the arches let into the new pier. The bottom is mud, good holding.

much of it and Sami was developed instead. In Maki's *Asteria Cafeneion* there is an old photograph of Ay Eufimia prior to 1953 showing a substantial village and a busy harbour. For years the village stagnated and few yachts visited here – in 1977 when I first tied up in Ay Eufimia there was one taverna and Maki's *Cafeneion*.

Near the village of Karavomilos on the road between Ay Eufimia and Sami is the Cave of Mellisani. From the entrance you go down through a tunnel to the cave and underground lake of deep inky water with turquoise patches where the sun manages to strike it. A boatman takes you around the cave, about a twenty minute trip, which I suppose gives one an idea of what entering Hades and encountering Charon must be like, though there are generally too many people to set the tone. The boatman will tell you

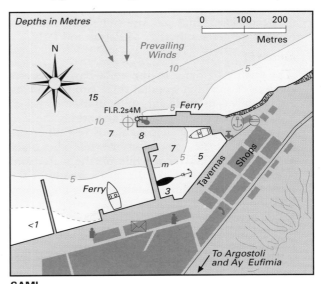

SAMI
⊕38°15'·3N 20°38'·8E

uncrowded as the locals and most visitors use the beach to the W. The ruins of ancient Sami are just outside the town, but there is little to see except a few sections of wall.

A village was built at the western end of the town for the filming of *Captain Corelli's Mandolin*. Yachts were banned from the sea area between Fiskardho and Poros so that no modern plastic fantastics upset the period characteristics of the movie set.

Ormos Andisamis

⊕ 38°16'·2N 20°41'·2E

A large bay immediately S of Ak Dekalia. A number of yachts have reported that shelter in here is adequate with the prevailing winds although a bit of slop does roll in. I suggest you have a look in here but be prepared to move out if the *maistro* hammers down into the bay. Ay Eufimia and Sami are not too far away. On the slopes above is the monastery of Moni Agrilion.

Poros

(Pronos)

A small harbour tucked into Ormos Poros 9M SE of Ak Dekalia.

Pilotage

Approach From the N the buildings of the village are easily identified. From the S the village and harbour will not be seen until you are around Ak Poros. Once into the harbour care is needed of an underwater rock reported to lie in approximately the position shown. Keep to the north of it when heading for the south quay.

Poros on Cephalonia

Sami

Facilities

Services Water at the foot of the mole. Fuel by mini-tanker.

Provisions Good shopping for provisions nearby in the town.

Eating out Tavernas and snack bars nearby.

Other PO. OTE. Bank. ATM. Hire cars and motorbikes. Bus to Argostoli that connects with the ferries. Ferries to Patras and Italy.

General

The setting of Sami in the wide bay under the shadow of the high wooded ridge running NE to Ak Dekalia is magnificent, so Sami itself comes as a bit of a disappointment. It is an entirely modern town built with the help of the British after the 1953 earthquake. Yet after a while the place grows on you. Sit for a while on the waterfront with a cold beer and like the locals watch for the ferry arriving – nothing much disturbs this sleepy little hollow until the ferry comes when there is hectic activity getting people and vehicles on and off and then everything settles back to a more sedate pace.

There are some wonderful walks along the coast to the NE of the town where there are rocky coves suitable for swimming which are usually

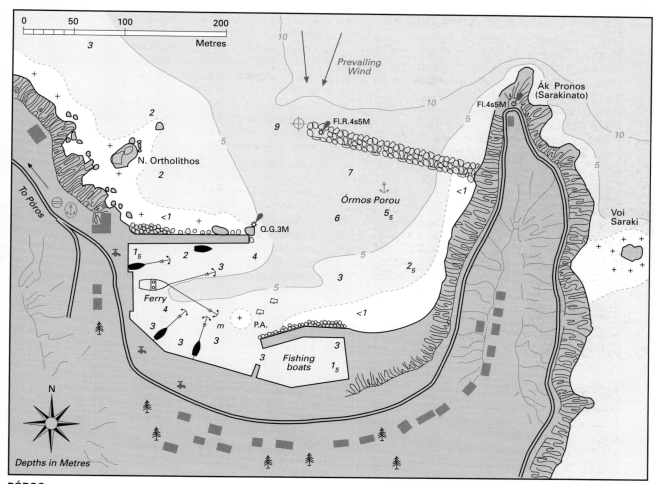

PÓROS
⊕38°09′·0N 20°46′·9E

Mooring Berth stern or bows-to the quay on the S or under the short breakwater on the east side. The bottom is mud and weed, good holding. The prevailing wind tends to push a chop into the harbour, uncomfortable but usually tenable although it has to be said shelter is not brilliant in here. At night when the wind dies down things are calmer.

You can also anchor under the breakwater on the NE side though it is not the most comfortable here with the prevailing wind. Make sure you are clear of the channel used by the ferry.

Facilities

Services Water on the quay.
Provisions Most provisions can be found in the village.

Eating out Good local taverna by the harbour and others in the village.
Other PO. OTE. Bus to Argostoli that connects with the ferry. Ferry to Killini and to Zakinthos in the summer.

General

Poros is often stated to be one of Cephalonia's major tourist resorts, but it seems to me that most people arriving on the ferry are on the road to Argostoli before they even blink twice at Poros. While Poros does attract numbers of tourists, many local, it is more in the mould of a ferry port like Sami. The setting is spectacular, it sits at the foot of a valley cutting down through the high mountains, on the edge of the sea, but the village itself wins little kudos from most people though I quite like it.

Ak Mounda and Kakova Shoal

Off Ak Mounda, the SE tip of Cephalonia, Kakova shoal runs out in a SE direction for around 1¾M. There are several 2m patches although there are mostly 4m depths in the inner and outer part. In calm weather a yacht can, with care, pass around ¼M and less than ½M off the coast where there are mostly 4m plus depths. However keep a lookout on the bows. With the prevailing wind a swell heaps up over the shoal water and a yacht should keep well off.

On the old Admiralty chart 203 a number of transits are given. Ak Kapri in line with the W side of Nisos Atoko leads clear of the shoals, however with any haze it can be difficult to see Atoko clearly. The other transit is Ay Yeoryios (Georgis) Castle in line with Ak Koroni which leads clear of the shoal water, but it depends on you being able to identify the castle.

Using WP26 you are outside the shoals on a N to S transit.

⊕26   2¼M E of Ak Mounda (Cephalonia SE end)
38°03'·20N 20°49'·97E WGS84

Ormos Kateleios

Under Ak Mounda there is a large bay extending around to Ak Kateleios. With light westerlies a yacht can anchor on the N side of the bay. The prevailing wind tends to blow down the E side of Cephalonia from the N to NW and along the S coast from the W. Directly under the cape there is a small rock-bound *caique* harbour where a small yacht may find room. Great care is needed in the approach and a lookout should con you in from the bows. The area to the W of the breakwater is littered with above and below-water rocks. The approach should be made from a SE direction passing between the end of the breakwater and a withy. There are 2m depths in the immediate approach and at the outer end of the breakwater. Ashore there is the village of Kato Kateleios where some provisions can be found and there are several tavernas.

Note Anchoring and fishing is prohibited between Ormos Kateleios and Ak Skinari on Zakinthos, presumably due to submarine cables. Observe the no-anchoring signs where shown.

On the slopes behind in the village of Markopoulo a remarkable phenomenon occurs in August. Between August 6th and 15th, or at least before the Feast of the Assumption on the 15th, small snakes migrate or emerge around and in the church. The snakes are said to have miraculous properties, conferred to whoever catches one, and the ceremony attracts the ill and infirm or whoever is looking for a miracle. It is difficult to know where the association comes from. In Kirkpinar in Anatolian Turkey water snakes appear in early summer and are said to have healing properties. The locals drape them over the afflicted part to cure it. The Christian religion normally associates snakes with Chaos and disorder, but a snake was the symbol of Askeplios, the Greek god of healing, and there are fragments here and there of snakes being used in ancient Greek medicine. Perhaps the ceremony here is one of those distant folk memories of an ancient practice, absorbed by the church because it could not entirely eliminate it.

Pessades

On the W side of Ormos Lourdha there is the small ferry port of Pessades for the ferry running across to Ay Nikolaos on Zakinthos. The *caique* harbour here is miniature, but a yacht may find a berth on the south side of the mole. Anchor and take a long line ashore. You will need to use your dinghy to get ashore. There are plans to develop the ferry quay and to built an extension to the mole to provide more shelter. At present there is reasonable shelter from the prevailing wind but no protection from southerlies.

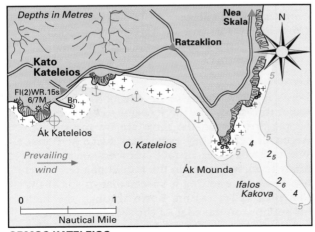

ORMOS KATELEIOS
⊕38°03'·8N 20°44'·6E

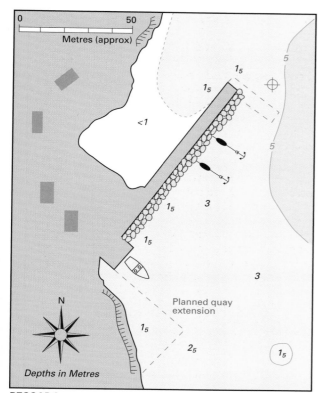

PESSADA
⊕38°06'·2N 20°34'·5E

Argostoli

(Argostolion)

The capital and principal harbour of the island tucked into a bay in Kolpos Argostoliou, the gulf in the SW of Cephalonia.

Pilotage

Approach From the W the tall white lighthouse on Ak Yero Gombos is conspicuous. From the E Nisis Thionisi and a large white hotel on Ak Pelagia are conspicuous. Care is needed of the reef SE of Ak Pelagia and of the reef W of Ak Ay Nikolaos.

Once into the immediate approaches to Kolpos Argostoliou, Nisis Vardianoi, although low-lying, can be identified. A yacht can pass between Nisis Vardianoi and Cephalonia where there are 5·5m least depths in the fairway. On Ak Ay Theodoroi a Doric style lighthouse is conspicuous. Proceed down into the bay where the buildings of Argostoli will be seen. Leave the beacon marking a rocky patch to starboard.

Mooring Berth stern or bows-to the S side of the ferry quay or on the N end of the W quay. Although the prevailing wind blows down into the harbour, there is a good lee under the ferry quay. The bottom is mud and good holding.

Facilities

Services Water on the quay. Fuel by mini-tanker.
Provisions Good shopping for provisions in the town.
Eating out Numerous tavernas in and near the town square immediately W of the ferry quay.
Other PO. OTE. Banks. ATMs. Hospital. Dentists. Hire cars and motorbikes. Buses to most places on the island. Ferry to Lixuri. Ferry to Killini. Internal and international flights from the airport nearby.

Argostoli Marina

Note At the time of writing the marina is not open to yachts.

Pilotage

Approach The marina is on the east side of the arm running south to Argostoli docks. The lights at the entrance are conspicuous.

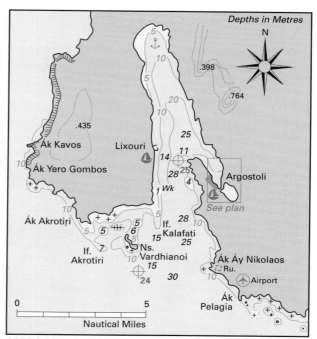

APPROACHES TO KOLPOS ARGOSTOLI

⊕24 1M S of N.Vardhianoi light (Cephalonia SW end)
38°06'·9N 20°25'·6E
⊕25 ½M W of Ak Ay Theodhoroi (Kolpos Argostoliou)
38°11'·5N 20°27'·5E

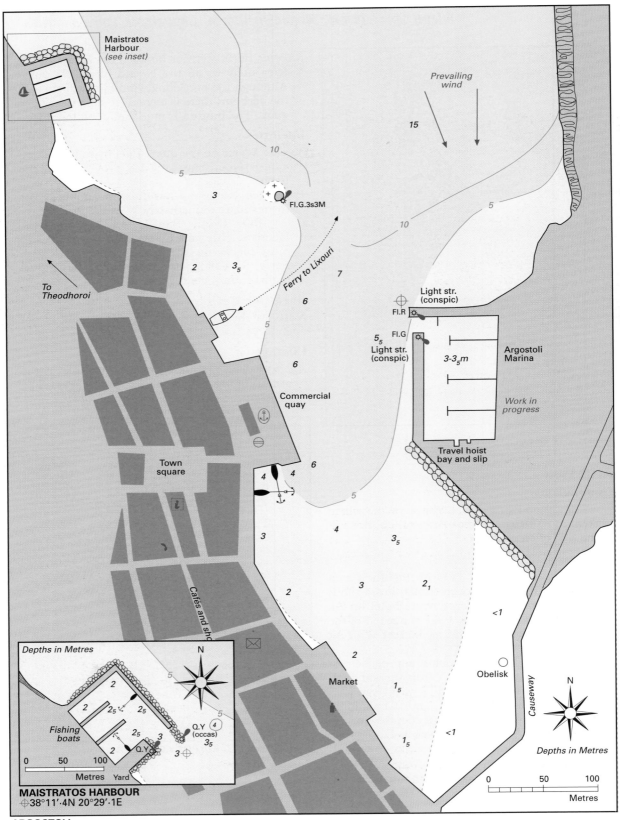

Maistratos
Harbour
(see inset)

*Prevailing
wind*

15

10

5

3

+

+

Fl.G.3s3M

3

5

2

3$_5$

*To
Theodhoroi*

Ferry to Lixouri

7

10

5

6

Light str.
(conspic)

Fl.R

Fl.G

5$_5$
Light str.
(conspic)

3-3$_5$*m*

Argostoli
Marina

*Work in
progress*

6

6

Commercial
quay

Town
square

6

Travel hoist
bay and slip

4 *4*

5

4

3$_5$

3

4

Cafés and sho

3

2$_1$

2

3

<1

Obelisk

MAISTRATOS HARBOUR
⊕38°11'·4N 20°29'·1E

Depths in Metres

N

2

2

5

2$_5$ *2*$_5$

5

Q.Y ④
(occas)

2$_5$

3$_5$

*Fishing
boats*

2$_5$ *3*

2   Q.Y

3

3 ⊕

0   50   100

Metres   Yard

⊠

2

Market

1$_5$

<1

1$_5$

Causeway

N

Depths in Metres

0   50   100

Metres

ARGOSTOLI
⊕38°10'·90N 20°29'·76E WGS84

The new marina at Argostoli looking across to Argostoli town.

Mooring Berth where directed when the marina is open. Laid moorings will be tailed to the quay. All-round shelter.

Facilities

Water and electricity to be installed. Most other facilities are also planned.

Maistratos Harbour

Pilotage

Approach This small harbour with a mix of fishing boats and yachts lies just over ½M north of the ferry quay in Argostoli. The breakwater and boats inside are easily identified when heading down towards the town.

Mooring There is little room for visiting yachts. The best policy is to head for Argostoli and come up on foot to enquire about a berth. Yachts go stern or bows-to on the NE and SE quay. Good all-round shelter.

Facilities

Water on the quay. Provisions and tavernas nearby. Argostoli town is a short walk away.

General

Argostoli, like 90% of the rest of Cephalonia, was flattened in the 1953 earthquake and the present city was entirely rebuilt after the event. Argostoli became the capital in 1765 when the Castle of St George on the heights to the SE, the Venetian

The Doric-style lighthouse conspicuous on Ak Ay Theodoroi in the approaches to Argostoli

The celebrated water wheel at Argostoli. The 1953 earthquake altered the terrain to such an extent that the flow of sea-water is now much reduced

In recent years the pedestrianised main street has become all *caffè latte* and *ciabattas*, with outdoor cafés in between fashionable boutiques and jewellery shops. The residents take their coffee and conversation in a relaxed atmosphere and the hum of conversation lends the place an Italianate feel which is not out of place.

Within the town there are two interesting museums. The Archaeological Museum just S of the main square has an interesting collection of artefacts from Mycenean through Greek and Roman to Byzantine times. The Folklore Museum in the basement of the library is interesting for its exhibits and photographs showing the town before the devastating earthquake.

At the end of the peninsula to the N of the town, close by the Doric style lighthouse, is the Katavotheres water wheel, now clasped in the grasp of a taverna. Prior to the 1953 earthquake seawater poured into a subterranean chasm and a water wheel was built to harness the power for grinding wheat. The earthquake reduced the flow and although the sea still flows underground, it is barely enough to turn the wheel. The seawater seeping into the underground passages finds its way right across the island to the Cave of Mellisani between Ay Eufimia and Sami. To the S of Argostoli at Metaxata, Byron spent the winter of 1823–24 before he went to Mesolongion and his death for the Greek cause. Like so much else the house was destroyed by the 1953 earthquake.

Lixouri

(Lixurion)

A town and small harbour nearly opposite Argostoli on the W side of Kolpos Argostoliou.

Pilotage

Approach The harbour is easily identified and the approach is straightforward. Keep a good lookout for the ferries crossing between Argostoli and Lixouri which have right of way in the harbour.

Mooring Berth stern or bows-to the N or W quay keeping clear of the ferry berth. The bottom is soft mud, poor holding until the anchor digs in. Good shelter although strong NW winds cause a surge.

capital, was considered beyond repair after a series of earthquakes. The small fishing village developed through the 18th and 19th centuries into what was apparently one of the most beautiful cities in the Ionian, rich in ornate public buildings in the Venetian style and later in a Georgian-Mediterranean style under British rule.

It is difficult to imagine today. The causeway across the lagoon was built under British rule and was one of the few things to survive the earthquake. For the rest, Argostoli seems to have been slapped together as quickly as possible after the earthquake and is a nondescript place that here and there is relieved by a reconstructed church or an old stone wall. I should add that year by year the town mellows, and the situation on the edge of the lagoon with high mountains on the other side is so wonderful.

Facilities

Services Water on the quay although it is not always turned on in the summer. Fuel in the town.

Provisions Good shopping for provisions.

Eating out Tavernas in the town close to the harbour.

Other PO. OTE. Bank. Hire motorbikes. Ferry to Argostoli.

General

Lixouri is an agricultural town serving the flat farmland around it, terrain that is a rarity on the island. It is a pleasant workaday place that sees a few tourists though most prefer to stay on the other side. The harbour is unfortunately next to the main sewer outlet and gets very smelly in the summer heat. Escape by taking a wander around the back-streets where there are all sorts of interesting workshops.

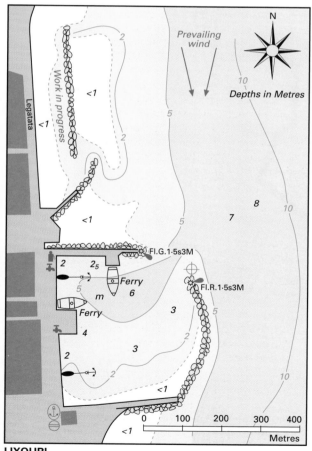

LIXOURI
⊕38°12'·1N 20°26'·6E

The West Coast

The west coast has little to offer the yachtsman apart from spectacular scenery and delightful coves and beaches that cannot be used because the prevailing NW to W winds send a heavy swell in. Even in the morning before the afternoon breeze has set in there is invariably a considerable ground swell setting onto the coast. In calm weather a small yacht could use Ay Kiriakis and larger yachts can get into Assos. However neither of these two places should be entered with the prevailing NW wind.

The west coast of Cephallonia was also used for some of the filming of *Captain Corelli's Mandoli*n.

Ormos Athera

A large bay about 13M N of Ak Yero Gombas. It is open to the prevailing wind and I mention it only because it looks a wonderful spot to explore in calm weather.

Ay Kiriakis

A small harbour in Ormos Ay Kiriakis, the large bay W of Athera in the crook of Cephalonia. In the SW corner of the bay there is a miniature fishing harbour where a small yacht could find a berth. It should only be approached in calm weather and not in the prevailing wind which blows straight down onto the entrance.

Considerable caution is needed in the immediate approach and the entrance which is bordered by underwater rocks. Berth under the outer breakwater with a long line ashore where shown on the plan. Care is needed as the depths inside the harbour are irregular.

Two tavernas ashore which often have excellent fresh fish caught by local boats. The situation under steep mountains and the rocky coast bordered by clear, clear waters is superb, but the harbour should only be used by a small yacht in calm weather.

Assos

A small harbour on the N side of a short headland lying 6M S of Ak Dafnoudhi on the N tip of Cephalonia. It should only be used in calm weather or light westerlies.

Ay Kiriakis

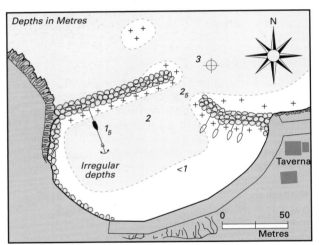

AYIOS KIRIAKIS
⊕38°18′·6N 20°28′·6E

Pilotage

Approach The massive fort on the steep headland partially sheltering Assos is not as easy to pick out as it might appear, but can usually be identified from the distance. Closer in yachts coming from the N will see the houses on the isthmus and the short mole.

Mooring Go stern or bows-to the mole with a long line ashore as it is bordered by rocks for most of its length. There are one or two spaces where smaller yachts can go close enough so you can get ashore. Alternatively anchor off. It is mostly quite deep in the bay, 7–10m, so

ensure you let out enough scope. The bottom is mud, shingle and weed, not everywhere good holding. Shelter in here is adequate in light northwesterlies, but a yacht should leave in moderate or strong northwesterlies which push a swell in.

Facilities

Some provisions can be found. Numerous tavernas in the village. Infrequent bus to Fiskardho and Argostoli.

General

The little hamlet snuggling into the hillside is

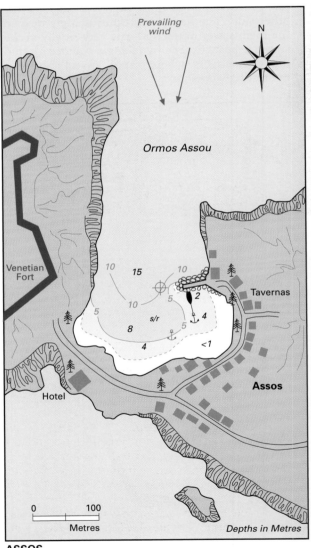

ASSOS
⊕38°22′·8N 20°32′·2E

Assos

nearly always mentioned as a popular tourist resort or resort-to-be, but as yet Assos entertains only a few visitors and remains an intimate spot with a small hotel and village rooms. It is difficult to reach by land down the winding road from the mountain ridge and its small harbour is not big enough nor safe enough for many yachts or tripper boats. It is a wonderfully picturesque place crammed into the gap between the fort and peninsula and the high cliffs and mountains around it.

The fort on the peninsula is massive and enclosed a large town, but little is known about it. An ancient Greek fort existed here and parts of it have been incorporated into the Venetian fort. This latter fort was built around 1595 and sprawls across the peninsula enclosing an area that is recorded to have included sixty public and over two hundred private buildings. Large water cisterns ensured it could last out a long siege.

In the 20th century a prison was established on the peninsula and though little is known about the type of prisoners sent here, it would have been an ideal location to exile political offenders to. The abandoned prison in the centre of the peninsula is a melancholy place, its watchtowers intact but deserted now, the roof destroyed, the cells abandoned, with only a few goats for inhabitants. The lonely setting casts a gloom over the decaying buildings and perhaps the ghosts of prisoners unjustly kept here linger on. The old fort is a fascinating place to wander around though care is needed of the crumbling masonry and of the underground cisterns. The rough dirt road leads to the cliffs at the W end of the peninsula and the limit of the old stone walls guarding it. Needless to say there are wonderful views from parts of the fort.

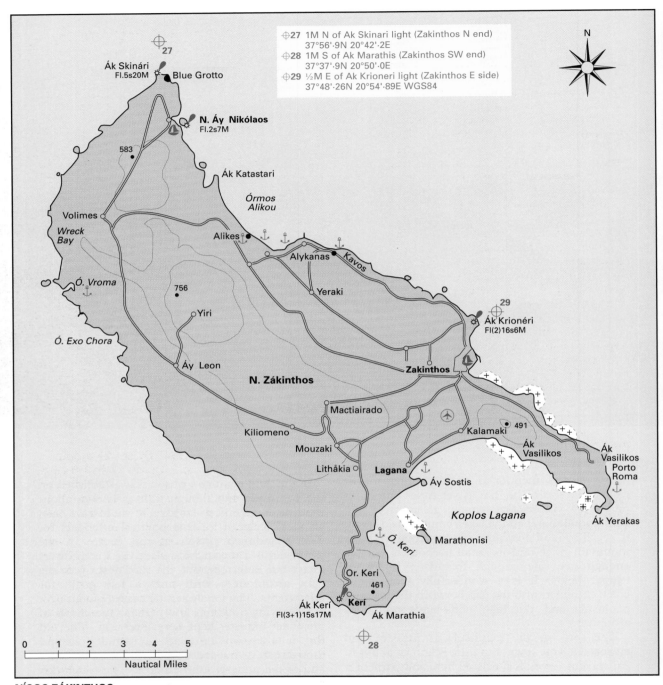

⊕**27** 1M N of Ak Skinari light (Zakinthos N end)
37°56'·9N 20°42'·2E
⊕**28** 1M S of Ak Marathis (Zakinthos SW end)
37°37'·9N 20°50'·0E
⊕**29** ½M E of Ak Krioneri light (Zakinthos E side)
37°48'·26N 20°54'·89E WGS84

N

⊕
27

Ák Skinári
Fl.5s20M ☼ ● Blue Grotto

N. Áy Nikólaos
Fl.2s7M

583

Ák Katastari

*Órmos
Alikou*

Volimes

*Wreck
Bay*

Alikes ⚓

Alykanas

Kavos

Ó. Vroma

756

Yeraki

29

Yiri

Ák Krionéri
Fl(2)16s6M

Ó. Exo Chora

Áy Leon

N. Zákinthos

Zakinthos

Mactiairado

Kiliomeno

491

Kalamaki

Mouzaki

Ák
Vasilikos

Ák
Vasilikos
Porto
Roma

Lithâkia

Lagana

Áy Sostis

Ák Yerakas

Koplos Lagana

Ó. Keri

Marathonisi

Or. Keri
461

Kerí

Ák Kerí
Fl(3+1)15s17M

Kerí

Ák Marathia

⊕
28

| 0 | 1 | 2 | 3 | 4 | 5 |

Nautical Miles

NÍSOS ZÁKINTHOS

Nisos Zakinthos

(Zakynthos, Zante)

Zakinthos is the southernmost of the Ionian islands although Kithera at the bottom of the Peloponnese used to be included in the Heptanisoi for administrative purposes. Geographically it is quite different from its northern neighbours, Cephalonia and Ithaca, which are really mountain tops in the sea with little flat land suitable for cultivation. Zakinthos has a huge central plain surrounded by a horseshoe range of mountains that catch the winter and spring rains and funnel them down to water it. The fertile soil responds to give Zakinthos a huge swathe of green, in marked contrast to the barren slopes of Cephalonia and Ithaca and in this it resembles Corfu – indeed there is an age-old rivalry between the two islands over which is the more beautiful. To this bounteous island add its strategic position in the southern approaches to the Gulf of Patras and it is obvious why it has long been historically important and consequently colonised by anyone who wished to control the sea routes to the south around the Peloponnese and into the Gulfs of Patras and Corinth.

Being close to Ithaca it is naturally enough mentioned by Homer in the *Odyssey* where it is called 'wooded Zakynthos', a description that not only mentions it by the name it bears today, but describes its principal asset. Homer also tells us that the name of the island comes from a son of Dardanos, an ancestor of the Kings of Troy, who was called, inevitably, Zakinthos. He arrived with ships and men from Arcadia and built an acropolis he called Psophida, and so gave his name to the island. There are other versions of

Spinning on Zakinthos

where the name comes from including a derivation from the Greek word for the hyacinth which grows everywhere.

Little is known of the ancient period until the Peloponnesian War when the Athenian fleet under Tolmidis sacked the island and the Zakinthians had little choice but to support Athens during the war. Later it came under Philip of Macedon and passed in turn to the Romans. After the end of Roman rule the island was subject to neglect and to the depredations of every passing pirate and invader. It was sacked by the Goths, the Vandals under Gizarich who left the island with 500 aristocrats who were systematically butchered and thrown overboard on the way home, the Saracens who regularly plundered Zakinthos, the Normans who razed the island, and then the Turks who in 1479 depopulated the entire island.

This catalogue of disaster and carnage ended in 1489 with the arrival of the Venetians who needed Zakinthos to safeguard their trade route

Getting around inland

The road system on Zakinthos is well developed except in the very north. Most of the major roads are paved and minor roads are usually in good condition. Like some of the other islands the local maps are not entirely truthful about the road network or the grade of the road. Some just do not exist and some marked as major roads are not.

The interior is served by a rudimentary bus service, but you really need a hire car/jeep or motorbike to get around. Hire cars and motorbikes are available from a number of hire firms in Zakinthos town. The interior is well worth exploring, especially parts of the southwest where it is impossible or difficult to get to by boat.

around the Peloponnese and on to the E. The Venetians restored order and immediately settlers flocked to the island such that by 1515 the formerly depopulated island had a population of more than 20,000 people. The Venetians remained until 1797 and the fall of the Republic. When the French took Zakinthos they were the beneficiaries of what has been described as one of the most beautiful cities in the Ionian. Their version of the name of the island, Zante, has stuck right up into the 20th century. The English arrived in 1809 and did what they were best at, building roads and public buildings, until in 1864, along with the other Ionian islands, Zakinthos became part of Greece.

As with many of the other islands, the enduring architectural legacy has been Venetian. The city of Zakinthos was flattened in the 1953 earthquake, but was rebuilt along the lines of the old city and so it is possible to get a glimpse of what old Zakinthos looked like. Some who saw the old city are harsh on the modern one, Lawrence Durrell described it as a '. . . beautiful woman whose face had been splashed with vitriol. Here and there, an arch, a pendant, a shattered remains of arcade, all that is left of her renowned beauty', though I think this goes a bit far. If you search out some of the old buildings, ignore the reinforced concrete, wander through the reconstructed arcades and then make an effort of will, you can see, only just, the old city.

The Venetians left another legacy which endures to this day: the currant. The Venetians supervised the transplantation of the currant from the Peloponnese to Zakinthos with the hope of cashing in on lucrative European trade. It worked and currant cultivation spread throughout Zakinthos, even today more than half of the island is cultivated with the currant vine although today's recipes do not call for the quantities used in Victorian recipes. On this theme when Edward Lear was on Zakinthos he penned a few lines on the view from the village of Galaro.

'The old nursery rhyme –
If all the world were apple-pie,
And all the trees were bread and cheese –
supposes a sort of food-landscape hardly more remarkable than that presented by this vast green plain, which may be, in truth, called one unbroken continuance of future currant-dumplings and plum-puddings.'

Limin Zakinthos

(Zakynthos, Port Zante)

The capital and major port on the E side of Zakinthos.

Pilotage

Approach From the N the SE peninsula dominated by Mount Skopos and separated by the central plain looks like an island. Closer in the hotels on Tsilivi Beach N of Ak Krioneri will be seen. The buildings and harbour of Zakinthos will not be seen until you are around the cape. From the S the buildings of Zakinthos stand out well against the eroded cliffs behind. In the approach from the S and E care is needed to avoid Ifalos Dhimitris, a reef and shoal water lying approximately 900m ESE of the harbour entrance; it is marked by a red conical buoy (Fl.R). In the immediate approaches and the harbour itself keep an eye open for the numerous ferries coming or going to Killini.

Mooring Berth stern or bows-to on the NE or NW quays. The NE quay is the base for many of the large trip boats which use the top half of the quay. There is usually space to go south of them, clear of the ferry berth marked on the

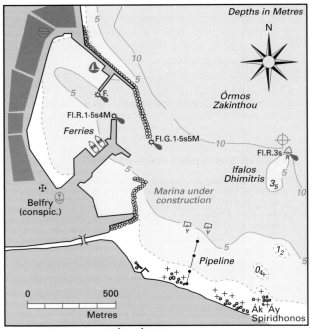

APPROACHES TO LIMÍN ZÁKINTHOU
⊕ 37°46'·84N 20°54'·91E WGS84

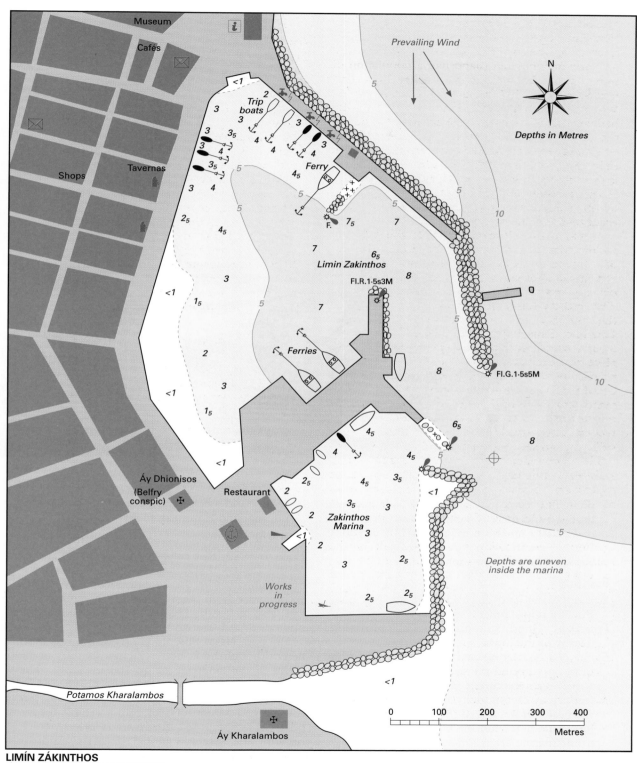

Museum

Cafés

Shops

Tavernas

Áy Dhionisos
(Belfry
conspic)

Restaurant

Trip
boats

Ferry

Ferries

Limin Zakinthos

Fl.R.1·5s3M

Fl.G.1·5s5M

Zakinthos
Marina

Works
in
progress

Depths are uneven
inside the marina

Prevailing Wind

N

Depths in Metres

Potamos Kharalambos

Áy Kharalambos

0   100   200   300   400
Metres

LIMÍN ZÁKINTHOS
37°46′·69N 20°54′·36E WGS84

Zakinthos harbour looking out to the entrance   *Lu Michell*

plan. The town quay on the NW side has been dredged and there is plenty of room to go stern or bows-to on the northern half of the quay. Further south has not been dredged and it is too shallow for most yachts.

Facilities

Services Water and electricity on the NE quay. Fuel by mini-tanker.

Provisions Good shopping for all provisions nearby in the town.

Eating Out Numerous tavernas of all types in the town and around the square near the harbour. *Komi's* fish restaurant at the foot of the main ferry quay is especially recommended. I had the best *barbounia* (red mullet) I have had in a long time here, and the tables at the waterside in the marina are wonderful.

Other PO. OTE. Banks. ATMs. Hospital. Dentists. Hire cars and motorbikes. Ferry to Killini and occasional service to Katakolon. Internal and European flights.

General

Prior to 1953, that catastrophic date in this part of the Ionian, Zakinthos was one of the most beautiful cities in the Ionian, rich in Venetian architecture from the 17th and 18th centuries. It was also a centre for the arts. It produced a number of well known men of letters.

The poet Hugo Foscolo (1778–1827) was born here although he is better known in Italy as he wrote in the language of his Italian father. The best known is Dionysis Solomos (1798–1857), who like Foscolo initially wrote in Italian, but then forged demotic Greek into a vehicle for his poetry. He composed the *Hymn to Liberty* which became the Greek national anthem. Andreas Kalvos (1792–1863) was born here, but lived most of his life in England with his English wife, though his remains were later shipped back to be buried on Zakinthos. These are only the best known of a whole panoply of writers that marked Zakinthos out as the cultural capital of this part of the world – it can even be seen in the locally produced guide book which instead of snatching likely looking words from a dictionary to enthuse about beaches and hotels, by contrast with others is well written with a solid chunk of text on the arts, past and present.

After the earthquake the city elders decided not to clear away the rubble and build a totally modern city, but to rebuild the old city as best they could. Some would say they failed utterly with the project, but for me the new city at least gives glimpses of the old. The streets parallel to the waterfront are in the arcaded style for which it was previously known. Some of the landmarks such as the church of Ay Dionissiou which survived the earthquake at the W end of the harbour and the buildings around the town square are in the old style, but perhaps because too many obviously modern buildings intrude or perhaps because the reinforced concrete used in the reconstruction does not weather like old Venetian mortar and plaster, the city needs years yet to mellow and acquire a distinct character of its own.

There are several interesting museums in the town should you need to enquire into the past of the town and island.

Zakinthos Museum Situated in Solomos Square right by the harbour, it houses an impressive collection of church art, especially Byzantine and post-Byzantine icons rescued after the earthquake, as well as other items relating to the island.

Solomos Museum In Ay Markou square just N of Solomos Square. Contains exhibits relating to Solomos, Kalvos, and Foscolo, as well as other

Port Zakinthos town quay

writers, painters and musicians from the island.

Resistance Museum Situated in the library in Solomos Square, it contains exhibits relating to the resistance in the Second World War as well as exhibits on folklore.

Zakinthos Marina

The marina has been 'Under construction' for many years now, but finally things appear to be reaching completion. The quays are in place, although mooring rings and bollards are scarce. Light structures guard the almost finished breakwaters, but rusting hulks hog much of the quay space. There is still work to be done before it is 'open', but this rush of activity suggests things have got off the ground again.

Ormos Ay Nikolaos

(Korynth)

A bay on the east side of the north tip of Zakinthos. Nisis Ay Nikolaos lies in the entrance to the bay and a yacht can pass on either side of it though care is needed in the north entrance. As well as a reef extending out from the north side, blocks have been laid out from the islet to improve shelter inside the bay, although some blocks are now under the surface. The end of the blocks is marked with a small stick beacon.

A large concrete apron has been built around the southern side of the bay, where yachts can berth stern or bows-to on the northwest end. The southern end is used by the larger trip boats and the ferry to Cephalonia. The south side of the southern quay and the quayed area in the north of the bay is full of fishing boats. The depths drop off quickly in the bay so make sure you have plenty of scope. Any swell entering the bay and all the trip boat and ferry wash rebounds off the quays making berths uncomfortable. There can be severe gusts into the bay with the afternoon breeze, so make sure your anchor is well in.

One enterprising family with a restaurant, a minimarket, the petrol station and several trip boats can arrange water, fuel by mini-tanker and fresh bread. Some provisions are available ashore and several tavernas open in the summer. The ferry from Pessades on Cephalonia runs across to here in the summer. Local boats run trips to the local 'Blue Grotto' on Ak Skinari which is said (don't they always) to rival that on Capri. Much of what goes on in Ay Nikolaos revolves around

Áy Nikolaos harbour tucked under the islet of the same name on the northeast corner of Zakinthos   *Lu Michell*

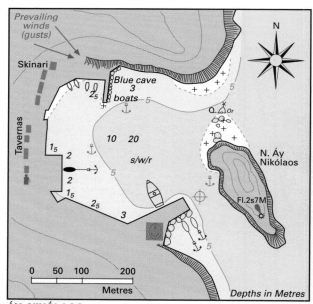

ÁY NIKÓLAOS
⊕37°54'·33N 20°42'·57E WGS84

running trip boats to the caves and the touts can be pretty aggressive. Like most places where people are not really staying too long, there is not a lot in the way of good food and I had one of the worst meals of the season here. If you are taking a boat trip to the caves it would be best to make the trip in the morning before the afternoon breeze sets in.

Alykanas

(Alikes)

A small harbour at the southern end of Ormos Alikon. Yachts must go bows-to with a long line to the rough stone mole as depths come up to less than 1m some distance off. Alternatively anchor off outside the buoyed swimming area. Excellent shelter in the north hook of the harbour otherwise the bay is open to the N. Hotels around the beach and Alikes village further to the north.

This stretch of coast is pretty much a rash of purpose built resorts and is more English breakfast than Moussaka, more Quiz night at Jimmy's than rembetiko, more fluffy turtle toys than a turtle protection policy; you really could be almost anywhere except they do advertise authentic Greek nights in case you forget where you are. You guessed: I don't much like the place.

Alykanas harbour on the east coast of Zakinthos *Lu Michell*

ALYKANAS (ALIKES)
⊕37°50'·68N 20°46'·83E WGS84

Kavos

A small fishing harbour about 2M ESE of Ormos Alikon. The miniature harbour is only really suitable for very small yachts drawing less than 1·5m. Berth where convenient taking care of uneven depths inside the harbour. Excellent shelter if you can get in amongst the local boats.

Porto Roma

A beautiful anchorage under Ak Vasilikos suitable in calm weather. Taverna on the beach and others a short walk away.

Ak Yerakas

On the W side of the cape there is a large bay suitable in calm weather. The entrance is fringed by reefs on both sides, so every care is needed when threading a way through them. Entry

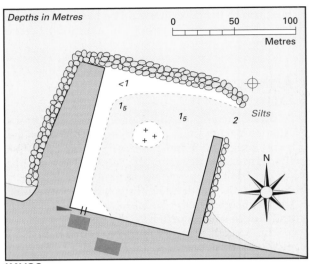

KAVOS
⊕37°50′·41N 20°49′·18E WGS84

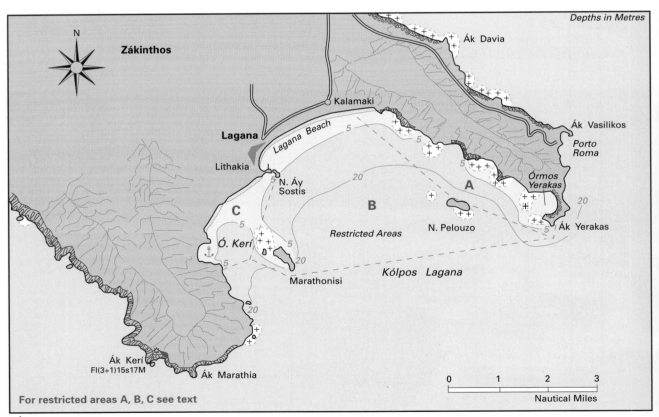

KÓLPOS LAGANA

Kavos harbour   *Lu Michell*

should be made on approximately 040° towards the beach. Anchor off the beach where convenient. Reasonably good protection from the prevailing wind.

Ashore there are several tavernas. The beach is a turtle breeding area and the restrictions above should be stringently heeded.

Ormos Lagana

The wide bay fringed by a long sandy beach on the N side of Kolpos Lagana. In settled weather a yacht can anchor off here outside of the restricted time period from May to end of October. The sandy bottom shelves gently to the shore. Numerous tavernas and most provisions can be obtained in Lagana village. The restrictions above should be stringently heeded.

The area has been much developed for tourism with hotels along the beach and tavernas, bars and discos to service the large numbers that arrive here in the summer. Lagana village/resort has little to recommend it and has little to do with things Greek on Zakinthos. The small village has expanded into an unwieldy resort lined with bars and souvenir shops that resounds to the monotonous beat of disco music and the equally monotonous chatter of those listening to it.

One of the casualties of the development along the beach has been the loggerhead turtle, *Caretta caretta*, which comes ashore in June to lay its eggs.

Boating restrictions in Kolpos Lagana

Reproduced below is the advice note from the Greek authorities restricting navigation and mooring in Kolpos Lagana. I have reproduced the advice note and zones rather than my interpretation of it so there can be no doubt regarding the wording and advice given.

Boating restrictions in the Bay of Laganas

The Bay of Laganas on Zakythnos is the most important·nesting area for the loggerhead sea turtle (*Caretta caretta*) in the Mediterranean. Apart from specific legislation (Presidential Decree of 5/7/90, Government Gazette 347/D) that has been enacted to protect the nesting beaches and a broader surrounding area, the Coast Guard of Zakythnos has issued two Local Port Regulations (Ref. Num. 19/91 and 20/94 Government Gazettes 585/B/91 & 591/B/94). According to these, the Bay is divided into three zones, in which the following laws are effective from 1 May through to 31 October each year.

Maritime Zone A: It is forbidden for any boat vessel to enter or moor within this zone. Fishing with any kind of fishing gear is prohibited.

Maritime Zone B: It is forbidden for any boat or vessel to travel at a speed greater than 6 knots, and to moor or anchor within this zone.

Maritime Zone C: It is forbidden for any boat or vessel to travel at a speed greater than 6 knots, within this zone.

The protection of sea turtles is the responsibility of us all!

Help us to ensure the effectiveness of the protective measures!

What this effectively means is that Yerakas, Ormos Lagana and Lithakia cannot be used from 1 of May to 31 October. Yachts should observe the restrictions diligently as there have been a number of fines (around £200) for infringements of the regulations.

Now the sea area is effectively policed it is to be hoped that the beach development will be policed as well so the turtles get a chance to breed safely without interference from the lager louts and their like who tend to inhabit parts of this resort area.

I have left the plan and notes on the anchorages in this restricted area intact in this edition in case any yachts want to go there out of the restricted times between May and the end of October. Even outside of the restricted period yachts should exercise caution and it may be prudent to enquire with the authorities at Limin Zakinthos on the legality of navigating and anchoring in these zones outside the time limits given.

171

Unfortunately the same thing that draws turtles here, the fine white sand in which they dig a nest to lay their eggs, is the same stuff that attracts tourists. The turtles are scared off by loud noise from the discos and bright lights in the hotels and tavernas. The egg nests themselves can be damaged by people digging in the sand. And worst of all the young turtles which hatch on a night of the full moon can lose their direction when distracted by bright lights. Instead of heading for the light of the moon over the water they head for the bright lights of hotels and tavernas and consequently never make it to the water.

If you are swimming around and you come across a lot of jellyfish, then reflect on the fact that the loggerhead eats large numbers of jellyfish and the decline in numbers, they are currently half what they were in 1973, may be responsible for the rise in the number of jellyfish in the Mediterranean. Thankfully access to the beach is now prohibited at night, but there is still much to be done. In the summer a Turtle Information Centre operates on the beach and organises volunteers to guard the nests and the turtles. You can contribute by getting in touch with the Sea Turtle Protection Society of Greece, PO Box 511, 54 Kifissia, 14510 Greece.

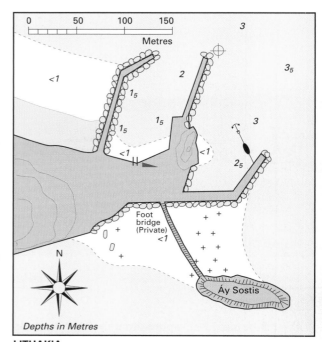

LITHAKIA
⊕37°42′·97N 20°51′·88E WGS84

Lithakia

(Ay Sostis)

At the W end of Lagana beach a small headland juts out towards a small islet, Nisis Ay Sostis. There is a small *caique* harbour on the E side of the headland. There are 1·5–2·5m depths in the harbour, but even a small yacht will have problems finding a berth amongst the local boats. Care is needed of long mooring lines stretching underwater across the harbour. Tavernas and discos on the beach nearby.

Ormos Keri

(Kieri)

A large bay lying under Nisis Marathonisi, the island lying on the W side of Kolpos Lagana. A yacht should pass outside the island as above-water rocks and a reef partially connect it to Zakinthos. On the W side of Ormos Keri there is a cove, Port Keri, where there is reasonable shelter from the prevailing wind. The restrictions

Kerí looking W   *Nigel Patten*

Ormos Keri   *Lu Michell*

above on speed limits should be stringently heeded.

Anchor in 2–8m on either side of the rough stone mole. The mole has underwater ballasting extending out from it in most places, but it is possible to anchor and take a long line to the outside of it. The bottom is mud and weed, good holding once through the weed. Mini-markets ashore and numerous tavernas.

In ancient times Keri was famous for its pitch wells mentioned by no less an authority than Herodotus:

'There are a number of lakes – or ponds – in Zacynthus, of which the largest measures seventy feet each way and has a depth of two fathoms. The process is to tie a branch of myrtle on to the end of a pole, which is then thrust down to the bottom of this pond; the pitch sticks to the myrtle, and is thus brought to the surface. It smells like bitumen, but in all other respects it is better than the pitch of Piera.'

The Histories Book IV

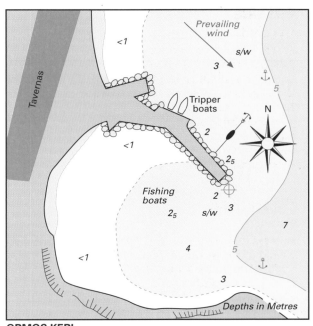

ORMOS KERI
⊕37°40'·95N 20°50'·19E WGS84

173

Today there is a concrete pool by the quay though this is claimed not to be pitch. In a marshy lake nearby you can go and poke a pole into the bottom after the method described by Herodotus. The pitch used to be much in demand for caulking boats, but I suppose modern synthetic alternatives have all but usurped the old-fashioned product. In recent years visitors have claimed there is more oil on the beach from the large numbers of RIBS here in the summer than there is in the lake.

Ormos Vroma

(Port Vromi)

An inlet close to the NW corner of Zakinthos under the islet of Nisis Ay Ioannis. It is difficult to make out the location of the inlet until close to it. It affords reasonable shelter from the prevailing wind but is untenable in southerlies. Anchor and take a line ashore on the N side on the dogleg of the inlet. The bottom is sand and rock, poor holding in places. Care needed to avoid permanent moorings used by trip boats. There can be a katabatic wind off the mountains at night.

A road has been cut down to it and its remote and savage charm has thus been eroded. A taverna opens in summer. Tripper boats visit on their route around the island.

Vroma looking W   *Nigel Patten*

In a bay just N of Vromi is a beautiful white sandy beach with the wreck of a coaster half-covered by sand that is much featured in the publicity photos of the Greek Tourist Organisation. The bay is much visited by tripper boats and others. The wreck is said to be an old smuggling boat that was apprehended and beached here, but others say it was just a coaster that happened to go ashore in the bay.

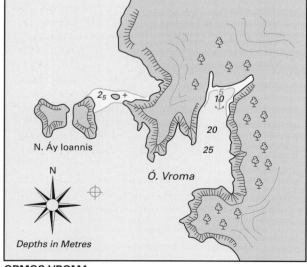

ORMOS VROMA
⊕37°48'·9N 20°37'·4E

4. The mainland coast
Levkas Canal to Nisis Oxia and adjacent islands

Quick reference guide

	Shelter	Mooring	Fuel	Water	Provisions	Tavernas	Plans
Vathi Vali	B	C	O	O	O	O	
Ormos Varko	C	C	O	O	O	C	
Pagonia	C	C	O	O	O	C	
Palairos (Zaverda)	A	A	B	A	B	B	•
Vounaki Marina	A	A	A	A	C	C	•
Mitika	C	AC	B	B	B	C	•
Kalamos							
Port Kalamos	B	A	O	B	C	C	•
Port Leone	B	AC	O	O	O	O	•
Episkopi	B	AB	O	O	O	O	•
Ak Aspro Yiali	O	C	O	O	O	O	
Kastos							
Port Kastos	B	AC	O	B	C	C	•
Anchorages around Kastos	BC	C	O	O	O	O	
Nisis Atoko	C	C	O	O	O	O	•
Dhragonera and Echinades							
Ormos Aspro Yiali	C	C	O	O	O	O	
Port Marathia	B	C	O	O	O	O	
Boulder Bay	C	C	O	O	O	O	
Astakos	B	A	B	A	B	B	•
Port Pandelimon	A	C	O	O	O	O	•
Plati Yiali	B	C	O	O	O	O	•
Nisis Petalas	B	C	O	O	O	O	•
Ormos Oxia	O	C	O	O	O	O	
Ormos Skrofa	C	C	O	O	O	O	
Nisis Oxia	O	C	O	O	O	O	

Like the mainland coast to the N this is a remote and lost area, even more so than the area N of it. From Levkas the coast rises abruptly to high mountains, the Akarnanika Oroi some 1590m (5167ft) high, which drop sheer into the sea. The mountains are mostly barren and rocky, little vegetation escapes the browsing of sheep and goats, and are cut by deep gorges and gullies that become torrents with the winter rain. Further S, below the agricultural town of Astakos, the coast flattens out around a huge river delta from the Akheloos, the longest river in Greece, to marshland and lagoons. This combination of inhospitable terrain, the precipitous mountains and swamp land, made it difficult to settle and even more difficult to control, so it is not surprising that it was little colonised by anyone over the ages.

Near Neokhorion in the middle of the marshland are the ruins of ancient Oiniadai, established sometime in the 6th century BC. At the time it was probably built on the coast, but the silting of two and half thousand years has locked it into the middle of this water land. It is the only major ancient site. This area has always been the domain of the dispossessed and of hardy farmers and fishermen. It is little changed to this day and despite a number of new roads winding up and over the mountains or across barrages in the swamp land, retains a feeling of isolation and supports only small communities who can put up with the rigours of life here. Even the two major islands off the coast, Kalamos and Kastos, are rugged places with small populations, though swelled by numbers of noisy campers in noisy inflatables in July and August.

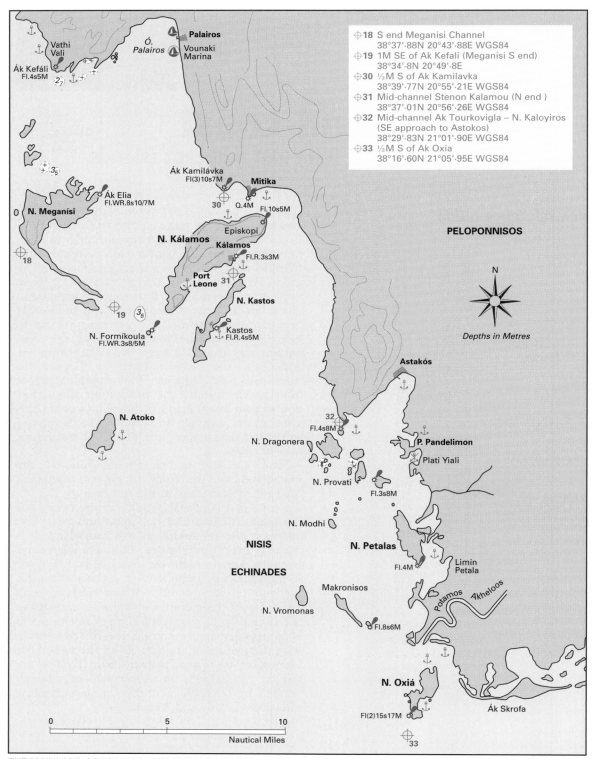

⊕**18** S end Meganisi Channel
38°37'·88N 20°43'·88E WGS84
⊕**19** 1M SE of Ak Kefali (Meganisi S end)
38°34'·8N 20°49'·8E
⊕**30** ½M S of Ak Kamilavka
38°39'·77N 20°55'·21E WGS84
⊕**31** Mid-channel Stenon Kalamou (N end)
38°37'·01N 20°56'·26E WGS84
⊕**32** Mid-channel Ak Tourkovigla – N. Kaloyiros
(SE approach to Astokos)
38°29'·83N 21°01'·90E WGS84
⊕**33** ½M S of Ak Oxia
38°16'·60N 21°05'·95E WGS84

Vathi
Vali
Palairos
Ó.
Palaíros
Vounaki
Marina

Ák Kefáli
Fl.4s5M
2₇

3₅

Ák Kamilávka
Fl(3)10s7M
Mitika

30   Q.4M

Fl.10s5M

Ák Elia
Fl.WR.8s10/7M

0 **N. Meganísi**

Episkopi

N. Kálamos **Kálamos**

Fl.R.3s3M

PELOPONNISOS

18

**Port
Leone** 31

N
Depths in Metres

N. Kastos

19 3₅

N. Formíkoula
Fl.WR.3s8/5M

Kastos
Fl.R.4s5M

Astakós

N. Atoko

32
Fl.4s8M

N. Dragonera

P. Pandelimon

Plati Yiali

N. Provati
Fl.3s8M

N. Modhi

N. Petalas
Fl.4M

Limin
Petala

NISIS

ECHINADES

Makronisos
Potamos Akheloos

N. Vromonas
Fl.8s6M

N. Oxiá

Ák Skrofa

Fl(2)15s17M

0   5   10

Nautical Miles

33

THE MAINLAND COAST AND ADJACENT ISLANDS
(Kalamos to Nisís Oxiá)

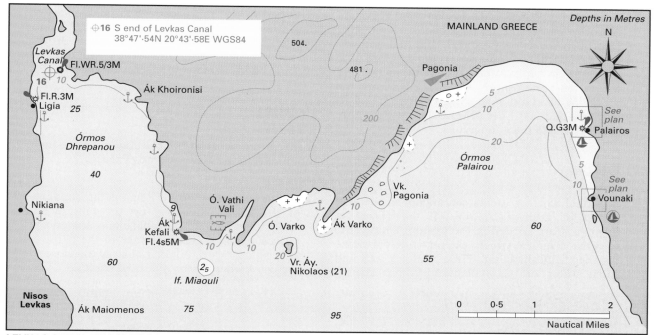

⊕16 S end of Levkas Canal
38°47'·54N 20°43'·58E WGS84

MAINLAND GREECE

Depths in Metres

N

504.

481.

Pagonia

Levkas
Canal   Fl.WR.5/3M
16   10

Ák Khoironisi

Fl.R.3M
Ligia   25

200

5

10

Q.G3M   Palairos
See
plan

Órmos
Dhrepanou

20

Órmos
Palairou

40

20

5

Nikiana

9

Ó. Vathi
Vali

Vk.
Pagonia

See
plan
Vounaki

Ák
Kefali
Fl.4s5M

10

10

Ó. Varko

+ Ák Varko

10

60

10

20

Vr. Áy.
Nikolaos (21)

55

2₅

If. Miaouli

Nisos
Levkas

Ák Maiomenos   75

95

0   0·5   1   2

Nautical Miles

LEVKAS CANAL TO PALAIROS

Levkas Canal to Palairos

Along the coast from the S end of the Levkas
canal to Ak Kefali there are a number of attractive
coves that can be used depending on the wind
and sea. With light northwesterlies blowing out of
Ormos Dhrepanou there are several coves
affording adequate shelter, but with strong
northwesterlies they become untenable. Care
needs to be taken of the isolated reef (2·7m least
depth) lying approximately ½M SSE of the light
structure on Ak Kefali.

Vathi Vali

⊕ 38°45'·3N 20°45'·55E

This inlet immediately E of Ak Kefali is now
mostly obstructed by a fish farm and although
you can still anchor in here, the ambience of the
place is dented by the ramshackle fish farm.

Ormos Varko

⊕ 38°45'·60N 20°47'·85E

The next bay east of Vathi Vali is a wide bay open
south, with the islet Ay Nikolaos in the middle of
the entrance fairway. The islet may be left to

Vathi Vali

Nigel Patten

177

either side on entering the bay but care is needed of rocky shoals off the headlands either side. Depths in the fairway exceed 30m and you will only find depths suitable for anchoring close in to the shore and it may be prudent to anchor and take a long line ashore. Good shelter from the prevailing wind although some swell does find its way around Ak Parathira, but it is more uncomfortable than dangerous.

Pagonia

⊕ 38°47'·05N 20°50'·25E

In settled weather yachts can anchor in the NW corner of Ormos Palairou off the village of Pagonia. Care needed in the western approaches of Vrak Pagonia which extends out for some distance from the coast. There is also a rock and shoal water off the village but it is readily identified in the approaches. Reasonable shelter from prevailing winds although a katabatic wind off the high land on the east side of Ormos Palairou means it is not really suitable to overnight here. Hotel and taverna ashore.

Palairos

(Zaverda)

A village and small harbour sitting under the high mountains in the NE of Ormos Palairos.

Pilotage

Approach Once into Ormos Palairos the buildings of the village straggling up the hillside are easily identified although haze may sometimes reduce visibility. The entrance to the harbour is straightforward, but do not stray too close to the coast where there is a shoal bank.

Palairos under the bare rocky slopes of the Arkananika mountains behind   *Lu Michell*

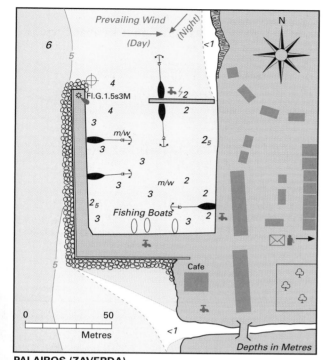

PALAIROS (ZAVERDA)
⊕38°46'·94N 20°52'·64E WGS84

General

Like Mitika and Astakos further down the coast, the village here has mostly concerned itself with the farming population in the area, only in the last 20 years have yachts and its adoption by a charter company turned it to the sea. It remains a predominantly agricultural village and one can see the local inhabitants metaphorically scratching their heads in bewilderment at these foreigners paying lots of money to go sailing on the sea. Behind the village the high mountains rise steeply from the sea and at times evening thunderstorms hover around the peaks. It is an impressive setting and all in all a convivial corner of the inland sea.

Vounaki Marina

A small marina, the home of *Sunsail* charter boats, situated just south of Palairos.

Pilotage

Approach The hotel complex associated with the marina is easily identified just south of Palairos. Make the final approach to the marina from the west to avoid the dinghy

Mooring Go stern or bows-to on the west side of the harbour or on either side of the new pontoon. There is sometimes room to go stern or bows-to on the east side although you may be taking a fishing boat berth. The harbour is used as a base by a charter company and at times can be crowded with yachts on turn-around. The bottom is mud and good holding. Good shelter from the prevailing breeze although a katabatic wind may blow down off the mountains from the NE at night making it uncomfortable for a few hours.

Facilities

Services Water on the quay. Water and electricity boxes on the pontoon. Fuel by mini-tanker.

Provisions Good shopping for provisions in the village.

Eating out Several tavernas near the harbour. The *Old Mill* restaurant run by the effervescent Kitty is now located in the village and not at the top of the hill – the food is still good although the location is not quite as pleasing.

Other PO. OTE. Bank. Taxis. Infrequent bus to Vonitsa.

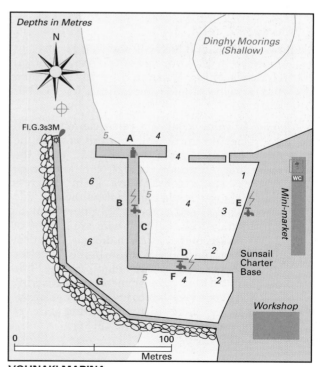

VOUNAKI MARINA
⊕38°46'·16N 20°52'·62E WGS84

mooring area immediately north of the entrance. The marina listens out on VHF Ch 10.

Mooring Berth where directed. There are laid moorings tailed to the quay. Good shelter inside although strong westerlies might cause some bother.

Facilities

Services Water and electricity at every berth. Shower and toilet block. Fuel on the T-pier.

Provisions Mini-market. Palairos is not too far away with better shopping.

Eating out Taverna ashore. Other tavernas in Palairos.

General

Vounaki is a major *Sunsail* charter base and the hotel is used as a Sunsail Club for shore-based holidaymakers. Visitors are free to use the marina facilities, taverna and shops, but cannot use the hotel facilities which are for *Sunsail* clients.

Mitika

(Mytikas)

An agricultural village and now a small ferry port for the islands in the Inland sea.

Pilotage

Approach The buildings of the village are not easily seen until you are into Ormos Mitika. However Nisos Kalamos is easily identified and a yacht should simply head for the NE end.

Mooring In calm weather a yacht can anchor off the village on the W side and this is quite the most pleasant place to be. But with the prevailing afternoon breeze the anchorage becomes quite rolly. Work is in progress improving the existing harbour on the east side of Ak Mitika, and completing a new harbour immediately SW of this. There are depths of 2–3m inside both basins, although I suspect that the primary use for the harbours is for small local craft rather than yachts. The harbours are both quite small so manoeuvering space inside is very limited. Go stern or bows-to wherever there is room, taking care of floating mooring lines. Good shelter.

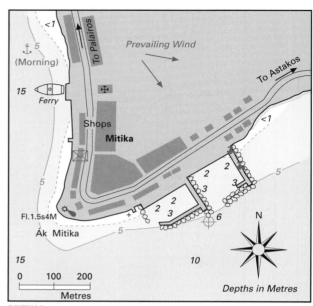

MITIKA
⊕38°40'·05N 20°56'·91E WGS84

Facilities

Services Water on the quay. Fuel is some distance out of town.

Provisions Good shopping for provisions.

Eating out Several tavernas on the waterfront. The *Glaros* at the N end of the waterfront has been around for ages and has good food and fresh fish.

Other PO. OTE. Ferry to Ay Eufimia. Local *caique* ferry to Kalamos and Kastos.

General

Like Palairos this village has traditionally been occupied with agriculture and only recently experienced a little tourism. It sits on a flat coastal plain hemmed in between mountains on either side and until the new road was built it was largely locked into itself. Now it plays host in July and August to a fleet of inflatables which occupy themselves, somewhat noisily, around Nisos Kalamos. It can get a bit dusty, but once you are safely tucked into the harbour then you can wander around to the west side for a drink and dinner in a setting which is just charming.

Nisos Kalamos

This high island looking like a colossal stranded whale off the mainland coast is easily identified from afar. It rises up from the tail in the SW to 750m (2438ft) at Oros Vouni near the NE end. The slopes drop mostly sheer into the sea and are covered sparsely in *maquis* at the S end, but surprisingly are thickly covered in pine at the N end. The name is said to be derived from the reeds (*kalami*) which used to grow here, but to anyone who has been to the island this is baffling as it has none of the marshy ground that reeds need. It may be that the name was transferred from the area around Mitika where there is swampy ground. Perhaps the inhabitants of the mainland were forced to flee to the island from pirates or invaders from the N. Now the process has reversed itself and the villages on the island are dying places and in the case of Port Leone (Kefali) in the S, entirely deserted.

Port Kalamos

The small village that serves as the island capital on the E side.

Pilotage

Approach Proceeding up Stenon Kalamou between Kastos and Kalamos, several mills on a short spit, including one on a rocky bluff by the sea, will be seen. Closer in the village and small harbour are easily identified. From the N the village will only be seen once you are around the N end of the island.

Mooring Berth stern or bows-to on the breakwater wherever there is room. There are laid moorings at some berths. If using your own anchor the bottom is mud, sand and weed, mostly good holding. Although the small harbour is popular at the height of summer you can usually find somewhere to berth, especially since the breakwater has been extended.

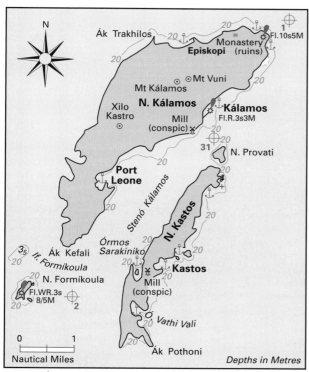

NISOI KÁLAMOS AND KASTOS

⊕1   38°39'·28N 20°57'·78E WGS84
⊕2   38°34'·00N 20°52'·30E WGS84

⊕31 38°37'·01N 20°56'·26E WGS84

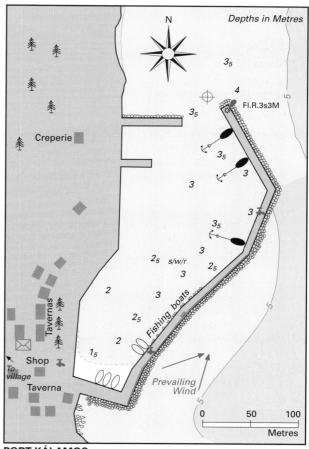

PORT KÁLAMOS
⊕38°37'·41N 20°55'·94E WGS84

Facilities

Several tavernas open in the summer, but don't expect lightning fast service – after all, as the old lady in one of them explained, 'it's difficult to cook and add up the bill as well'. Small grocery shop and a bakery in the village. PO.

General

The small village is a wonderful place that somehow handles its summer visitors entirely on its own terms. One of the last trading *caiques* in the Ionian still putters across from the mainland to supply the island. But the population is decidedly skewed to the older age group and I fear for the survival of villages like this except as some sort of summer resort. Recently I watched a funeral procession here and of the forty or so mourners, there were only a couple under late middle-age and the bulk of them were sixty or older. The young leave for the fleshpots of Athens and once there, few return to the simple life on the island.

One of the last trading *caiques* in Kalamos harbour

Port Kalamos   *Nigel Patten*

Port Leone

(Kefali)

A large deep bay on the S of the island. The entrance is difficult to see from the S, but if you head for the general vicinity of the bay it is difficult to miss. From the N two old mills will be seen on the E side of the entrance and closer in the houses and the church of the deserted village.

The bay is very deep and you will have to anchor in 10–15m of water. A few yachts can go bows-to the short stone jetties with a long line ashore. The bottom is sand, mud and weed, good holding. Good shelter in here although gusts may occasionally swirl down off the high slopes.

Recently a bar-cum-taverna has opened here after several failures in the past. Many of us feel that the sputtering of a noisy generator and Zorba's theme should not invade the special peace and quiet of this place.

The village was deserted after the 1953 earthquake which destroyed the water supply. The inhabitants decided not to rebuild the village,

Port Leone and the village deserted after the 1953 earthquake

but moved to the mainland or migrated. The village church is still in good repair and every Sunday a few villagers come from Kalamos village to clean it, renew the oil in the lamps and put fresh flowers on the altar. The village, the ruined houses, the abandoned olive press, the cisterns now empty, the church still cared for, all contribute to a poignancy that cuts through the crackle of cicadas and rustling wind.

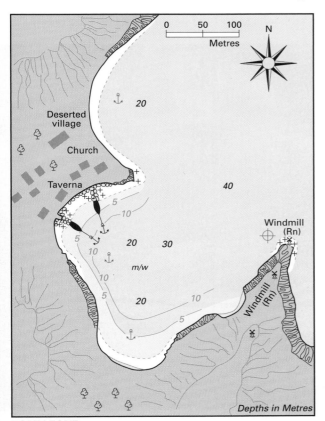

PORT LEONE
⊕38°35′·96N 20°53′·36E WGS84

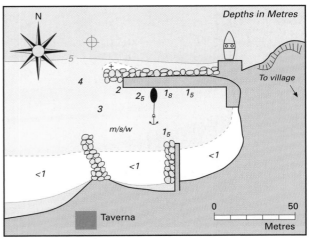

EPISKOPI
⊕38°38′·92N 20°55′·57E WGS84

Episkopi

A small village and harbour on the N side of Nisos Kalamos. The houses of the hamlet can be seen and also a ruined monastery further E of the hamlet. Closer in the breakwater will be seen. The harbour has been improved with extensions to the quay and a separate ferry ramp built on the north side of the breakwater. Berth stern or bows-to on the north quay where there is room. The bottom shelves gradually to the beach and is reasonable holding on mud, sand and weed. Good shelter. From the village there is a pleasant walk along the little-used road to the ruined fortified monastery with wonderful views over the strait to the mainland.

Ak Aspro Yiali

Around the cape on the N end of the island there are several anchorages protected from the prevailing winds. It is mostly quite deep here. In July and August campers with inflatables base themselves here creating noise pollution, littering the area with rubbish, and defiling the cemetery though it clearly has a notice up saying: No Camping. I can understand why they flock here: the water is a wonderful turquoise and cobalt, the rocks and cliffs are eroded into fantastic shapes, and the whole area is thick with green pine providing cool shade.

Nisos Kastos

The scraggly sister island lying parallel to Kalamos. Although it is nearly as long as its neighbour, it is thinner and lower. The only village on the island is Kastos on the E side, but there are a number of anchorages that can be used in the summer.

Port Kastos

Pilotage

Approach From the S the exact location of the village and harbour is difficult to make out until you are close to it. A mill on the S side of the village and the harbour will be seen before

Kastos harbour

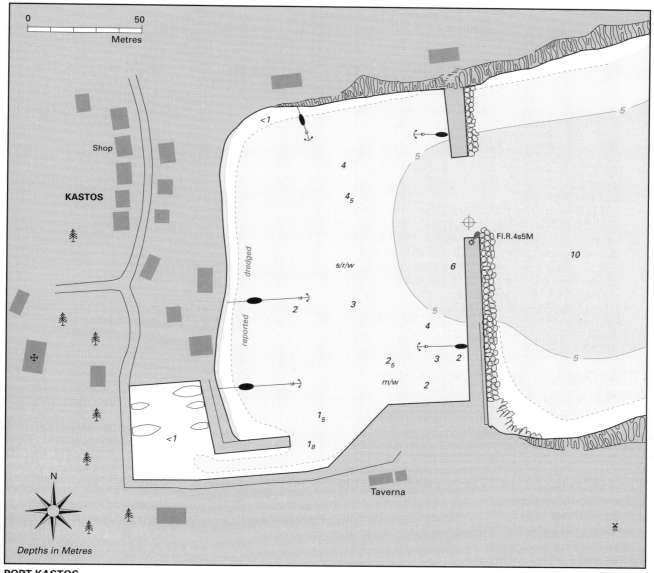

0   50
Metres

Shop

KASTOS

dredged

reported

<1

s/r/w

m/w

4

4 5

6

10

<1

5

5

Fl.R.4s5M

5

2

3

4

3 2

2 5

2

1 5

1 8

N

Depths in Metres

Taverna

PORT KASTOS
⊕38°34'·12N 20°54'·73E WGS84

the village and tiny harbour. From the N the islet of Prasonisi is easily identified and closer in the houses of the village, a mill on a ridge above the village and another on the S side will be seen.

Mooring Go bows-to off the mole if there is room. Alternatively anchor in the bay although this can be a bit rolly from the ground swell that works its way around. With care you can anchor off the beach with a long line ashore or

a kedge out the back where you escape the worst of the ground swell. The bottom is mud and weed, good holding once through the weed. Good shelter from the prevailing winds. At night a katabatic wind may blow but the harbour is usually tenable.

Facilities

Three tavernas, one by the harbour, *Belos* has been here the longest, *The Windmill* bar and restaurant has wonderful views out from the headland, and *Chef Johns* is tucked up the hill in the village.

General

The small village is a charmer. It is gradually coming back to life after the population dwindled to some 20 souls or so. When I first visited in 1977 the population was probably around 30 or so. I have written before that the population had been evacuated in 1976 because of a suspected typhoid outbreak (that's what I was told on the island), but the locals here now contest that. Who knows, but certainly its economy has revived by yachties visiting it.

It is a wonderful little place. The inner harbour shelters a few fishing boats and the adjacent square has a few trees for shade so the fishermen can sit around talking about the fishing and the visitors while they mend their nets. Outside the village the land shimmers in the heat and there are only a few olive groves and a lot of prickly pear cacti to support the surprising array of livestock, including cows, sheep and the ubiquitous goats. Good snorkelling in the waters around the island.

Anchorages around Nisis Kastos

Port Sarakiniko

The indented bay on the west side of the island. In calm weather you can anchor in the bay in 5–10m. When the prevailing NW–W wind is blowing a swell is sent into here. At night a katabatic wind may blow down off the mainland coast. At the head of the bay is a short mole where a yacht may be able to go bows-to and take a long line ashore.

South Bay
On the S tip of the island there is a bay that also provides an attractive early lunch stop. By afternoon the prevailing breeze pushes a sizeable swell into it.

Southeast Bay
On the E coast near the S end of the island there is a deep bay suitable for an overnight stay in settled conditions. It is quite deep so you will be anchoring in 10–20m.

Prasonisi Cove
The rocky islet northeast of Kastos harbour. In the channel between the islet and Kastos there are least depths of 4m in the fairway at the north end of the channel and least depths of 7m at the southern end in the fairway. In calm weather you can anchor in the bay opposite the islet.

Northeast Coves
On the E coast at the N end of

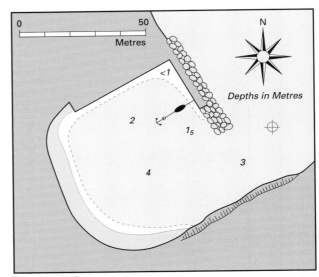

SARAKINIKO
⊕38°34'·0N 20°54'·2E

the island there are several coves that make attractive lunch stops in settled weather.

Nisis Atoko

This large lump of an island sits almost in the middle of the Inland sea. It is easily identified from some distance off because of its height (303m/985ft) and because it sits by itself away from the other islands. It has two anchorages that can be used in settled weather.

Cliff Bay
At the S end there is a wide double-ended bay suitable in calm weather or light westerlies. With strong westerlies a swell penetrates. It is everywhere very deep and you will have to anchor in 10–15m at either end. The steep cliffs and rocky pinnacles provide an imposing backdrop, fine for a lunch stop in calm weather but, I imagine, threatening in bad weather.

One House Bay
On the SE side there is a bay providing reasonable shelter with the prevailing westerlies. Anchor in 5–12m on sand, good holding. In settled weather yachts stay overnight here although a katabatic wind off the mainland coast may push some swell in at night.

The anchorage is a wonderful place with high cliffs and huge eroded rocks on the S side and a fine beach at the head of the bay. A single house stands on the shore used occasionally by a fisherman and his family.

One House Bay on Atoko   *Nigel Patten*

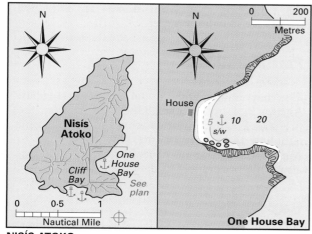

NISÍS ATOKO
⊕38°28'·4N 20°49'·1E

Nisoi Dhragonera and Echinades

This group of islands and islets scattered down the coast nearly to the entrance of the Gulf of Patras (Patraikos Kolpos) hide the low mainland coast and call for some attentive eyeball navigation to get you safely through them. They are all uninhabited and there are few safe anchorages in the islands – though luckily there are several down the adjacent mainland coast. The name echinades means sea urchin and in this it is accurate as these are spiky rocky islands sitting in the sea and looking just like their namesake.

Anchorages around Nisoi Dhragonera and Echinades

Nisis Dhragonera The comparatively large island lying close off Ak Tourkoviglas. On the N side there are two coves suitable in calm weather, but open to the prevailing westerlies. On the SE tip of the island there is a miniature crack of an inlet that a small yacht can use. Take a long line ashore to the W side.

Nisis Karlonisi Lies close E of Nisis Dhragonera. With care a small yacht can tuck itself into the cove lying in the narrow channel separating the island from Nisis Provati immediately S of it. Care needs to be taken of a reef running out on the W side. Take a long line ashore.

Nisis Provati Lies close S of Karlonisi. On the S end there is a small inlet suitable for an overnight stay. Take a long line ashore.

Navigating around the islands

For the most part navigation around the islands and rocks is straightforward so long as you keep tabs on which island is which by diligent eyeball navigation. Most of the islands are steep-to and easily identified. Most of the reefs and shoal water are either close to the islands or not of consequence for most yachts.

The two shallowest isolated patches of shoal water have 9m (Ifalos Praso) and 8m (Ifalos Dei/Day Rock) over them. Ifalos Pondikou lying midway between Pondikonisi and Stenigonia also has 8m over it though it is really an extension of the shoal water bordering the coast. Vrakhonisos Navayion (Wreck Rock) and Vrakhonisos Xeropoula (Shag Rock), two above-water rocks lying S of Nisis Provati and Pondikonisi, can be identified with care. Shag Rock, as the old Admiralty name implies, invariably has shags sitting on it and is white with their droppings. Wreck rock is sometimes marked with a pole beacon.

NISÍS DRAGONERA AND ECHINADES AND ADJACENT COAST

⊕**32** Mid-channel Ak Tourkovigla – N. Kaloyiros (SE approach to Astokos)
38°29'·83N 21°01'·90E WGS844
⊕**33** ½M S of Ak Oxia 38°16'·60N 21°05'·95E WGS84

Ormos Aspro Yiali

⊕ 38°32'·3N 21°00'·7E

A large bay on the mainland coast lying just under 2½M N of Ak Tourkoviglas. It is entirely open to the prevailing wind, but makes an attractive anchorage in calm weather.

Port Marathia

⊕ 38°30'·2N 21°02'·2E

The bay immediately under Ak Tourkoviglas. Anchor in 4–6m on mud. Good shelter from the prevailing wind. The anchorage is pleasant although the traffic on the new coast road to Mitika removes some of its remoteness and has also brought campers to the bay.

Boulder Bay

An attractive bight just under the legend 'boulder' on the old Admiralty chart 3496 (now deleted) and near the church marked Ay Yeoryios on Imray-Tetra chart G121 just under a mile SW of

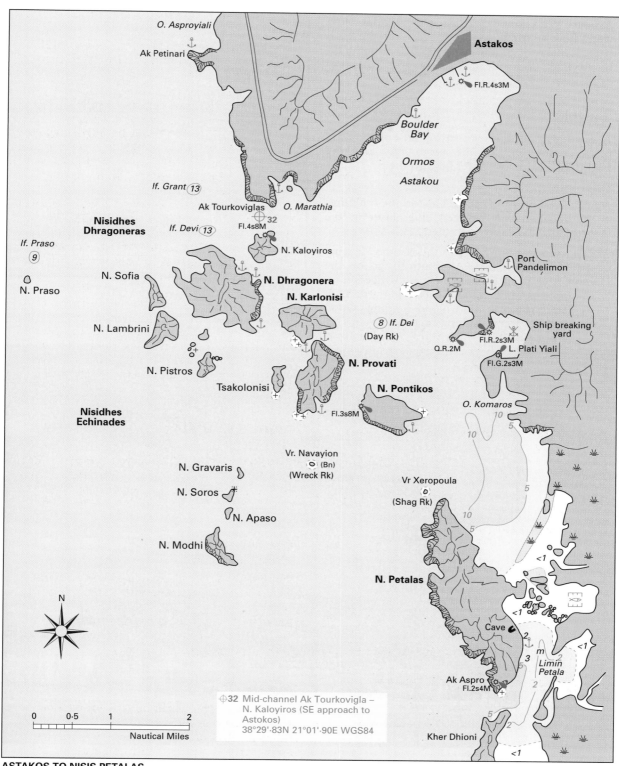

O. Asproyiali

Ak Petinari

Astakos

Fl.R.4s3M

Boulder Bay

Ormos Astakou

If. Grant (13)

Ak Tourkoviglas

O. Marathia

If. Devi (13)

Fl.4s8M

⊕ 32

N. Kaloyiros

Nisidhes Dhragoneras

If. Praso (9)

N. Praso

N. Sofia

N. Dhragonera

N. Karlonisi

(8) *If. Dei* (Day Rk)

Port Pandelimon

Ship breaking yard

N. Lambrini

Q.R.2M

Fl.R.2s3M

L. Plati Yiali

Fl.G.2s3M

N. Pistros

N. Provati

Tsakolonisi

N. Pontikos

O. Komaros

Fl.3s8M

10

Nisidhes Echinades

10

5

Vr. Navayion

(Bn)

(Wreck Rk)

Vr Xeropoula

(Shag Rk)

10

5

N. Gravaris

5

N. Soros

N. Apaso

N. Modhi

<1

N. Petalas

<1

Cave

2

<1

m

Limin Petala

3

2

Ak Aspro

Fl.2s4M

2

N

⊕**32** Mid-channel Ak Tourkovigla –
N. Kaloyiros (SE approach to
Astokos)
38°29'·83N 21°01'·90E WGS84

5

Kher Dhioni

2

<1

0   0·5   1   2

Nautical Miles

ASTAKOS TO NISIS PETALAS
⊕38°29'·83N 21°01'·90E WGS84

Astakos. With light westerlies, which tend to blow alternately from the SW and gust off the land here, it makes a good lunch stop before going on to Astakos itself. Beach ashore and pine and cypress on the slopes.

Astakos

A small agricultural town sitting on a flat coastal plain at the end of the mountains and the beginning of the low water land to the S.

Pilotage

Approach Once into Ormos Astakou the buildings of the town will be seen and closer in the breakwater is easily identified.

Mooring Go stern or bows-to the N quay, leaving the ferry quay clear. Alternatively go on the mole if you can find room. Care is needed on the mole as underwater ballast fringes parts of it. The bottom is mud, good holding. Good shelter from the prevailing breeze.

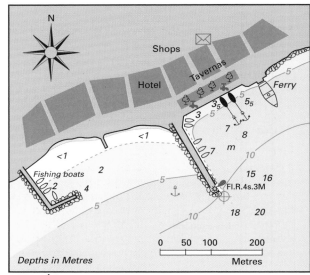

ASTAKÓS
⊕ 38°31′·91N 21°04′·94E WGS84

Astakos

Facilities

Services Water on the quay. Fuel delivered by mini-tanker.

Provisions Good shopping for provisions. A good baker behind the waterfront.

Eating out Several tavernas on the waterfront and in the town.

Other Banks. PO. OTE. Ferry to Ithaca and Cephalonia.

General

Astakos has long been locked into this remote part of Greece, cut off by the mountains and the swamp land and away from the sea-routes, it still feels a remote and insular sort of place. There are only a few concessions to the Greek holiday-makers who come here in July and August and the yachts which turn up through the summer.

It remains very much an agricultural town dealing in shovels and hoes, fertiliser and weed-killer, baggy denim overalls rather than designer jeans. As well as the farmers it has a sizeable fishing fleet which harvests the rich waters around the Dhragonera and Echinades islands. The name of the town, *Astakos*, means lobster, but I have never seen any on offer in the tavernas or even brought ashore, though the rocky islets appear to be an ideal habitat for the rare crustacean.

The town was known as Dragomestre in the 19th century. In 1828 Richard Church made it the base for his operations during the Greek struggle against their Turkish masters. Church was one of many eccentric British Philhellenes, (Byron was only the most famous), who came to help the Greeks in one way or another. By all accounts Church was an arrogant man with a desire for pomp and power, but not a commander who led his troops from the front. In the battle for the Acropolis at Athens he and Cochrane commanded the land troops from the safety of a ship anchored off and not surprisingly the attack was a fiasco. Despite his blunders Church lived to a ripe old age in Athens in a free Greece.

Port Pandelimon

(Panteleimon, Pandelemona)

A twin-headed inlet now partially obstructed by fish farms but still usable with care.

Pilotage

Approach The inlet lies 2½M almost due S of Astakos. The exact location of the entrance is

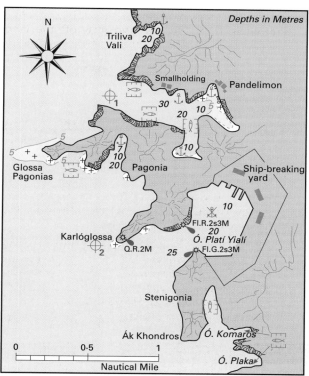

PANDELIMON AND PLATÍ YIALÍ
⊕1 38°29′·52N 21°04′·81E WGS84
⊕2 38°28′·38N 21°04′·82E WGS84

difficult to make out from the distance, but is easy enough to see when closer in. Care needs to be taken of the fish farms shown on the plan. The perimeter of the farms is marked by small plastic buoys.

Mooring Anchor in the NE or S creek, the latter affords the better shelter but is largely obscured by the fish farm. The bottom is mud and weed, good holding once through the weed, though this can take some doing. Good shelter from the prevailing wind although the E creek can be uncomfortable from the chop pushed in by the westerlies, though rarely dangerous.

General

There are no facilities here although you may be able to negotiate for a fish or two from the fish farm. Personally I am suspicious of fish reared in this artificial way. Until the fish farms were recently established there was only the small farm on the N which seems to have been abandoned. The anchorage still has a remote feel to it despite

Pandelimon   *Nigel Patten*

the muffled sounds of heavy machinery at Platiyialos and the debris of the fish farms littering the rocky slopes.

Note
The fish farms are moved around the bay from time to time, mostly I suspect because of the toxins and debris which build up on the sea bottom after a period and aggravate diseases in the fish. Consequently the position of the buoyed-off areas will vary and I have not moved the positions of the farms in the plans because they may well be situated back in the original positions by the time this is printed. Prudence is needed wherever fish farms are located as their exact locations in a bay will change from time to time.

Glossa Pagonias

The tongue of land separating Pandelimon and Plati Yialos. Care needs to be taken of the reef and shoal water running out from the tip of it. In the past it was possible to anchor and take a long line ashore in the inlet on the south side, but most of the coast here is obstructed by fish farms.

Plati Yiali

⊕ 38°28'·36N 21°05'·61E WGS84
(Plateali)

The large bay lying immediately S of Pandelimon. For some time now a massive project has been underway to make it a ship-breaking yard. At least that has been the story put around. Why you would build a ship-breaking yard in a place miles from anywhere that could use bits of old ships and with no good transport links is a bit of a mystery. At one time it was believed this was going to be the site for reprocessing medium level toxic waste and it would seem that this is more likely. All around the bay huge concrete aprons slope into the water and there are quays and piers right around the bay. The amount of concrete used to ring this large bay with quays, aprons and hard-standing is difficult to comprehend. Effectively it has demolished any charm the bay had and in any case berthing is now prohibited. A patrol boat now operates here preventing yachts from berthing or even approaching the installations too closely.

If it does come about that this place is going to be used for storing or processing toxic waste of some level and you find out about it, I suggest you contact Greenpeace or Friends of the Earth in Greece or your own country and let them know. Hopefully we can stop this wonderfully remote area being polluted by whatever is planned for it.

Ormos Komaros

A small inlet immediately S of Platiyiali that is now so obstructed by a fish farm that it is virtually unusable.

Nisis Petalas

The large, quite high island (250m/815ft) lying close off the coast 2½M S of Plati Yiali. It is connected to the swampy coast by several lower islets and shallow water which is home to a large fishery.

A yacht can find a solitary anchorage around the S tip (Ak Aspro) tucked under the E side of the island. The bottom slopes very gradually up so you can putter in slowly and anchor in 1·75–2·5m. The bottom is mud and thick weed, good holding once through the weed. Shelter from the prevailing wind is good and the anchorage is useful in strong southerlies when you can anchor at the S end of the bay under Khersonisos Dhioni.

There are no facilities nearby and nor should there be. On the slopes of Petalas there is a large cave. On one visit with an ornithologist friend we spied a huge bird sitting outside the cave at dusk. From a pinion feather retrieved from the cave he later identified it as a tufted vulture with an estimated wing span of around eight feet. They are shy birds, much reduced in numbers since some of the remote places have been opened up, and it is unlikely you will see one except in early spring or late autumn.

Ormos Dhioni

Around the S end of Khersonisos Dhioni a yacht can find some shelter from moderate westerlies tucked under the peninsula. Shelter is better at Petalas.

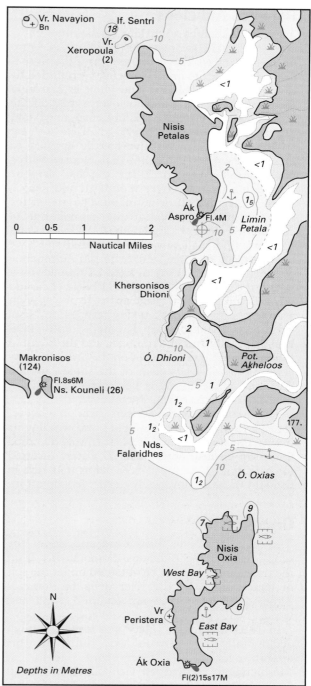

NISIS PETALAS TO NISIS OXIA
⊕ 38°23´·49N 21°06´·00E WGS84

Potamos Akheloos

The river Akheloos (Acheloos or Aspropotamos) empties into the sea just over 3M S of Ak Aspro on Nisis Petalas. The exact mouth of the river is difficult to identify precisely being surrounded by sandbanks and low islets. The whole area around the delta is low-lying and for over a mile off the mouth the sea is shallow and obstructed by banks just under the water.

The shoal water off the mouth appears to extend for a greater distance than charted with a considerable area of 2–3m depths. Anyone proceeding past the river mouth should keep a prudent distance off or he might, like me on the last occasion I lazily cut the corner full of confidence that I knew these waters well, suddenly find shallow water all around and have to thread a passage out with an adrenaline overload. It is very easy to keep cutting across if taking the inside passage around Nisis Oxia and the only thing to do is make an acute dogleg right around the river mouth taking transits on Nisoi Vromonas, Makronisos, Kounelli, and Oxia. Keeping the N end of Vromonas and the S end of Makronisos in line as shown on the old Admiralty chart 3496 still leads clear of the shoals, though the limit of the shoals is not correct and today they extend further than shown.

The Akheloos is the longest river in Greece, starting in the Pindus Mountains and winding its way to the sea here for 135M. It is now dammed for hydro-electric power and its waters diverted for irrigation. Like most river deltas it is rich in fish and there are invariably *caiques* fishing off it.

Ormos Oxia

The wide bay N of Nisis Oxia and under the sandy delta of the Akheloos. Some shelter from the prevailing wind can be obtained under the spit of land formed by the river delta of Potamos Akheloos. Anchor in 4–6m on mud, sand and weed.

In 1823 this remote place was visited, though accidentally, by Byron en route to his appointment with fever and death at Mesolongion. He had left Cephalonia in a small fast ship in company with a larger one for the baggage and equipment, both local boats and therefore sailing under the neutral Ionian flag. In the night the two ships lost contact and in the dawn found they were close to another ship, a

The anchorage under Nisis Petalas looking out from the cave
Nigel Patten

Turkish brig. The skipper decided to run into Ormos Skrofa and anchor to escape from the Turk. At some point he decided the anchorage was unsafe and fled N to Astakos. Three days later three ships sent by Mavrocordato found him and escorted the small boat and its occupants to Mesolongion, though not without incident as David Howarth records in his excellent *The Greek Adventure*.

'The passengers in this boat were a landlubberly lot, except perhaps Tita the gondolier, and the crew seem not to have been much better. Fletcher the valet had caught a cold and had to lie down on the only mattress on board, Dr Bruno was prone to wring his hands and weep at any threat of disaster, and Loukas could not swim. Byron himself liked boats, but had never learned much about them. And as they returned through the Oxia channel, the boat missed stays and ran aground in a squall. Two thirds of the crew climbed out on the bowsprit and jumped ashore, Byron told Loukas he would save him, and Dr Bruno stripped to his flannel waistcoat and running about like a rat (it was Byron's description) shouted 'Save him indeed! By God, save me rather – I'll be the first if I can.' Thereupon, after striking twice, the boat blew off again. The crew was removed from the rocks by one of the escort ships, and that evening, without any more alarms, Byron reached the entrance to Missalonghi.'

Ormos Skrofa

Under Ormos Koutsilapis, the high land enclosed by the river delta E of Nisis Oxia, there is a small bay with Nisis Skrofa in the entrance. It is used by local fishing boats, but offers only indifferent shelter from strong westerlies. With gales from the W or S the boats are run up on the beach, so it is best avoided by yachts.

Immediately S of Ormos Skrofa work is in progress reclaiming land and constructing a huge rock barrage. Running out from the reclamation work is Ifalos Skrofa, a huge shoal patch extending up to a mile off the coast. Like the shoal water off the mouth of the Akheloos, it is prudent to keep well off and take a dogleg course around the shoal water.

Nisis Oxia

The high island with a jagged ridge running down the spine at the entrance to the Gulf of Patras. Once seen, its spiny outline is unmistakable. The lighthouse on the southern end is conspicuous from east and west. There are only two anchorages, both very deep.

North Bay The bay at the N end of the island. Unfortunately it is now occupied by a fish farm and effectively unusable. A shame as it was a spectacular anchorage in a beautiful remote location.

East Bay On the E side at the narrowest part of the island there is a bay affording reasonable shelter from moderate westerlies. Again it is very deep and you will have to anchor in 15–20m with a long line ashore. A fishfarm occupies the lower side of the bay.

The island itself is impossible to mistake once seen. The craggy razor-ridged island is just the sort of sentinel you would expect to find at the entrance to a gulf. I imagine the lighthouse keeper on Ak Oxia at the southern end has a lonely job and must be cheered to see the new aquatic travellers mad enough to go to sea for pleasure – I know on several windswept trips around the cape that he has emerged to give me a wave, and little things like that do a lot for your spirits.

Note Nisis Oxia has reputedly been sold privately to an Australian Greek, although apparently there are no plans to do anything with the island. . .yet.

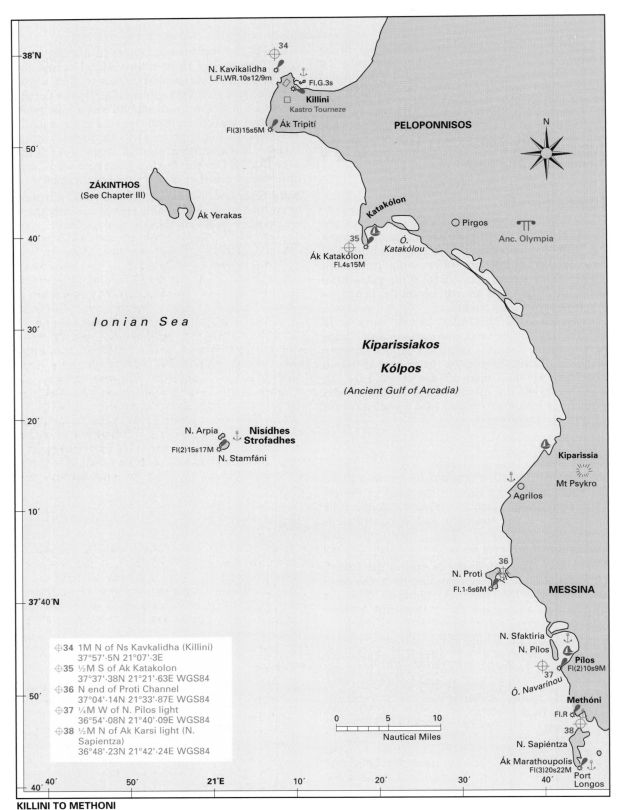

38°N

N. Kavikalidha
L.Fl.WR.10s12/9m

34

Fl.G.3s

Killini
Kastro Tourneze

PELOPONNISOS

N

Fl(3)15s5M   Ák Tripití

50′

ZÁKINTHOS
(See Chapter III)

Ák Yerakas

Katakólon

40′

35

Ó.
Katakólou

○ Pirgos

Anc. Olympia

Ák Katakólon
Fl.4s15M

Ionian Sea

30′

Kiparissiakos

Kólpos

(Ancient Gulf of Arcadia)

20′

N. Arpia

Nisídhes
Strofadhes

Fl(2)15s17M

N. Stamfáni

Kiparissia

Mt Psykro

Agrilos ○

10′

N. Proti

36

MESSINA

Fl.1·5s6M

37°40′N

N. Sfaktiria

N. Pílos

Pílos
Fl(2)10s9M

⊕34 1M N of Ns Kavkalidha (Killini)
　　37°57′·5N 21°07′·3E
⊕35 ½M S of Ak Katakolon
　　37°37′·38N 21°21′·63E WGS84
⊕36 N end of Proti Channel
　　37°04′·14N 21°33′·87E WGS84
⊕37 ¼M W of N. Pilos light
　　36°54′·08N 21°40′·09E WGS84
⊕38 ½M N of Ak Karsi light (N.
　　Sapientza)
　　36°48′·23N 21°42′·24E WGS84

37

Ó. Navarínou

50′

Methóni

Fl.R

38

N. Sapiéntza

0   5   10

Nautical Miles

Ák Marathoupolis
Fl(3)20s22M

Port
Longos

40′

40′   50′   **21′E**   10′   20′   30′   40′

KILLINI TO METHONI

5. The southern Ionian
Killini to Methoni

Quick reference guide

	Shelter	Mooring	Fuel	Water	Provisions	Tavernas	Plans
Killini	B	AC	B	A	C	C	•
Katakolon	A	AC	B	A	B	B	•
Kiparissia	C	AC	B	A	B	B	•
N. Strofades							
Ormos Tavernas	C	C	O	O	O	O	•
Ormos Limani	B	C	O	O	O	O	•
Ormos Panayia	C	C	O	O	O	O	•
Agrilos	C	A	O	B	C	C	•
Ay Kiriaki	C	AB	O	B	C	C	
N. Proti Channel	C	C	O	O	O	O	•
Marathoupolis	B	A	B	B	B	B	•
Vromoneri	B	C	O	B	O	C	•
Voidhokoilia	C	C	O	O	O	O	•
O. Navarinou	B	C	O	O	O	C	•
Pilos	A	AB	B	A	B	A	•
Methoni	B	C	B	B	C	B	•

This chapter covers the western coast of the Peloponnese from Killini to Methoni. Around the southern entrance to the Gulf of Patras much of the land is low-lying and shoal water fringes much of the coast. At the southern end of the Gulf of Kiparissia the land rises abruptly from the coast to the edge of the Aigaleon mountain range. Like the other sea areas in the Ionian further north, the prevailing wind is the *maistro* blowing from the northwest although it gradually turns to blow from a more westerly direction further south. Often it will get up a little later than in the northern Ionian, although by noon it has usually started to blow and it then blows strongly at Force 4–5 through the afternoon before dying down in the evening. Because there is a significant fetch from the southern shores of Zakinthos wave heights can be higher than amongst the islands, although rarely more than a couple of metres.

This area comes within the ancient regions of Ellis (Elis, Ellia) and Messinia (Messenia, Messene) and it is still divided pretty much along ancient lines. Ellis covers the area from Patras to Kiparissia and Messinia the southwestern part of the Peloponnese. In the Middle Ages the area around Kiparissia received a lot of refugees from the central region known as Arcadia and consequently Kiparissia became known as Arcadia and the gulf was called the Gulf of Arcadia until comparatively recently.

It makes an interesting cruising ground for yachts hovering around the southern edges of the Inland Sea and apart from a bit of planning and some early mornings to get back north, it is really no more demanding than cruising around the islands.

Killini

Killini is the mainland ferry port for Zakinthos sitting just behind Ak Glarentza in the southern approaches to the Gulf of Patras. For the most part the coast is flat except for the hilly hummock between Ak Glarentza and Ak Tripiti. On the slopes of the hummock sits Kastro Tornese which can be seen from miles away even at night, when it is floodlit.

Pilotage

Approach The approaches to Killini are littered with rocks and reefs. From the south you need to keep well clear of Nisis Kavkalidha which is easily identified by the lighthouse on it. Keep a good distance off as you round the headland as a reef fringes the coast for some distance out. Once around Ak Glarentza the harbour and town will be seen.

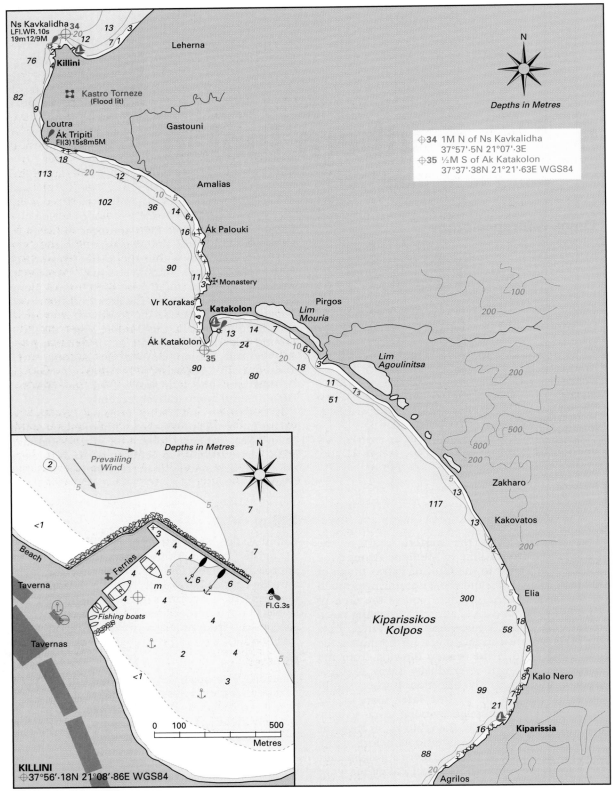

Ns Kavkalidha **34**
LFl.WR.10s
19m12/9M

13

3

7 1

12

Leherna

76

Killini

82

9

Loutra

Ák Tripiti
Fl(3)15s8m5M

18

113

20

12 7

102

36

14 6 4

Amalias

Gastouni

Kastro Torneze
(Flood lit)

10 5

16

Ák Palouki

90

11

3

Monastery

Vr Korakas

Katakolon

Pirgos

*Lim
Mouria*

14 7

13

Ák Katakolon

24

35

90

80

20

18

3

10 6 4

*Lim
Agoulinitsa*

11

7 3

51

7 3

N

Depths in Metres

⊕**34** 1M N of Ns Kavkalidha
37°57'·5N 21°07'·3E
⊕**35** ½M S of Ak Katakolon
37°37'·38N 21°21'·63E WGS84

100

200

200

500

800

200

5

Zakharo

13

117

13

Kakovatos

200

7 2

*Kiparissikos
Kolpos*

5

Elia

300

20

18

58

8

8 7 Kalo Nero

99

7 3

21

16

Kiparissia

88

5

20

Agrilos

2

*Prevailing
Wind*

Depths in Metres

N

5

5

7

<1

Beach

5

3

4

4

7

Taverna

Ferries

4

4

6

6

m

Fl.G.3s

4

4

4

Tavernas

Fishing boats

<1

2

4

5

3

0	100		500

Metres

KILLINI
⊕37°56'·18N 21°08'·86E WGS84

KILLINI TO KIPARISSIA

Care is needed of the ferries constantly coming and going on the Zakinthos route though they also help pinpoint where the harbour is.

Mooring Berth stern or bows-to under the outer breakwater where shown. The bottom is mud and good holding. Shelter is generally good although a strong *maistro* sets up a bit of a surge in here and the coming and going of the ferries also creates some uncomfortable wash.

Yachts can also anchor off the beach clear of the port area proper. The bottom shelves gently to the shore and is shallow for some distance off it. Anchor in 2–3 metres on mud. Good holding although there may be a bit of chop rolling around the end of the mole until the prevailing northwesterlies die down.

Facilities

Services Water on the ferry quay although you may need to find the 'waterman' to turn it on. Fuel by tanker.
Provisions Most things can be found in the village, but it is not a place to stock up.
Eating out Most of the tavernas here serve soulless reheated or grilled food to the captive ferry clientele. Try one of the tavernas on the beach rather than those clustered around the port.
Other PO. ATM. Bus to Patras. Ferries to Zakinthos (around 10 a day in the summer) and also to Poros and Argostoli in the summer.

General

Killini is a sorry little place whose only function is as a conduit for the ferry traffic to and from Zakinthos. This was not always so. It is difficult to think of this little ferry port as the centre of Frankish life in this part of the world, but for two hundred years in the 13th and 14th century Killini, or Glarentza as it was then known, was the most important city in the Ionian. When the Franks under Villehardouin conquered the Peloponnese they established their capital at Andravidha or Andreville a bit inland from present-day Killini. At Killini they built a port and the fort to protect it called Clairmont. (Over time Clairmont was corrupted by the Venetians and Genoese to Chiarentza and then Clarentza.) Very soon the harbour town became one of the most important commercial towns in Medieval Europe. Merchant ships from all nations used the harbour, merchants sold everything and anything from the east or the west, banks were established

and the ultimate accolade was bestowed by Louis IX who granted permission for the Franks to mint the French 'Tournois' or 'Tornesi'. Tornesi from the Peloponnese mint became one of the most trusted currencies in the eastern Mediterranean.

The harbour town had its own castle but the Franks needed something bigger and better. On the slopes of Khlemoutsi they built an imposing fortified castle that still looms over the approaches to Killini. The castle is still one of the most formidable pieces of French military architecture in Greece. Its walls rise sheer from the slopes and command views across to Zakinthos and to Cephalonia. It was largely self contained with giant cisterns for water and two defensive rings to fall back to. It also had its own little tragedy. After Guillame de Villehardouin and the rest of his family had died, his youngest daughter Marguerite, heiress to the throne, was imprisoned here so others might rule. She died here in 1315, although her unjust treatment was later avenged by Ferdinand of Majorca who captured the castle and killed the conspirators. Eventually the castle became known as Castel Tornese (Kastro Torneze) after the coins minted here.

The castle was later captured by the Byzantines and then the Turks who held it off and on until 1826 when Ibrahim Pasha blew up parts of the castle and most of the fort down by the port. The castle is open daily 0830-2000 in the summer and it's worth making your way up to the village of

Killini

Kastro and the Kastro Torneze. After a walk around the vast ramparts there are a couple of good tavernas in the village.

Katakolon

Around 25 miles south of Killini lies Katakolon tucked under Ak Katakolon. Much of the coast is still low and featureless and although Ak Katakolon is not very high, it is easily identified when coming across from Zakinthos or coming north through the Gulf of Kiparissia.

Pilotage

Approach Ak Katakolon and the lighthouse on it are relatively easy to identify. Coming from the north you will not see the harbour which is tucked under the cape. Care is needed of the reef and shoal water running out from the cape and you should keep at least 700 metres off. It is tempting to head straight for the harbour when you round the cape but this will take you close to the reef off the shore. From the south the approach is straightforward and the high rock breakwater is easily identified.

Mooring Head for the old quay on the north side of the cruise ship pier and go stern or bows-to. Alternatively go alongside under the new breakwater for the marina or on the town side quay of the marina. The majority of berths on the pontoons are taken up by small local boats although you may still be able to find a berth here.

Note It is uncertain whether visiting yachts will have to berth in the marina in the future or whether all the small local boats will remain on the berths. The marina has been dredged to mostly 3–4 metres and it is difficult to believe this was only for small local boats drawing less than a metre.

Anchorage You can anchor out in the bay where there is good protection from the prevailing westerlies. Anchor in 2–4 metres on mud and sand, excellent holding. The water off the beach is fairly clean and although the beach is popular in the summer, most people have gone home by evening and it is relatively peaceful compared to the noisy bars that hammer music out over the harbour.

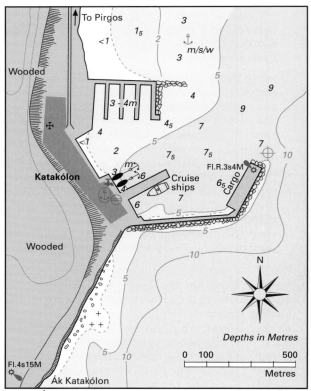

KATAKÓLON
⊕37°38'·81N 21°19'·66E WGS84

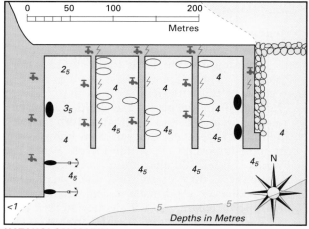

KATAKOLON MARINA

Facilities

Services Water on the town quay. Water and electricity boxes on the pontoons although they have not yet been connected. Fuel by mini-tanker.

Katakolon looking over the town quay to the new 'marina'

Provisions There are several minimarkets in the village where most provisions can be found. Also a butcher, greengrocer and bakery.

Eating out There are a number of tavernas along the waterfront and a lot of pizzerias. A couple of the tavernas near the car-park have good fish.

Other PO. Bank. ATM. Bus to Pirgos where you can connect to get to Olympia. Taxis. Hire cars and motorbikes.

General

Katakolon is a bit of a chameleon of a place. You arrive at this huge commercial port with freighters and the odd cruise ship tied up. Ashore it is all discarded bits of ships and trawlers and a dilapidated embarkation area for the cruise ships. (Although cruise ships have been coming here for years the inhabitants always look a bit surprised when they turn up.) Most of the passengers are hustled off the ship into coaches for a quick tour of Olympia and then get back on board without

seeing too much of Katakolon, though I guess there is not really that much to see. The port was originally built to ship currants from the hinterland, although today there does not seem to be much of that going on.

In the early evening take a walk along to the lighthouse on the cape and back, a leisurely hour's stroll, by which time you will be ready for a drink on the waterfront. The village sprawls along the waterfront intertwined with the old warehouses and by day it seems there is nothing happening. But by evening it is all humming and the bars and tavernas fill up, seemingly from nowhere, and it can get quite noisy. The setting is all very convivial and most people end up liking this funny harbour town.

To get to Olympia you can hire a car or a scooter. Alternatively get a bus to Pirgos where you can get a train or bus to Olympia.

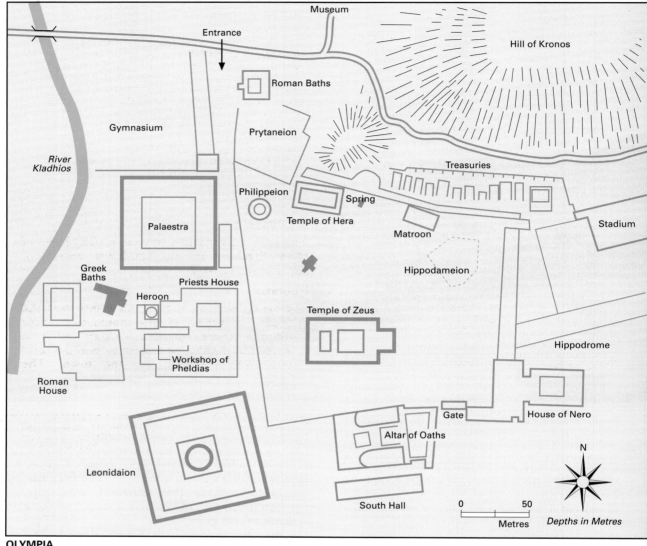

OLYMPIA

Kiparissikos Kolpos

This gulf is closer to a straight coastline than to any sort of large bay extending inland for some distance. The long straight coast around the edge of Kiparissikos Kolpos is low-lying in the north and gradually rises to higher land behind Kiparissia. Long sandy beaches front much of the coast and although there has been some development, much of the coastline is not built up. Loggerhead turtles nest on parts of the beach as at Lagana on Zakinthos. Salt marsh and *étangs* are lodged behind the northern part of the gulf and at one of these, Lake Kaiafas, there is a spa resort. There are a number of hotels and both hydrotherapy and hot springs are on the spa menu. At the southern end of the gulf Kiparissia straggles up the slopes behind the harbour to yet another Frankish castle. Above the town is the first peak of the Aigaleon mountain range.

Note For yachts heading north from Kiparissia or anywhere further south it pays to leave early in the morning and motor for a while before the *maistro* gets up around midday. Generally winds are light to moderate in the afternoon and tend to curve into the gulf from a more westerly direction so you can happily make it up the gulf to Katakolon close hauled on port tack.

OLYMPIA

When you get to Olympia it can be a bit dispiriting. Everywhere there are tour coaches, tour groups milling around, shops and stalls selling tacky souvenirs, and fast food stands. All you want to do is get out of there and somehow experience the site itself. If you think about it, the crowds all help to recreate the scenes that went on here for more than a millennium when this site hosted the Panhellenic games and competitors and spectators came from all over Greece to Olympia. It must have heaved and throbbed with the crowds then.

The site itself is spectacular, lying in a wooded valley beside the River Kladhios and overlooked by the pine-clad slopes of Mt Kronos. The ruins lie all around the valley and although it takes a bit of time to sort out what is where, the impression of the site is powerful and without getting all dewy eyed, it is worth sitting down and contemplating what the games here were all about.

The origins of the games are rooted in ancient mythology and Pelops goes down as the first cheat in the games. He was competing for the hand of Hippodamia against her father Oenomaus and bribed the charioteer to removed the pins from the wheels of the chariot of the father of his intended. He won and married Hippodamia. Heracles was also a competitor, although the big lad was never accused of cheating. The games probably started around the 11th century BC and over the next few hundred years expanded from a local affair to include all the Greek states. A code was established for the Olympics which included the *Ekeheiria*, a sacred truce, whereby warring states had to put aside their differences and for the duration of the games there was a period of peace. It recalls those wonderful moments in the First World War when the British and Germans laid down their arms and played a game of football over Christmas.

The Olympic games encompassed most athletic events including running, jumping, wrestling, discus and javelin and other events like chariot racing. The prize for winning was a simple olive wreath. Later some commercialisation crept in and under the Romans large sums of money and property were awarded to victors. New events were also added and some were a bit fanciful. The Emperor Nero added a singing event in 67AD which he won (along with the chariot race, even though he didn't finish it). They were different times and the spirit of the sacred truce got lost along the way. The games were held until AD393 when the Emperor Theodosius converted to Christianity and was encouraged to close down this long-running pagan event. The early Christians were a canny lot and knew that the ancient sites needed to be converted or destroyed if the new monotheism was to succeed. So Theodosius

ordered the destruction of the temples and other holy sites.

The games were resurrected through the passion and foresight of Baron Pierre de Coubertin who staged the first modern Olympics in 1896. Such was his love for the ancient games and the site that he ordered his heart to be buried at Olympia when he died. Now in 2004 the Olympics have returned to Greece, though not to Olympia but to Athens. The contrast between the ancient site and the modern city could not be greater.

Olympia is open from 0800–1900 from May till mid-October and from 0800–1700 (earlier at weekends) from mid-October to May. A charge is made for admission.

Kiparissia

The town of Kiparissia lies under the slopes of Oros Aigaleon in the southeast corner of Kiparissikos Kolpos.

Pilotage

Approach The town is easily identified from the north. From the south you should keep a little distance off the coast to avoid reefs and shoal water and working your away around the coast you will eventually see the town. The

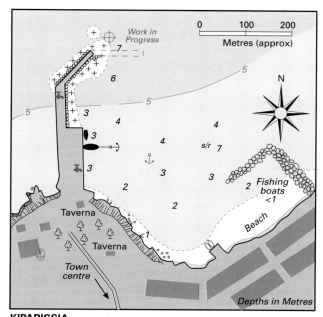

KIPARISSIA
⊕37°15´.51N 21°39´.76E WGS84

Disneyesque castle at Agrilos is easily identified some 5 miles southwest of Kiparissia.

Note At the time of going to press works were reported to be underway extending the breakwater to the east. The underwater ballast is marked with a buoy. When finished the extension should improve the shelter here.

Mooring The harbour provides only mediocre shelter in settled conditions. With bad weather don't even think about staying here. Go alongside or stern-to the quayed section of the breakwater taking care of uneven depths close to it. If alongside pay attention to your fenders. Alternatively anchor off to the east of the harbour. The bottom is hard sand and weed and not the best holding. Make sure your anchor is well in. Care needs to be taken of large rocks (bits of the ancient harbour of Messene?) and old mooring chains. Shelter is adequate when the prevailing winds are light but only mediocre when the prevailing northwest to west winds are stronger and push some swell around the end of the breakwater making it uncomfortable alongside or stern-to. Things get a bit better when the wind dies down in the evening, but there always seems to be some swell in here. In unsettled weather it is not a good place to be and you should head for Pilos or Katakolon.

The small fishing harbour under the breakwater is full of local boats and all berths are jealously guarded.

Kiparissia castle above the old town
Lu Michell

Kiparissia harbour

Facilities

Services Water on the quay. Fuel in the town about 500 metres away. A mini-tanker can deliver.

Provisions Good shopping in the town which has minimarkets, butchers and bakers.

Eating out There are a couple of tavernas by the harbour that are quite OK and at least let you keep an eye on the boat. There are others around the main square in town and in the old town under the castle.

Other PO. Banks and ATMs. Bus and train to Pirgos and to Kalamata. Bus to Pilos. Hire cars.

General

Kiparissia is such a likeable place that it's just too bad it doesn't have a good safe harbour. There has been talk for years of building a new harbour here, especially after the storms in the winter of 1990 which reputedly sank every boat in the harbour. There is nothing you really have to do here. Wander up to the town and have a coffee in the main square. Carry on up to the old town and have a coffee there. Have a look around the castle. And then wander back down to the harbour.

The town has an ancient pedigree and an interesting medieval confusion over names. It was established in the 4th century BC and was the principal harbour of ancient Messene, though there had been a town here earlier than this. There are the remains of the ancient harbour on the foreshore and scattered around the shallow waters. On the shore is a spring which is said to have been opened by Dionysios striking his staff on the rock to provide drinking water for the inhabitants.

In the Middle Ages the town received large numbers of refugees from Arcadia in the centre and east when the Slavs pushed down into the Peloponnese. The town lost it's ancient name and was rechristened Arcadia, a name that stuck until the 19th century. A lot of the credit or the blame for the whole notion of an Arcadia is due to Virgil who in his poems replaced the tough geographical region of Arcadia with a virtual poetic and more bucolic Arcadia peopled by shepherds and country maidens frolicking around the countryside. Later in the Middle Ages and after this new Arcadia (aka Kiparissia) became the focus of this translation of the real to the unreal, of establishing a rural paradise on the slopes of a barren mountain on the western Peloponnese, poems and treatises on poems were written about the place. This literary Arcadia had almost nothing to do with the real Kiparissia which although a prosperous port in the Middle Ages, was no doubt peopled by rufty-tufty sailors, prostitutes, beggars and greedy merchants raking in the lucre. Today this backwater in the Peloponnese is probably closer to Arcadia than in the Middle Ages, though the clubs and bars and the deep boom of dance music beloved by young Greeks is moving ever closer.

The castle above the old town was built largely by the Byzantines, although an older structure had stood here. Later the Franks and then the Genoese moved in, followed finally by the Turks. It has one tower, made of huge blocks, that is said to be the work of giants, as no human could lift such stones. The castle is usually open and you can wander up there at will to look around.

Nisidhes Strofadhes

These lonely islands in the southern Ionian lie approximately 32 miles west of Kiparissia. The anchorages around them are not secure and passage to them should be made only in settled weather.

Pilotage

The islands are the only speck on the horizon once you head out this way and if you miss them the next stop is Sicily. The islands are not that high and can be difficult to pick up in the summer haze until closer to.

Pilotage

Approach The islands should be visible around 5 or more miles off and when closer to the fort-like monastery on Nisis Stamfani is easily recognised. Most yachts will head for Ormos Tavernas on the south side of Nisis Arpia. Some care is needed of the reefs scattered around and in between the islands and it is a good idea to have someone up forward keeping an eye out.

Mooring Yachts can anchor in several places although Ormos Tavernas is the best choice in settled conditions. In the event of bad weather yachts should vacate the area immediately and head for Pilos or Katakolon.

Ormos Tavernas The bay on the south side of Nisis Arpia. The approach should be made from the east to avoid the isolated rocks and reefs on the west side of the islands. Anchor in 4–10 metres where convenient, good holding once the

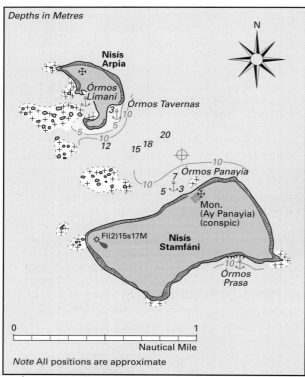

Depths in Metres

NISÍDHES STROFADHES
⊕37°15'·4N 21°00'·7E

The monastery on Nisís Stamfáni   *Nigel Patten*

anchor is in. Good shelter from the prevailing NW–W winds although a bit of swell is pushed around the island.

Ormos Limani On the west side of Arpia there is a crescent bay fringed by above and below-water rocks. Small yachts may be able to get in here and anchor near the north end of the bay with a long line ashore to get some shelter. Reconnoitre first by dinghy.

Ormos Panayia In calm weather you can anchor off the north side of Nisis Stamfani to go ashore and look at the monastery. Anchor in 5–6 metres on sand and rock. When the prevailing northwesterlies get up this is not a good place to be. There is a well ashore at the monastery.

Ormos Prasa A bay on the south side of Nisis Stamfani. It is not really recommended as an anchorage as the shore is a low cliff and the sea bed is littered with huge boulders which may foul your anchor.

General

The monastery of Ay Panayia was constructed in the 13th century by an order of Byzantine monks.

It is as much a fort as a monastery, not surprising given the parlous times it was built in and its lonely situation in the middle of the sea. For a lengthy period the monastery was a wealthy place served by a whole community of monks and it's cliff-like walls ensured its safety through the Middle Ages. The monastery is said to have once possessed the body of St Dionysios and the story goes that in the 18th century the pirate Kanka Moustis sacked the island and 'mangled 20 hermits, Saint Dionysios' body and robbed the monastery'. After this the body of the saint was transported to Zakinthos where he was made the patron saint of the island. The problem with the story is that other accounts don't mention the

Órmos Tavernas on the S side of Nisís Arpia. The monastery on Stamfáni is conspicuous behind *Nigel Patten*

Strofadhes at all and he is supposed to have lived on Zakinthos all his life. Anyway, his relics are in Zakinthos town and miraculously the body has not decayed – though I can't verify that.

Today there is just one monk here who farms the island and lives alone in the monastery, although recent reports are that this lonely hermit may have left too. The islands are part of the marine reserve that includes most of Lagana Bay on the south of Zakinthos. These tiny specks have important bird colonies and serve as a staging post for migrating birds. Cory's Shearwater, various passerines, Turtle Doves and quail number among the important species. And those of a nervous disposition may not want to know that the islands have been near the epicentre of several recent earthquakes with the last in 1997. This last earthquake didn't do much for the structure of the monastery and it is now braced with thick steel girdles in an attempt to prevent further damage.

Agrilos

A small harbour lying approximately 5 miles southwest of Kiparissia. It is easily recognised because the Disney-esque castle nearby is conspicuous from some distance off. The harbour lies a short distance south of it. Only small yachts 8 metres or less and drawing less than a metre should attempt to look for a berth in here and only in a flat calm. And don't rely on finding a berth in here. Try to go alongside the south mole where shown. The prevailing wind tends to send some swell in. Depths in the harbour are uneven and it is very small to manoeuvre in.

Ashore you can get some provisions and there are some wonderfully situated tavernas nearby. The taverna on the north side built into an old windmill should be visited just for the location.

The castle and other follies close by were built by a local boy made good. Harry Fournier emigrated to the USA and made a lot of money as a doctor. When he retired he returned to his birthplace and began building his follies. At first he contented himself with smaller projects: he built a mini-Eiffel tower illuminated at night and a replica of the globe from the 1964 New York Exposition in the village. Then he decided to build his Castle of the Legends (*Kastro ton Paramythion*) by the sea. The castle with its turrets and battlements is built right by the sea and it would have warmed Disney's heart to see

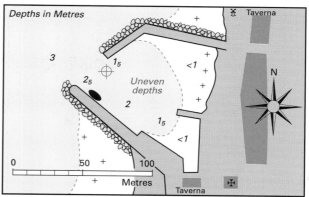

AGRILOS
⊕ 37°12'·74N 21°35'·68E WGS84

it. Outside there are huge kitsch statues of Poseidon's horse and Athena. It's easy to laugh at his creations, but I have a soft spot for rich eccentrics who decide to do something different with their money and good old Harry has done just that. It's open 0900–1400 and 1700–2000 in the summer.

The Disney-esque Castle of the Legends on the coast near Agrilos

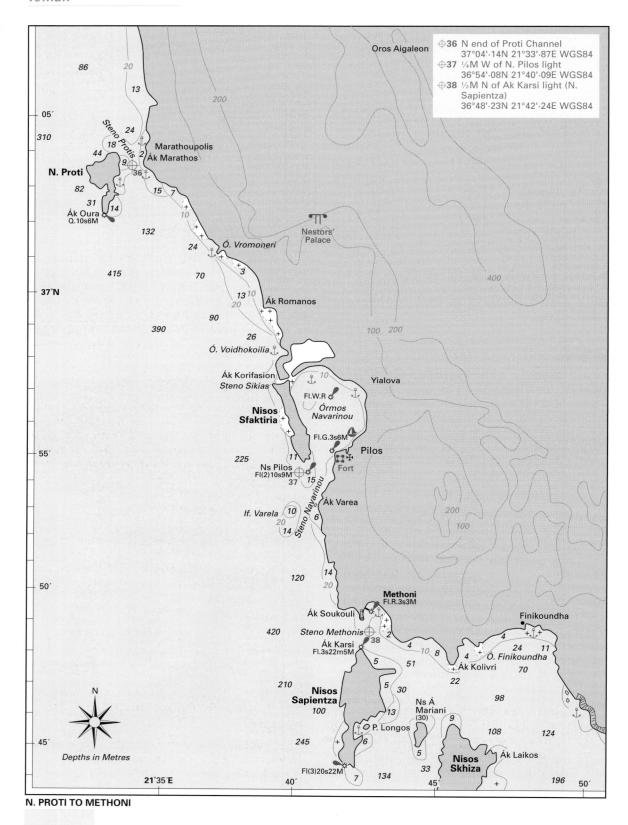

⊕**36** N end of Proti Channel
37°04'·14N 21°33'·87E WGS84
⊕**37** ¼M W of N. Pilos light
36°54'·08N 21°40'·09E WGS84
⊕**38** ½M N of Ak Karsi light (N. Sapientza)
36°48'·23N 21°42'·24E WGS84

Oros Aigaleon

86

20

13

310

05´

Steno Protis

24

18

44

9

2

N. Proti

36

82

Marathoupolis

Ák Marathos

31

14

Ák Oura
Q.10s6M

15

7

10

132

+

24

+

Ó. Vromoneri

Nestors' Palace

415

70

3

37°N

390

90

13 10

Ák Romanos

20

26

Ó. Voidhokoilia

100 200

Ák Korifasion
Steno Sikias

10

Yialova

Fl.W.R

**Nisos
Sfaktiria**

*Órmos
Navarinou*

400

Fl.G.3s6M

55´

225

11

Ns Pilos
Fl(2)10s9M

Pilos

Fort

37 15

Ák Varea

If. Varela

10

6

20

Steno Navarinou

14

200

100

120

14

20

50´

Methoni
Fl.R.3s3M

Ák Soukouli

Finikoundha

420

Steno Methonis

38

2

4

4

24

11

Ák Karsi
Fl.3s22m5M

4

8

10

4

Ó. Finikoundha

5

51

Ák Kolivri

70

210

5

22

98

**Nisos
Sapientza**

5

30

100

Ns Á
Mariani
(30)

13

9

108

124

N

245

6

P. Longos

5

**Nisos
Skhiza**

Ák Laikos

Depths in Metres

45´

Fl(3)20s22M

7

134

33

196

50´

21°35'E

40´

45´

Ay Kiriaki

⊕ 37°07'·11N 21°34'·52E WGS84

A small fishing harbour off the village of Ay Kiriaki. Depths are mostly less than 1 metre and the picturesque little harbour is not well protected at all. You could get in here with the tender, but little else. Several tavernas ashore.

Nisis Proti and Channel

Most yachts heading south sail through the passage between Nisis Proti and the mainland. There are good depths in the fairway and although the prevailing wind is funnelled down through the channel, the seas are relatively flat and you don't need to reef to get through. Yachts heading north through the channel should keep tucked well in on the west side close to the island which, although prone to gusts, will usually have flatter seas.

There are a couple of fairly indifferent anchorages in the channel.

Nisis Proti east side Anchor in the cove under the restored house and monastery. Depths here are considerable and the holding patchy. You also need to be careful of floating lines from moorings and old moorings on the bottom. Reasonable shelter from the prevailing wind, although you never seem to sleep easy here.

Ashore there is a monastery which seems to have been undergoing some restoration, and what appears to be a private villa but may just be very nice accommodation for the monks.

Marathoupolis channel Local fishing boats moor on the east side of the channel in the bight under the village. There is a good lee from the prevailing northwest wind here although a sloppy swell is pushed into the anchorage.

Marathoupolis

A small *caique* harbour on the northeastern corner of Proti Channel. Only yachts around 10 metres or less should attempt to enter.

Pilotage

Approach The immediate approaches to the harbour are encumbered with shoal water and rocks on either side of the channel. Enter from the north on a course of due south keeping the end of the breakwater in line with the church conspicuous in the village. Care is needed as

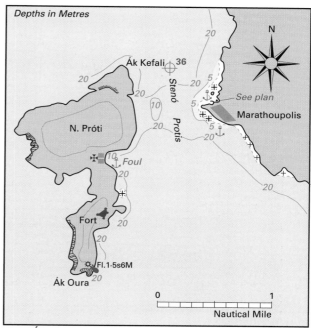

STENÓ PROTIS

⊕36 N end of Proti Channel
37°04'·14N 21°33'·87E WGS84

the outer part of the breakwater was partially destroyed in a recent storm and bits are underwater or just above. The prevailing wind blows straight down into the immediate approaches and the entrance so some care is needed.

Mooring Try to go bows-to under the east mole. The little harbour is full of local boats and you may have difficulty finding a berth here. There is some debris on the bottom close to the quay so bows-to is better than stern-to. Good shelter from the prevailing northwesterlies although there is a bit of swell until the wind dies down in the evening.

Facilities

Services Water nearby. Fuel is about 1km away, but a mini-tanker can deliver.
Provisions Most provisions can be found in the village.
Eating out Tavernas in the town and around the coast looking out over the channel.

General

The village tends towards pour-and-fill architecture, but although not the prettiest place around, it is a convivial place. The locals see little

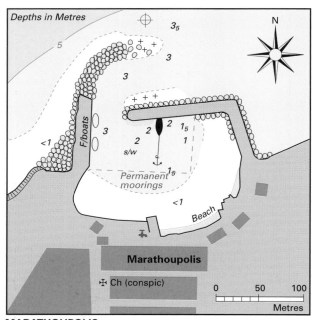

MARATHOUPOLIS
⊕37°03′·69N 21°34′·42E WGS84

Vromoneri

A miniature cove lying 3½ miles south of Marathoupolis. It is barely 100 metres across and the entrance has some nasty rocks on either side, so some care is needed when entering and anchoring. Small yachts (10 metres or less) can anchor on the north side with a long line ashore in calm weather. There are a laid moorings with local boats on them, but still room for a couple of small yachts in here. With the prevailing northwest winds some swell is pushed into the cove, but dies down at night when the wind drops.

The little oval bay is a delightful spot that attracts a few locals in the summer, but not too many. A sandy beach runs around the head of the bay and a beach-café-cum-taverna opens in the summer.

in the way of tourism and are eager to know what is going on in the big resorts – a very Greek sort of place and I like it. Walk around to the beach on the channel and find somewhere to sit in one of the bars and contemplate the passage north or south.

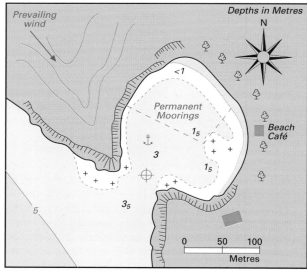

ORMOS VROMONERI
⊕37°01′·01N 21°37′·21E WGS84

Ormos Voidhokoilia

The oval bay located just before you get to the north end of Nisos Pilos. In calm weather anchor off at the north end of the bay clear of the shoal water which fringes the coast here. The bottom is sand and good holding. With the prevailing northwest winds a swell is pushed into the bay so you need to gauge how tenable it is depending on the strength of the wind. Above Force 3–4 or so it is uncomfortable and in real terms untenable. So basically a calm weather anchorage.

Marathoupolis looking towards the entrance   *Lu Michell*

Vromoneri   *Lu Michell*

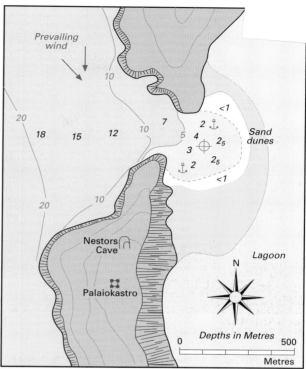

VOIDHOKOILIA
⊕36°56'·97N 21°39'·64E WGS84

Around the bay is a beautiful sandy beach. The salt marsh behind has been designated as a conservation area under Natura 2000 though I believe it has not yet been established as such as cars keep driving around the edge of the lagoon in the summer. The beach is popular in the summer, mainly with local Greek tourists who drive here.

The bay has been identified as the harbour of Nestor and artefacts around it point to its use during the Mycenean era. It has to be remembered that the galleys of this time were comparatively shallow draught, probably a metre or less, and that it was common practice to beach them at night to let the wood dry out. Consequently the requirements for a Mycenean harbour are much different to the requirements of later ships with greater draught. What was needed was just this sort of bay with a gently shelving bottom and a sandy beach to pull the galleys out.

Close south of the bay is a cave, inevitably dubbed Nestor's Cave. It is definitely worth a visit, with an opening in the roof which lets in some natural light. The cave has been identified as the one mentioned in the *Odyssey* where Nestor and Neleus kept their cows and also as the cave where Hermes hid Apollo's sacred cattle.

From the cave you can walk up to the imposing Palaio Kastro (or properly Kastro Navarinou as Palaio Kastro simply means 'Old Castle') standing on the ridge above. It is worth the steep walk up as it remains largely intact, with

Voidhokoilia   *Lu Michell*

211

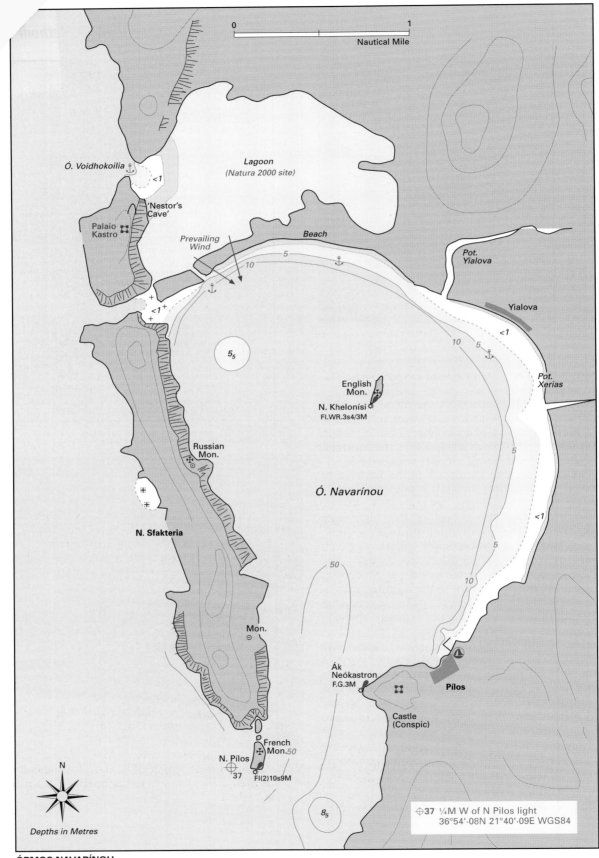

0   1

Nautical Mile

Ó. Voidhokoilia

Lagoon
(Natura 2000 site)

'Nestor's
Cave'

Palaio
Kastro

Prevailing
Wind

Beach

Pot.
Yialova

Yialova

<1

<1

5

10

5₅

10   5

<1

Pot.
Xerias

English
Mon.

N. Khelonísi
Fl.WR.3s4/3M

Russian
Mon.

Ó. Navarínou

5

N. Sfakteria

5

<1

50

5

Mon.

10

N

Depths in Metres

Ák
Neókastron
F.G.3M

Castle
(Conspic)

Pílos

French
Mon.*50*

N. Pílos

37

Fl(2)10s9M

8₅

⊕**37** ¼M W of N Pilos light
36°54'·08N 21°40'·09E WGS84

ÓRMOS NAVARÍNOU
⊕**37** 36°54'·08N 21°40'·09E WGS84   1/4M W of N.Pilos light

courtyards and cisterns inside. Built on the site of an ancient Acropolis, the present fort is a bit of a gallimaufry from the Frankish and Venetian periods with a bit of Turkish mixed in. The view, as you would expect, is just stupendous. The large enclosed bay of Navarinou takes its name from here as in the early Middle Ages Slav groups migrated here and one of these groups, the Avaroslavs, settled in the vicinity. The castle and the area was then called Avarino and later Navarino.

Ormos Navarinou

This large natural harbour is a spectacular place with a spectacular entrance around the southern end of Nisos Sfakteria. Here the rocks have been weathered into pinnacles and spires and through one there is a natural arch. As you bomb down from the north with a building swell in the afternoon breeze, it is a bit of a relief to do a handbrake turn into Ormos Navarinou where there is still some wind but much less swell than outside.

The large bay is used by merchant ships changing crews and picking up supplies and there are usually one or two anchored in the bay. There are several anchorages around the bay which are not as good as you might think when looking at a chart.

Navarinou north end You can anchor off the beach at the north end of Ormos Navarinou where convenient. The bottom comes up quickly to the beach so you will have to anchor in 10–12 metres. The bottom is sand and mud, good holding once the anchor is in. Good shelter from the prevailing northwest wind. At night when the wind dies down a residual swell somehow finds its way into the bay and up to the north end. It is not dangerous but makes it uncomfortable. Ashore a few snack bars open in the summer.

From here you can take the dinghy to the northwest corner to climb up to Palaio Kastro and to visit Nestor's Cave. The northern entrance to Navarinou around the northern end of Sfakteria was apparently once navigable by galleys. It may also have been another Mycenean harbour.

Yialova On the east side of Navarinou it is possible to anchor off the village of Yialova. If the prevailing wind is strong this is not a good place to be. Otherwise anchor in 5–6 metres off the beach. It is shallower on this side than the north

The Sfakteria Incident

On the island protecting the western side of Ormos Navarinou there occurred one of those incidents in ancient times which proved to be the exception to the rule. Thucydides recorded how in 425BC during the Peloponnesian War between the Athenians and the Spartans, a Spartan force did that most un-Spartan of things by surrendering. 'Nothing that happened in the war surprised the Hellenes as much as this', Thucydides wrote. The *hoplite* warriors of the Spartans were taught from birth that to surrender was not a thing to be contemplated. A good Spartan died in battle.

Athens had seized Pilos after the inhabitants revolted against Spartan rule and the incensed Spartans sent an army to quash the usurpers. The Spartans decided that a pincer movement from the land and from the sea would do the trick and consequently based a force on Sfakteria to control the seaward entrance to Pilos. The Athenians simply sent a naval force in and quashed the Spartans on the mainland and cut off the 400 strong force on Sfakteria. The Athenians then sent over archers and javelin throwers and picked off nearly 300 of the Spartan force by simply refusing to engage in the hand-to-hand combat the Spartans were so good at. When the Spartans advanced the Athenians retreated far enough to fire off arrows and javelins and bit by bit the *hoplites* were cut down. Then instead of moving in and crushing the remaining Spartans, the Athenians left them to stew for a bit and then sent an envoi over to see if they wanted to surrender. To the Athenians' surprise, they did, and 120 Spartan *hoplites* were taken to Athens and paraded around the city. The Spartan myth of invincibility had been shattered.

end of Ormos Navarinou so watch the depths as you close the shore. Anchor in 3–5 metres off the beach. Yialova is a straggling resort, not unpleasant, just spread out around the coast. Tavernas and hotels ashore.

Pilos

The town of Pilos sits in the southeast corner of Ormos Navarinou, just inside the entrance.

Pilotage

Approach Once through the entrance of Ormos Navarinou head for the large fort conspicuous on the southern side of the bay and then follow the coast round to Pilos. The marina sits immediately east of the town harbour. A bit of care is needed when approaching the entrance to the marina as you head straight for the cliffs and then do a tight turn to starboard to get into the harbour.

Mooring The 'marina' is much used by local boats and fishing boats that have occupied many of the berths on the piers jutting out from the south quay. At present yachts must find somewhere to go alongside on the outer breakwater quay or on one of the stub piers if there is a space. Shelter inside is good although the prevailing northwesterlies push a swell onto the cliffs at the entrance which rebounds into the marina and makes some of the berths near the entrance a bit uncomfortable. After the wind dies down the reflected swell disappears.

Note When the marina is up and running, and this could take some time, laid moorings and ancillary services will be installed. At present a small charge is made in a haphazard fashion.

Facilities

Services Water at the root of the marina breakwater. Fuel can be delivered by mini-tanker.
Provisions Good shopping for provisions in town.
Eating out Restaurants and bars around the central square and on the steep road leading up to the slopes above the marina. Have an aperitif in the square and then wander up the hill to the *1930* taverna near the entrance to the marina or to others in this general location.

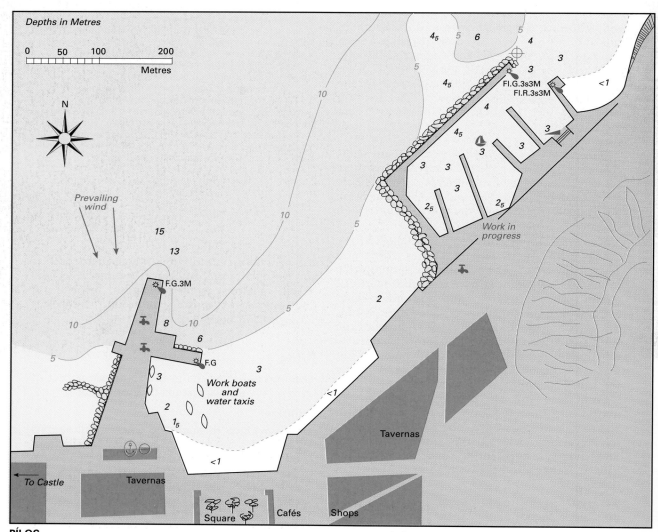

PÍLOS
⊕ 36°55'·16N 21°42'·02E WGS84

Pilos Marina looking out over the pier at Pilos town to the entrance to Ormos Navarinou

Other PO. Banks. ATMs. Hire cars and motorbikes. Buses to Methoni, Kalamata and Kiparissia.

General

Pilos is a sympathetic little place where it is well worth tarrying for a day or two. From here you can organise a trip to Nestor's Palace or to Olympia. Alternatively just sit around the central square and watch the comings and goings of Pilos. The town was built by the French in the 19th century after the Battle of Navarinon. Everything is laid out around the large central square shaded by limes and plane trees and with a view out over the harbour and Ormos Navarinou. Cafès, bars and restaurants are scattered around the square and it is really just a matter of finding a favourite and settling in. In the

Battle of Navarinon

After Missalonghi and the death of Byron, the Greek War of Independence rumbled on back and forth, with few gains to the Greeks and small advances by the Turks. It was not going well and when the Turks invited the Egyptians in under Mehemet Ali, things looked dire. In 1825 Mehemet Ali landed a large force on the Peloponnese and, backed up by his naval fleet, quickly secured the western Peloponnese. His base was Ormos Navarinou.

It looked as if the Greek cause was lost. The Turks and the Egyptians secured more territory and the Greeks were at their lowest ebb. So many of the Greek ships melted away to turn to piracy that the European powers decreed them an international menace that should be fired upon at will. By 1827 most of Greece was effectively under Turkish and Egyptian control except for a few areas in the hinterland which were difficult, if not impossible, to control.

In July 1827 the Treaty of London between Great Britain, France and Russia provided that Greece should be autonomous but under the administration of the Turks. This piece of legal chicanery was an attempt by the Great Powers to maintain friendly relations with both the Greeks and the Turks and to keep the sea routes open against the threat of the Turkish and Egyptian fleets and Greek pirates. The treaty also stated that the naval forces of the signatories were responsible for enforcing it, and Admiral Codrington was given wide powers of discretion in the policing of the treaty.

With winter coming on, the combined fleet under Codrington had to somehow contain the threat of the Turko-Egyptian fleet. Mehemet Ali was determined to turn the Peloponnese into a mini-Arab state and also

had a personal vendetta against the Hydriots who had harried his shipping so much. Admirals Codrington, de Rigny and von Heyden decided that the only thing they could do was sail into Navarino and anchor there to keep an eye on the Turco-Egyptian fleet and try to get Mehemet Ali to contain his army and navy.

The opposing fleet was anchored in a semi-circle with the largest ships in front and smaller ships behind. Near the shore were transports and fireships. Codrington knew that to sail in with the prevailing westerlies and anchor in the semi-circle was a huge risk. All his ships would be raked by cannon fire before they could beat out against the wind. And he was massively outnumbered: the allied fleet numbered 26 ships and 1270 guns whereas the Turko-Egyptian fleet numbered 89 warships, many of them new, and 2450 guns. Codrington led the fleet in, the bands playing on the deck and the gun ports half open, as was common practice in calm weather, and anchored in the middle of the semi-circle. Before entering he had instructed his captains not to fire unless fired upon, although he had also added that "In case of a regular battle ensuing, it is to be observed that, in the words of Lord Nelson, 'No captain can do very wrong who places his ship alongside that of an enemy'".

An Egyptian ship fired a cannon and so the battle began. 'The bloody and destructive battle was continued with unabated fury for four hours; and the scene of wreck and devastation which presented itself at its termination was such as has been seldom before witnessed', Codrington wrote in his dispatches. For much of the battle it was reported that the ships could hardly see each other because of the miasmic cloud of gunsmoke over the bay. The battle will not go down as a class act of naval strategy. It was fought at anchor and only proved that European gun crews could load and sight quicker and better than those on the Turko-Egyptian fleet.

Codrington was not officially censured over his actions. The British expressed regret, the French mopped up any remaining opposition in the Peloponnese, and the Russians warred with Turkey in Asia Minor. The end result was that Greece was free: ruined, starving, riven by feud and counter-feud, but it was free. The Battle of Navarinon forced Turkey and Egypt to negotiate and five years later Greece was formally given independence by the Sultan.

BATTLE OF NAVARINON
- Turkish and Egyptian Fleet
- English ships under Codrington
- Russian ships under Von Heyden
- French ships under de Rigny

Pilos town square and one of the cannons from the Battle of Navarinou under the monument to Admirals de Rigny, von Heyden and Codrington

centre is a memorial to the three admirals who commanded the fleet that destroyed the Turks in the Battle of Navarinon: Admirals Codrington, de Rigny and von Heyden.

On the west side of the town is the imposing bulk of the fort which is so prominent in the approach from seawards. The Neo Kastro ('New Castle') was built by the Franks and later the Venetians, but it was the Turks sometime after 1498 who extended the fort to the extent we see today. It is in relatively good repair and you can wander around much of it. It has a beautiful little mosque, later converted to a church, inside the walls. In the 18th and 19th centuries it served as a prison, especially for the feisty Maniotes further down the Peloponnese, and you can still see how it was divided up into little pens to hold the prisoners.

The Palace of Nestor lies north of the lagoon opposite Voidhokoilia. You really need a car or motorbike to get there – around 30 minutes' drive. The palace seems to have been abandoned after a fire around 1200BC and later covered over, so it is one of the best-preserved sites of a Mycenean palace. It is also unusual in that it was not heavily fortified and sits in a pastoral setting overlooking Ormos Navarinou. In terms of its position and evident wealth it has been identified as the palace of wise King Nestor described in Homer's *Odyssey* – and why not? It was beautifully decorated with frescoes and evidently had links with the gentler Minoan civilisation based on Crete, as tablets with Linear B script were found here. It is well worth taking the effort

to visit the site because it is so complete and just so wonderfully evocative of what seems to have been a pretty civilised life in the Homeric Age.

Methoni

The port and anchorage lie tucked under Ak Soukouli nearly 7 miles south of Ormos Navarinou. In the approaches from the north you will see the wonderful castle and Turkish tower guarding the approaches to the bay.

Pilotage

Approach Once the castle and Turkish tower are identified a yacht should keep well off the end of the Turkish tower and make a wide sweep into the anchorage. Once into the roadstead the town and breakwater of the harbour are easily identified. Under the lee of the cape the water will be comparatively calm.

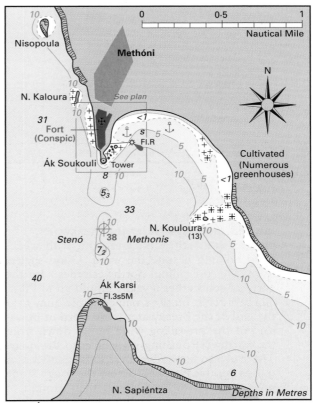

STENÓ METHONIS

⊕38 ½M N of Ak Karsi light (N. Sapientza)
36°48'·23N 21°42'·24E WGS84

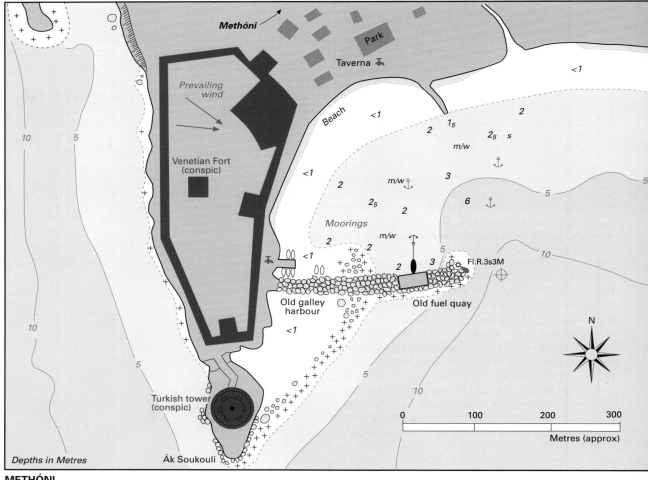

METHÓNI
⊕38°48´·83N 21°42´·58E WGS84

Mooring Anchor in the bay off the beach clear of the laid moorings under the breakwater. The bottom is mostly sand and mud with weed, good holding despite the weed. Good shelter from the prevailing northwesterlies. In the event of southerlies a yacht should go to Pilos. There is room on the small concrete quay near the end of the breakwater to go stern or bows-to, but the prevailing wind blows down from the northwest pushing a yacht onto the quay. There is also little advantage to be gained as it means you have to walk across the rough stone breakwater to the castle and then around to town, whereas in the anchorage it is a short trip ashore in the dinghy.

Facilities

Services Water on the beach and in the southwest corner of the harbour.
Provisions Most provisions can be found in the village.
Eating out There are several waterside tavernas and in the town the *Klimateria* has good food.
Other PO. Bank. Hire cars and motorbikes. Bus to Pilos.

General

The setting off the beach with the castle and Turkish tower on the eastern side is improbably romantic. It is one of my favourite places around the Peloponnese and although land-based tourism has increased, at least at anchor you are away from much of it. It has been a favoured region since ancient times. Homer mentioned that it was 'rich in vines' and under the Venetians it was renowned for its wine and pork. Today it is still a fertile region with a mild climate and you can hardly miss the giant plastic covered greenhouses around the coast that grow early season tomatoes. The village ashore is a modest place built relatively recently on a grid system and it is easy to gently accommodate to Methoni and dally longer than intended.

The Venetian castle on the headland, washed by the sea on three sides and cut off by a moat flooded with sea water at the landward entrance, looks every bit a proper castle. At the end on a rocky islet is Bourtzi, the Turkish tower, that adds to the charm of the place. Fortifications existed on this spit of land from ancient times, but the great castle we see today was built by the Venetians around the 13th century. It was an important harbour on the trading routes to the Levant and Venice called it the 'Eye of the Republic' along with Koroni a bit further down the coast. Inside there was a sizeable town and several churches. Cellars underneath housed supplies and gunpowder and were also probably there as anti-mining measures. An aqueduct was built to bring fresh water to the castle. Three gates lead into the inner courtyard and the main gate is as much an ornamental entrance as a defensive structure. The Lion of St Mark can be seen emblazoned all around the castle walls.

Around 1500 the castle was taken by the infamous Beyazid II, and the inhabitants massacred. The Turks lost it, only to retake it again in 1715. Cervantes was a prisoner here under the Turks and a tale in *Don Quixote* of the captive may relate to his experiences here.

The entrance to the castle is on the north wall and it is open 1000–1600.

Passage on around the Peloponnese

From Methoni yachts can cruise on down to Messiniakos Kolpos and Lakonikos Kolpos before rounding Cape Malea and continuing on into the Aegean. For details see *Greek Waters Pilot*.

The conspicuous Turkish tower at Methóni looking SW from the harbour. (It looks pretty much the same from all angles.)

Appendix

GLOSSARY

Common Greek terms and abbreviations used in the text and plans

Ákra (Ák)	Cape
Andí (Anti)	Opposite
Áyios (Áy)	Saint
Dhíavlos	Strait or channel
Dhiórix	Channel or canal
Dhrómos	Roadstead
Fáros	Lighthouse
Ífalos (If or I)	Reef
Isthmós	Isthmus
Kávos	Cape
Khersónisos	Headland
Kólpos	Gulf
Limín (L)	Harbour
Mólos	Breakwater or mole
Moní	Monastery
Nisáki, Nisidhes	Islet(s)
Nísos/Nisí/	
Nisía, Nisoi (N)	Island(s)
Nótios	Southern
Órmos (O)	Bay
Ormiskos	Cove
Óros	Mountain
Pélagos	Sea
Pírgos	Tower
Porto	Small harbour
Potamós (Pot)	River
Pounda	Cape or point
Stenó	Strait
Thálassa	Sea
Vórios	Northern
Vrakhonisis	Rocky islet
Vrákhos	Rock

A few useful words in Greek

General

yes	né
no	ókhi
please	parakaló
thank you	efharistó
OK	endaksi
hot	zeste
cold	krió
here	ethó
there	ekí
hello	herete
goodbye	adío
good morning	kaliméra
good evening	kalíspera
good night	kalíníkhta
good	kaló
bad	kakó
today	símera
tomorrow	ávrio
later	metá
now	tóra
I want	egó thélo
where is	poú inai
big	megálo
small	mikró
one	éna
two	dhío
three	tría
four	téssera
five	pénde
six	éxi
seven	eptá
eight	octó
nine	eniá, enéa
ten	dheca

Shopping

apples	míla
apricots	veríkoka
aubergines	melitzána
baker	foúrnos
beans	fassólia
biscuits	biscóttes
bread	psomí
butcher	hassápiko
butter	voútiro
carrots	caróta
cheese	tirí
chicken	kotópoulo
chocolate	socoláta
coffee	kafés
cucumber	angouri
eggs	avgá
fish shop	psaróplion
flour	alévri
garlic	scórdo
green pepper	piperiá
grocer	bakáliko
ham	zambón
honey	méli
jam	marmeláda
lamb	arnáki
lemon	lemóni
margarine	margaríni
meat	kréas
milk	gála
mutton	arní
oil	ládhi
onions	kremmídia
oranges	portokália
parsley	maïdanós
peach	rodhákino
pepper	pipéri
pork	khirinó
potatoes	patátes
rice	rízi
salt	aláti
sugar	zákhari
tea	tsái
tomatoes	domátes
veal	moskhári
water	neró
watermelon	karpoúzi
wine	krassí
yoghurt	yaoúrti

USEFUL BOOKS

Admiralty Publications
Mediterranean Pilot Vol III Covers the Ionian Sea.
List of Lights Vol E Covers the Mediterranean, Black and Red Seas.

Yachtsman's Pilots
Greek Waters Pilot Rod Heikell (Imray). Covers all Greek waters in a single volume.
The Ionian Islands to Rhodes H M Denham (John Murray). Covers the Ionian islands through Crete to Rhodes. Classic guides though no longer revised and kept up to date.
Imray Mediterranean Almanac Ed. Rod Heikell (Imray). Biennial publication covering all major Mediterranean harbours and marinas although of course not in detail.

Other Guides
Blue Guide to Greece Edited by Stuart Rossiter (A & C Black).
Yacht Charter Handbook Rod Heikell (Imray). Covers charter destinations worldwide.
Berlitz Guide to Corfu (Berlitz) Good compact guide.
Kefallonia and the South Ionian Islands John Fawssett Roger Lascelles.
Corfu & the Ionian Islands Grocs Candid Guides.
The Greek Islands Lawrence Durrell (Faber). Good photos and eloquent prose.
The Greek Islands Ernle Bradford (Collins Companion Guide).
The Rough Guide to Greece Ellingham, Jansz and Fisher (RKP). Down-to-earth guide.

Prospero's Cell Lawrence Durrell. On Corfu.
Fortresses and Castles of Greek Islands and *Fortresses and Castles of Greece* Vol II Alexander Paradissis (Efstathiados Group). Detailed guides available in Greece.
The Venetian Empire Jan Morris (Penguin). Readable account of the Venetian maritime empire.

General
A Literary Companion to Travel in Greece Edited by Richard Stoneman (Penguin).
The Ulysses Voyage Tim Severin (Hutchinson).
Eleni Nicholas Gage (Fontana/Collins).
Hellas Nicholas Gage (Collins Harvill).
Captain Corelli's Mandolin Louis de Bernieres (Penguin). A 'must' read.

Flora and Fauna
Flowers of Greece and the Aegean Anthony Huxley and William Taylor
Flowers of the Mediterranean Anthony Huxley and Oleg Polunin. Both the above have excellent colour photos and line drawings for identification.
Trees and Bushes of Britain and Europe Oleg Polunin Paladin.
The Hamlyn Guide to Birds of Britain and Europe Bruun, Delin and Svensson (Hamlyn).
The Hamlyn Guide to the Flora and Fauna of the Mediterranean A C Campbell (Hamlyn. Good guide to marine life.

Food
Greek Cooking Robin Howe
Food of Greece Vilma Chantiles
The Best of Greek Cooking Chrissa Paradissis

BEAUFORT WIND SCALE

B'fort No.	Wind Descrip	Effect on sea	Effect on land	Wind speed knots	mph	Wave ht (metres)
0	Calm	Like a mirror	Smoke rises vertically	less than 1		
1	Light	Ripples, no foam	Direction shown by smoke	1–3	1–3	–
2	Light breeze	Small wavelets, crests do not break	Wind felt on face, leaves rustle	4–6	4–7	0·2–0·3
3	Gentle breeze	Large wavelets, some white horses	Wind extends light flag	7–10	8–12	0·6–1·0
4	Moderate breeze	Small waves, frequent white horses	Small branches move	11–16	13–18	1·0–1·5
5	Fresh breeze	Moderate waves, some spray	Small trees sway	17–21	19–24	1·8–2·5
6	Strong breeze	Large waves form, white crests, some spray	Large branches move	22–27	25–31	3·0–4·0
7	Near gale	Sea heaps up, white foam, waves begin to streak	Difficult to walk in wind	28–33	32–38	4·0–6·0
8	Gale	Moderately high waves	Twigs break off trees, walking impeded	34–40	39–46	5·5–7·5
9	Strong gale	High waves, dense foam, wave crests break, heavy spray	Slates blow off roofs	41–47	47–54	7·0–9·75
10	Storm	Very high waves, sea appears white, visibility affected	Trees uprooted, structural damage	48–56	55–63	9·0–12·5
11	Violent storm	Exceptionally high waves, wave crests blown off, badly impaired	Widespread damage	57–65	64–75	11·3–16
12	Hurricane	Winds of this force seldom encountered for any duration in the Mediterranean.				

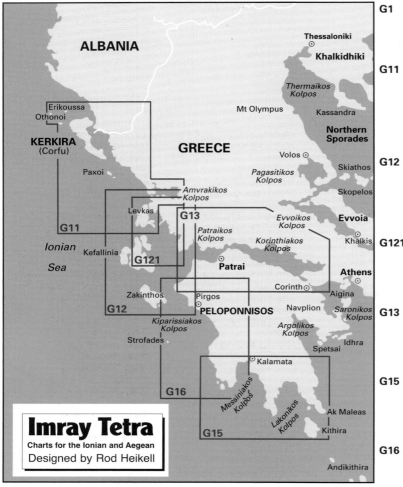

G1 Mainland Greece and the Peloponnísos
1:729,000 WGS 84
Plans Approaches to Piraeus and Ó. Falírou

G11 North Ionian Islands — Nísos Kérkira to Nísos Levkas 1:185 000 WGS 84
Plans Órmos Gouvíon, Vorion Stenó Kérkíras, Kérkíra (Corfu Town), Limín Alípa, Órmos Lákka, Órmos Párgas. *Insets* Amvrakikós Kólpos, Nísos Othonoí

G12 South Ionian Islands — Nísos Levkas to Nísos Zákinthos 1:190 000 WGS 84
Plans Kólpos Aetoú (N. Itháki), Dhíoriga Levkádhos (Levkas Canal), Órmos Argostolíou (N. Kefallínia), Órmos Zákinthou (N. Zákinthos)

G121 The Inland Sea 1:95 000 WGS 84
Plans Órmos Ayias Eufimia (N. Kefallínia), Órmos Frikou (N. Itháki), Órmos Fiskárdho (N. Kefallinia), Vasiliki (N. Levkas), Dhíoriga Levkádhos (Levkas Canal)

G13 Gulfs of Patras and Corinth
1:218,800
Plans Mesolongi, Ó. Loutrákiou, Kiato, Patrai, Ó. Andíkiron, Ó. Aiyiou, Krissaíos Kólpos, Dhíorix Korínthou (Corinth Canal)

G15 Southern Peloponnísos Ó. Navarínou to Nísos Kithíra and Akra Tourkovigla 1:189,700 WGS 84
Plans Kalamata, Ó. Navarínou, Yíthion, Monemvasía (Yefira), Methóni, Koróni

G16 Western Peloponnísos – Killini to Kalamata 1:189,000
Plans Killini, Kiparissia, Kalamata, Katakolon, Pilos, Steno Methonis

USEFUL CONVERSIONS

1 inch = 2.54 centimetres (roughly 4in = 10cm)
1 centimetre = 0.394 inches

1 foot = 0.305 metres (roughly 10ft = 3 metres)
1 metre = 3.281 feet

1 pound = 0.454 kilograms (roughly 10lbs = 4.5kg)
1 kilogram = 2.205 pounds

1 mile = 1.609 kilometres (roughly 10 miles = 16 km)
1 kilometre = 0.621 miles

1 nautical mile = 1.1515 miles
1 mile = 0.8684 nautical miles

1 acre = 0.405 hectares (roughly 10 acres = 4 hectares)
1 hectare = 2.471 acres

1 gallon = 4.546 litres (roughly 1 gallon = 4.5 litres)
1 litre = 0.220 gallons

Temperature scale
t°F to t°C : 5/9(t°F–32) = t°C
t°C to t°F : 9/5(t°C+32) = t°F

So 70°F = 21.1°C   20°C = 68°F
     80°F = 26.7°C   30°C = 86°F
     90°F = 32.2°C   40°C = 104°F

Index